THE PSYCHOLOGY OF

How and why does someone become a terrorist? Are there common causes? Is there a terrorist personality?

To understand the psychology of those who engage in terrorism, John Horgan draws on interviews with terrorists and analyses current evidence to argue that only by asking the right questions about this complex problem, and by answering them only with evidence, can we truly begin to understand the nature of terrorism and how to respond effectively to it. Consequently this book presents a critical analysis of our existing knowledge and understanding of terrorist psychology, and in doing so, highlights the substantial shortcomings and limitations of the nature and direction of current research. Building on this, the author presents a model of involvement and engagement in terrorism by considering it as a process and exploring three distinct phases of the making of a terrorist: becoming involved, remaining involved (or 'being' a terrorist), and leaving terrorism behind. Despite the ongoing search for a terrorist personality, the most insightful and evidence-based research to date not only illustrates the lack of any identifiable psychopathology in terrorists, but demonstrates how frighteningly 'normal' and unremarkable in psychological terms are those who engage in terrorist activity.

By producing a clearer picture of the complex processes that impinge upon the individual terrorist, a different type of terrorist psychology emerges, one which has controversial implications for efforts at countering terrorism in today's world.

The book concludes with what this new psychology of terrorism means for understanding the terrorist and highlights what both researchers and the broader community can do to realistically engage the terrorist threat.

The Psychology of Terrorism will be an invaluable reference text for students, researchers and practitioners in security studies, forensic psychology, legal studies and criminology.

Dr John Horgan is a lecturer at the Department of Applied Psychology, University College, Cork. He is widely published in the areas of terrorism and forensic psychology.

CASS SERIES: POLITICAL VIOLENCE
Series Editors: Paul Wilkinson and David C. Rapoport

Terrorism versus Democracy: The Liberal State Response
Paul Wilkinson

Aviation Terrorism and Security
Paul Wilkinson and Brian M. Jenkins (eds)

Counter-Terrorist Law and Emergency Powers in the United Kingdom, 1922–2000
Laura K. Donohue

The Democratic Experience and Political Violence
David C. Rapoport and Leonard Weinberg (eds)

Inside Terrorist Organizations
David C. Rapoport (ed.)

The Future of Terrorism
Max Taylor and John Horgan (eds)

The IRA, 1968–2000: An Analysis of a Secret Army
J. Bowyer Bell

Millennial Violence: Past, Present and Future
Jeffrey Kaplan (ed.)

Right-Wing Extremism in the Twenty-First Century
Peter H. Merkl and Leonard Weinberg (eds)

Terrorism Today
Christopher C. Harmon

The Psychology of Terrorism
John Horgan

Research on Terrorism: Trends, Achievements and Failures
Andrew Silke (ed.)

A War of Words: Political Violence and Public Debate in Israel
Gerald Cromer

THE PSYCHOLOGY OF TERRORISM

John Horgan

Routledge
Taylor & Francis Group

LONDON AND NEW YORK

First published 2005
by Routledge, and imprint of Taylor & Francis
2 Park Square, Milton Park, Abingdon, Oxon OX14 4RN

Simultaneously published in the USA and Canada
by Routledge
270 Madison Ave, New York, NY 10016

Routledge is an imprint of the Taylor & Francis Group, an informa business

© 2005 John Horgan

Reprinted 2006 (twice), 2007

Typeset in Times by BC Typesetting Ltd, Bristol
Printed and bound in Great Britain by
TJ International Ltd, Padstow, Cornwall

British Library Cataloguing in Publication Data
A catalogue record for this book is available from the British Library

Library of Congress Cataloging in Publication Data
Horgan, John, 1974–
The psychology of terrorism/John Horgan.
p. cm. – (Terrorism and political violence)
Simultaneously published in the USA and Canada.
Includes bibliographical references and index.
ISBN 0–7146–5262–8 (hdbk.) – ISBN 0–7146–8239–X (pbk.)
1. Terrorism–Psychological aspects.
I. Title. II. Series: Terrorism and political violence (Unnumbered)
HV6431.H667 2005
303.6′25′019–dc22   2004026154

ISBN 10: 0–714–65262–8 (hbk)
ISBN 10: 0–714–68239–X (pbk)

ISBN 13: 978–0–714–65262–7 (hbk)
ISBN 13: 978–0–714–68239–6 (pbk)

CONTENTS

About the Author   vi
Foreword by Xavier Raufer   vii
Preface   xi
Acknowledgements   xviii

1   What is terrorism?   1

2   Understanding terrorism   23

3   Individual approaches   47

4   Becoming a terrorist   80

5   Being a terrorist   107

6   Disengaging   140

7   Analysis, integration, response   158

Notes   169
Bibliography   184
Index   194

ABOUT THE AUTHOR

Dr John Horgan is a College Lecturer at the Department of Applied Psychology, University College, Cork. Born in 1974, he has an honours degree in Psychology and was awarded his PhD by University College, Cork in 2000. He is widely published in the areas of forensic psychology and terrorism and his previous work includes *The Future of Terrorism* (with Max Taylor). His research and teaching has taken him to many countries, where he lectures to police, intelligence, military and public audiences on terrorism and political violence.

FOREWORD

Terrorism, scientific methods and the fog of media warfare

Terrorism, a truly global phenomenon in all its different shapes and forms, had always been considered a marginal threat until the end of the 1960s. Since then, however, it has invaded global information networks to become what is today probably the top-choice subject for the media. Just one example of this is found in the *International Herald Tribune*, a newspaper published simultaneously across all the continents of the world. Now, every week, and sometimes for several days in a row, we find all the leading front page titles devoted to terrorism, the consequences of terrorism and the risks and dangers associated with it. It is hard to find an issue or theme capable of rivalling the level of media coverage enjoyed by terrorism. But how is it that topics such as the economy, pandemics or major catastrophes do not have the pulling power of terrorism?

During the historic interlude from 1989 to 2001, the nature and pace of terrorism changed significantly. Previously, the terrorist threat was heavy and slow moving, predictable and explicable. Take Abu Nidal's *Fatah* Revolutionary Council, for instance: the country giving it shelter and the weapons and explosives it used were known to one and all. It was child's play to decipher the makeshift signature used by the group to claim responsibility for its actions. By contrast, terrorism today is brutal, fleeting and often irrational, as with Al Qaeda, the Aum Shinri Kyo sect or the Armed Islamic Group (or GIA) in Algeria. Today, terrorism is a major component in warfare, which it has slowly but steadily contaminated over the past three decades. In the early twenty-first century, terrorism is now the central security concern for our governments. It may even be observed that today terrorism has *become* war. However, this all-pervasive terrorism – every single day, somewhere around the world, bombs explode for a thousand reasons – has also undergone a significant mutation. The State terrorism of the Cold War era, whether political or ideological, has almost disappeared. Moreover, since the Cold War ended, new players have emerged on the terrorist scene: the hard core are of course fanatics such as Islamist terrorists, but there are also non-political, criminal groups such as mafia gangs, doomsday sects and other such irrational and violent groups.

Let us see if any similarities may be detected between most of the groups mentioned thus far. In the first place, they have in common the fact that they are not really *organizations* at all, in our usual and Western connotation of the term, i.e. solid, even rigid structures. On the contrary these groups are fluid, liquid – when not actually volatile. By way of example, we may take what the United States Administration refers to as 'Al Qaeda', which it insists on presenting as a formal organization with a 'No. 2' and a 'No. 3' – with a hierarchy, in other words – and concerning which it alleges that 'two thirds of the command structure has been eliminated', again suggesting some sort of stable or permanent membership. Such fictions are spread further by various 'experts', who blithely estimate the 'membership of Al Qaeda' at (to quote one example) 1,200. It is, however, child's play to demonstrate that Al Qaeda is *not* an organization in the way that – to stick with terrorism – the Provisional IRA *is* an organization. To put it another way, it is equally easy to show that Al Qaeda is not simply a kind of Provisional IRA, only dedicated to Islamic militancy instead of being Roman Catholic. Since August 1998 and its first attacks against the US embassies in Nairobi and Dar es Salaam, Al Qaeda has seen unleashed against it the fiercest wave of repression in world history. According to our database, since 2001 some 5,000 individuals referred to as its 'members' have been interrogated in 58 countries around the globe, themselves nationals from as many countries again, if not more. Furthermore, in the Arab world especially, hundreds more arrests have been conducted in secret.

The worldwide freezing of 'Al Qaeda' funds

In a July 2003 report of the group of United Nations experts responsible for monitoring the application of UN resolutions on the fight against terrorism, it was noted that 59.2 million dollars held by 'Al Qaeda', through linked companies or entities (or by individuals identified as 'members'), have been frozen or confiscated in 129 countries worldwide: 70 per cent in Europe, Eurasia or North America, 21 per cent in the Middle East (Saudi Arabia, Emirates, etc.) and 8 per cent in South-East Asia. We might also note that all of the above took place *before* the Iraq war in spring 2003 and the subsequent attacks in:

- Riyadh (Saudi Arabia, May 2003, 35 killed; November 2003, 17 killed)
- Casablanca (Morocco, May 2003, 45 killed)
- Jakarta (Indonesia, August 2003, 12 killed)
- Istanbul (Turkey, November 2003, 69 killed)
- Madrid (Spain, March 2004, 202 killed)

Let us now consider the case of two major organizations, properly termed as such, which also have a global presence for professional reasons: a multinational corporation and an intelligence gathering service. Say, General Motors and the CIA. What would be left of these two giants if, at world level, 5,000 to 6,000 of their executive and salaried staff were thrown in prison, their offices closed down, their records pillaged, their working tools, bank accounts and financial resources confiscated? Quite simply, nothing. It should also be noted that the nature of terrorist groups is *hybrid*, part 'political', part criminal. Considerable exchanges between criminal and terrorist groups are currently being reported: the Neapolitan Camorra with the Basque group ETA and the GIA in Algeria, the Dawood Ibrahim gang in Karachi with Islamist groups close to Bin Laden such as Jaish-i-Muhammad and the Harakat-ul-Mujahideen. Similar contacts link the Provisional IRA with the degenerate, proto-criminal FARC guerilla movement in Colombia. These dangerous groups possess an ultra-rapid *mutation capability*, as a function of the now crucial dollar factor. In most cases and most frequently they are *nomadic*, de-territorialized (or located in inaccessible areas) and transnational. They are *cut off from the world* and civilized society. Their objectives may be criminal, fanatical, doomsday-driven or entirely spurious – in reality driven by a determination to hoodwink the world in general (e.g. in Liberia and Sierra Leone, the murderous bands led by Foday Sankoh under the name of the Revolutionary United Front or RUF); lastly, their goals may simply defy understanding (e.g. the Aum sect). These dangerous groups generally lack state sponsorship of any kind – which makes them still more unpredictable and uncontrollable. Finally, they inflict massacres widely, with the will to kill as many people as possible (examples being Bin Laden, the GIA in Algeria, and the Aum sect).

Talking about terrorism does not explain terrorism

An obvious paradox exists in the fact that the more talk there is about terrorism, the more reports of terrorist crimes grab the headlines – be it in the press, on television or in the media at large – the less experts and commentators feel they have a grasp of what is really happening. Just who are these groups with incomprehensible names that appear one day and vanish the next? What are we to make of the myriad small terrorist groups from Iraq to Afghanistan, not to mention Pakistan or Kashmir? Who *are* these *Abu* something-or-others cited almost daily in the headlines only to disappear as quickly as they emerged, in a bloody version of 'now you see me now you don't'? Even more importantly, *why* do these particular groups and hotchpotch entities, and these particular individuals, commit such crimes? What is going through the mind of a disciple of the Aum sect when he releases deadly nerve gas in the Tokyo subway? What psychological motive drove Timothy McVeigh to blow up a truck packed with explosives outside the federal building in Oklahoma City, killing nearly 200 innocent people? What does Abu Musab al-Zarqawi feel as he slits another human being's throat? What did Osama Bin Laden feel when he saw the twin towers collapse in Manhattan? Press coverage, let alone television coverage, says nothing about such issues. The press simply relates events. It does not seek to explain them and even less to instruct. But then, that is not its role. Explaining and instructing are the tasks of the academic world and it is true that a number of scientific disciplines are contributing and have already contributed to forging a better understanding of terrorism. Among the frontrunners in this respect are geopolitics and, albeit more indirectly, philosophy, which has tackled the subject at a deeper, more abstract level. We had some expectations of sociology but, in the Latin world at least, our disappointment can be said to be inversely proportional to our hopes. That leaves psychology.

When we mention psychology we are getting close to something crucial. We criminologists know full well that beyond all ideology, all plans, projects and conspiracies, beyond human greed, rage and fury, there lies that one essential ingredient: 'acting out', or behaviour. We criminologists are very well aware that human beings may sometimes feel the urge to strangle the person they are talking to – and what more legitimate reason for doing so than when faced with a nit-picking representative of French university bureaucracy – and that if we look for the source of the 'acting out' we will find a dark pool of silence that remains a secret sealed off from the conscious self. If we are to understand the secret nature of this 'acting out' and other decisive and central concepts, we need to turn to psychology. And there are few areas that one would wish to delve into or understand more than the psychology of terrorism and of terrorists. John Horgan has undertaken such a task helped by an important body of research carried out at the Department of Applied Psychology at University College, Cork. The title of this preface refers to the fog created by media warfare. John Horgan's book effectively cuts through that fog – at times even lifting it completely. We learn a great deal from it and we end up with a better understanding of situations and pattern shifts that were previously unfathomable. It is a book that 'instructs', and that to my mind is the greatest compliment one can pay a piece of academic work. I am proud to have been asked to write the preface to this book, which shows great promise for becoming a classic reference in its field.

Xavier Raufer
Director of Studies
Department for the Study of the Contemporary Criminal Menace
Paris Criminology Institute of the University of Paris II
September 2004

PREFACE

In early May, 2004, the website of *Muntada al-Ansar*, an Iraq-based terrorist group supporting pro-militant Islamic extremism, distributed videotape material which was to achieve worldwide notoriety within hours of its appearance. The clip was entitled 'Abu Musab al-Zarqawi shown slaughtering an American' and showed Nicholas Berg, a 26-year-old American civilian, who had gone to Iraq as part of the infrastructural reconstruction efforts. Berg had been reported missing since the previous month. The 14-minute clip began with Berg sitting on a chair, wearing an orange jumpsuit, similar to those worn by detainees at the Guantanamo Bay facility in Cuba. Berg identified himself to his interviewer, stating: 'My father's name is Michael, my mother's name is Suzanne. I have a brother and sister, David and Sarah. I live in Philadelphia'. The clip then skips to a scene during which Berg is seated on the floor, his arms bound behind his back, and his feet bound together in front of five masked men, one of whom (in the centre) reads aloud a statement in Arabic. The statement condemned the abuse of Iraqi detainees at the US-controlled Abu Ghraib prison in Baghdad, during which some American soldiers and civilian contractors engaged in the torture of prisoners. This man was later identified as al-Zarqawi, whom Western news media have continued to describe as an Iraq-based Al Qaeda 'commander'.

While the statement was read slowly and calmly, two men on both far sides of al-Zarqawi continuously fidgeted during the reading of the statement, glancing at Berg, and then al-Zarqawi, with both men subtly but regularly checking their weapons throughout. Berg himself sat motionless throughout the reading of the statement until it came to a sudden and abrupt end. There was a loud scream from what appears to have been the person holding the video camera, followed by al-Zarqawi who dropped his sheets of paper and pulled a long knife from his tunic. A scuffle ensued while two of the masked men pushed Berg over on his left side to the ground, sitting on his legs and back with their knees. At this point, Berg began screaming but his shouts were drowned out by a lowly drone of 'Allahu-Akhbar, Allahu-Akhbar' (God is great). In the seconds that followed, the chant became louder and more frequent as al-Zarqawi held Berg's head back by his hair and proceeded to cut his throat right through to the back of his neck. As Berg's decapitated head was held aloft before the camera, the chanting ceased. The clip then skips to another scene, showing Berg's head being placed on a bed, alongside his body.

Where do we begin to try to understand such an act? Indeed, why even *try* to understand it? Perhaps we might be better off just condemning it. Maybe attempts to understand such behaviour might detract from the sense of outrage and shock that seems a more appropriate and justifiable reaction than any supposed intellectual debate? When the eminent scholar George Steiner was asked how best to react to the horrors of the Holocaust, he said that the only appropriate reaction was silence. Language, words, opinions, arguments, Steiner suggested, were in themselves simply too corruptible (as the Nazis themselves demonstrated) to convey what had happened. The result, Steiner feared, would be revealed in a trifling simplification and a routinization that would only desecrate any accurate portrayal of the past's horrors.

Steiner's comment seems completely out of place in today's world. By mid-October, 2001, less than five weeks after the devastating Al Qaeda attacks in the United States, the first book on the attacks was already published. What followed, however, was surprising even for the cynic. The subsequent 12 months saw the emergence of over *800 texts* (in English alone) attempting to address the events of 11 September, or 9/11.

The drama surrounding terrorism, and the speed with which academics and scholars the world over have embraced the subject, has spawned a veritable industry. There are literally more books on terrorism in print than even the most eager student could read in a lifetime. Because of the flood of books, papers, articles, news items and many other sources, the prospect of assembling a literature review on any aspect of terrorism is disheartening even to the most dedicated student. Indeed, in spite of this mass of data, or even perhaps because of it, it is ironic then that even now a sound understanding of terrorism continues to elude us. It still surprises us that just because there is more information on terrorism than ever before, it does not necessarily follow that we understand it any better. On the one hand, part of this is easy to appreciate, and we can consider ourselves lucky as a result: because very few of us will ever be caught up in a terrorist attack, the reality of terrorism is still a very distant thing to us. Indeed, for the most part, it is the drama that derives from, and is constructed around, terrorism that dictates our perceptions of both the process of terrorism and those involved in it: the terrorists. Terrorism is one of the most obvious examples of the popular media's tendency to *personalize* the activity itself. Media portrayals of any form of politically motivated violence might sometimes be presented in a positive light if the terrorist cause appears to display some popular qualities, or represents itself as some form of political correctness, if conveying perhaps a sense (however vague) of nobility. On the other hand, however, such characterizations may present a group negatively if such appropriateness is perceived not to exist. Even despite this, there may be a grudging admiration for the technical sophistication (or conversely, its utter simplicity), the sense of determination or boldness of the terrorist, even within broadly negative comments.

Misinformed, politicized, short-sighted, incomplete and, above all, rushed analysis has now become such a reality of the discourse on terrorism that even academic analyses are straining under their own weight: in attempting to make sense of the torrent of debate surrounding Al Qaeda, Xavier Raufer[1] recently warned that we run the risk of 'drowning in a rising tide of misunderstood facts'. His point is equally valid at a much broader level. Within what some have suggested we call 'terrorism studies', our theories have become more abstract, our data increasingly unreliable (often second hand at very best), and most worrying of all in the present climate there are major difficulties in appreciating the value in what knowledge we currently possess and what strategies we have at our disposal for effective disruption and harassment of terrorist networks. Our perceptions, and ultimately our understanding both of the process of terrorism and the behaviour of its perpetrators, are influenced particularly by the recognizable characteristics of terrorism: its extreme violence and, in a slightly broader sense, its tactics we frequently label 'cowardly' in line with its subversive, illegal, covert and seemingly unpredictable nature. While not necessarily incorrect, such perceptions remain limited by the fact that little more than a paucity of verifiable data exists on all but the most prominent and over-researched terrorist groups. To the general reader, it may appear surprising, but despite the contemporary relevance of the phenomenon and its increased media coverage over the past 40 years, our knowledge and understanding of those we call the terrorists still remains seriously underdeveloped.

We do have some starting points, however. Although it may be unclear and inconsistently used, terrorism is still an accepted concept. If this book was about understanding what terrorism is, or how it ought to be defined, then we would probably start at the beginning of a lengthy, decades-long debate, and develop a systematic analysis to try to approach it objectively and critically. This book is not about defining terrorism however, so there is a sense in which we have to work within the kinds of frameworks we already have at our disposal. The main reason for writing this book is to try to explain not only why it is that psychology has played little or no role in analyses of terrorism, but to attempt to play a part in undoing some of the widespread confusion about what a 'psychology of terrorism' actually means (or could potentially offer). There is a widespread assumption that there may exist something like a terrorist 'personality', and there have been many efforts to engage psychology in a technical sense in terms of the development of profiles (e.g. of suicidal terrorists or hijackers, for instance), but as a discipline psychology has had little to say about terrorism, and the ways in which contemporary discussions feature 'the psychology of the terrorist' hide this gaping absence of empirical, data-driven analysis. In the main there appears to be a few principal reasons for this. In part, and as Chapters 1 and 2 will illustrate, a problem lies in its poorly delineated state – as above, even the simplest critical analyses of the concept of terrorism or 'terrorist' reveal a multiplicity of inconsistent and confusing uses. In addition, terrorism is illegal, and it is difficult to gain access to significant actors or situations from which more meaningful information for our analysis might emerge. The nature of terrorism is such that it impinges on the state in a potentially significant way, giving rise to a variety of security and other concerns. This necessarily limits the nature and scope of analysis possible. One other concern which will only briefly be mentioned at this point, but perhaps a more general problem of psychology, is that because the processes inherent in terrorism seem to relate to high-level activities, relating to both social movements and political processes, psychology has had little to say about such issues, and these seem to have always been the remit of other disciplines (in particular, political science).

The central aim of this book is to explore ways in which our knowledge of psychology and psychological processes might inform and improve our understanding of terrorism. At the outset, it must be said that there are a variety of ways in which such an endeavour might proceed. For instance, we can easily identify at least four principal areas that we can explore from a psychological perspective. First, there is the individual terrorist, and the processes that allow the emergence of and sustenance of violent behaviour (along with associated activities) that we identify as 'terrorism'. This is the focus of much of the psychological research to date, and in a sense this reflects the *individual* issues that maintain terrorist behaviour, the reinforcers, the lures and other supportive qualities that both create the impetus for involvement in terrorism as well as engagement in terrorist acts (this also necessarily impinges on the role of non-violent political or supportive behaviour in sustaining more violent behaviour).

Second, we can explore from psychological perspectives the relationship between the individual and the political, religious or ideological context in which he or she operates. This often involves the organizational aspects of terrorist movements, and particularly the ways in which the organization impinges upon the behaviour of the individual. That these two aspects form the focus of this book, it should be stated at this point, reflects a critical need to attempt to set the record straight on much of the confusion and misunderstanding around these issues.

Third, we could consider the effects of terrorist activity. In a way, this is the task inherent in all analyses of terrorism because it remains impossible to separate our reactions to terrorism from our attempts to understand and conceptualize it. All studies of terrorism and terrorists will reflect concern about 'effects' as such, but for the most part psychology has attempted to examine the effects of terrorism across two primary areas – at the level of the public (in terms of how we can be directly involved in victimization, through for instance, post-traumatic stress disorder after a terrorist attack and being involved more generally as an observer) as well as how the political system and those involved in it at higher levels (i.e. above the electorate) are affected.

A fourth, and final example of an important issue that we can explore from a psychological point of view is the broader issue of methodology, and the ways of studying terrorism we need to consider and develop. It is a central assertion throughout this book that we must not accept knowledge of terrorism based on authority or belief. In any endeavour, only evidence can settle disputes, and if terrorism research activity is to become rigorous, then we must align our analyses closely with the methodological rigour consistent with established academic disciplines. A special problem in existing studies of terrorists is a lack of a variety of important empirical datasets to support particular viewpoints. Most of the data available to researchers is made available through secondary sources – books, newspaper reports, terrorist communiqués, statements, speeches, sometimes even autobiographies, and then to the longer-standing terrorism researchers, information gained directly from the security services or government. Less effort has been put into listening to what the terrorists themselves have to say. Unpalatable as this may seem, it is inevitable that in order to understand the development and structure of terrorist behaviour, we eventually have to meet with and speak to people who have been, or are, involved in terrorist violence. To the academic reader, this point may appear moot, but the reality is not so clear, with academic reluctance to enter the violent field now more obvious than ever before. Given that for most of us, it is the drama surrounding terrorist incidents that drives our perceptions and understanding of both the process and its instigators, the need for a reliance on research-driven knowledge is all the more important.

In attempting to serve a clear set of interests, this book aims to educate and inform people of how psychological knowledge and theory can help us better understand this complex problem, but this can only be based on a clearer picture of what we know is the reality of terrorism. One senior scholar suggested that this be the principal role of the academic terrorism researcher – to help make it known. It is in this sense that a deliberate decision was made in the early stages of preparing this book that there would be no explicit focus on formulating guidelines towards 'responses'. Despite the implications for counter-terrorism of some of the chapters in this book, those expecting a manual or checklist of how to react to and control terrorism will be disappointed. It is, essentially, about *making the psychology of terrorism known* and providing a set of conceptual starting points that seem to be absent from the current nature and direction of psychological research on terrorist behaviour. To some, however, a psychological approach might still suggest a clinical diagnosis – given the nature of terrorism, it might logically suggest that the perpetrators of shootings and bombings are in some way special (if not some way different in some more discrete psychological way to the rest of us). This issue will be addressed in detail, but for the moment, it might be useful to qualify a 'psychology of terrorism' as taking a broad focus, suggesting more complex ways of appreciating involvement and engagement in terrorism. The structure of later sections of the book (particularly the decision to provide separate chapters on becoming a terrorist (Chapter 4), being a terrorist (Chapter 5) and disengaging from terrorism (Chapter 6)) is heavily influenced by this need to acknowledge the complexity of terrorism and what it means. It is only recently that we have begun to acknowledge that the factors that lead people to join terrorist groups have relatively little role in explaining what it is people subsequently do as terrorists (or something else), and are themselves distinct when we try to look at what helps keep members inside a terrorist group and what might happen to lead to eventual disengagement from terrorism altogether.

In addition, another decision was taken that in the development of this book, a significant priority would be not only to consolidate existing psychological knowledge on terrorists (the focus of which is presented in Chapter 3), which takes the primary focus of the book and consequently the book is structured accordingly, but also to identify gaps in our experimental, theoretical and conceptual analyses that need attention. An inescapable feature of this then is a serious consideration of how an interdisciplinary approach to studying terrorism can actually be constructed. Rather than simply paying lip service to existing efforts, a serious attempt is made to develop this idea through both the initial debate in Chapter 2 but more prominently via the development of a *process model* of terrorism, integrating both criminological and psychological perspectives in particular, the detail of which is provided throughout Chapters 4, 5 and 6, and the implications of which are discussed in the final chapter (7).

Although this book is written in such a way as to be relevant to a variety of audiences, the book was written particularly with the critical reader in mind – including those who may be less convinced about the merits of a psychological perspective on terrorism than of any attempt to make systematic sense of terrorist behaviour per se. The author has already participated in enough seminars and conferences on terrorism to realize that problems related to the misrepresentation of psychological analysis of terrorism owe as much to what little development we have had within a psychology of terrorism as opposed to any pre-existing tensions that exist between the disciplines. Even for seasoned researchers, a psychology of terrorism still implies something limited and obscure. The reader will hopefully be in a better position to understand how a psychological analysis of terrorism may make terrorism and terrorist behaviour somewhat less mysterious to the point that we might eventually be able to formulate more informed research agendas *and* ultimately, better-informed responses. That is not to say that we have clear or easy answers, but the fact that we have ways of asking the right questions about this difficult subject means that we can go about developing a realistic understanding of terrorism that will, in time, serve us better than we currently find following the confusion and panic of a terrorist attack. To some this may not be an optimistic outlook, but it reflects the reality of our current situation.

John Horgan
Cork, 2004

ACKNOWLEDGEMENTS

Without the assistance of many people, this book would still remain a half-finished draft sitting on the shelf in my office. I owe an incalculable debt to Professor Max Taylor, whose great knowledge and experience I have benefited from since I began at UCC. His encouragement and sound advice has played a large part in helping this book, and my career more generally, to develop. On a similar note, I have benefited from the support and encouragement of my friends and all my colleagues at the Department of Applied Psychology, UCC. Whilst it is not favourable to single out individuals, I am always grateful for the constant support and encouragement of Sean, Dave and Liz. As always, Noreen Moynihan makes that which seems difficult much easier to deal with.

I greatly acknowledge all the authors cited whose materials I have used to support arguments in this book. This book would simply not exist without the existence of a terrorism research community, and the persistent efforts of many researchers is difficult to overestimate. I must thank in particular Andrew Silke, Dipak Gupta, Orla Lynch and Lorraine Bowman for comments on early drafts of specific chapters. Andrew Humphreys at Frank Cass extended his patience and the deadline to unfeasible lengths, and I am grateful that he did.

Some of the material in Chapters 3 and 6 is reproduced from earlier articles (in particular, my contributions to Andrew Silke's edited collection *Terrorists, Victims and Society*) and although heavily altered here, appear kind courtesy of both the editor and John Wiley.

The friendship and support of Barry, Richard, Andrew, Louise and Yzabel was, as always, both constantly needed and appreciated. Laurent was always a good source of advice, while Martin and Ruth kept me in good spirits during difficult final phases. I would also like to thank collectively students from the various classes of AP3015 Forensic Psychology and AP3016 Terrorism and Political Violence for their input over the years, and for providing me with a perfect audience for some of the arguments that have finally been put down on paper.

ACKNOWLEDGEMENTS

Finally, the opinions expressed in this book are solely my own, and do not necessarily reflect those of University College, Cork, or the individuals whose research I have cited throughout.

1

WHAT IS TERRORISM?

Introduction

Any debate surrounding the concept and phenomenon of terrorism is so assured to be shrouded in controversy, emotion, inaccuracies and such downright confusion that terrorism expert Louise Richardson confidently announced that the only certainty regarding terrorism is the pejorative nature in which the word is used.[1] Given this, it is worth recalling Wittgenstein's aphorism 'let the use of a word teach you its meaning', since it seems particularly applicable to the words 'terrorism' and 'terrorist'. While we may hear of youths who terrorize old people with taunts or threats, or of groups of young children who terrorize and torture helpless animals, we are unlikely to refer to any of these as *terrorists*. This we reserve for something else.

Generally speaking, what we think of as terrorism involves the use or threat of use of violence as a means of attempting to achieve some sort of effect within a political context. Despite the general tone of such a description, this is the broadest (and most acceptable) level of consensus we can reach on what terrorism is – it is when we try to go beyond this description that problems arise. Perhaps from a psychological perspective, an important characteristic even in the simplest analyses distinguishing terrorism from other kinds of crime involving murder, or violence committed for some personal reasons (as for example, sexually motivated murder, or rape), is the *political* dimension to the terrorist's behaviour. The point may be obvious on reflection, but it is one that poses significant implications for psychological analyses.

Most terrorist movements are relatively small, (semi-)clandestine collectives built on anti-establishment political or religious ideologies, seeking to overthrow or at least effectively destabilize some target regime or influence (be it a domestic or foreign-based power), using violence or the threat thereof to carry influence. In this sense terrorism is evidently instrumental in character. Very often, it seems that the goal of terrorism is simply to create widespread fear, arousal and uncertainty on a wider, more distant scale than that achieved by targeting the victim alone, *thereby* influencing the political process and how it might normally be expected to function. How terrorist movements do this, however, is determined by a variety of factors, notably the ideology of the group, their available resources, knowledge, expertise and a host of other factors. For most terrorist groups around the globe, the gun and the bomb serve symbolically to epitomize their struggle for freedom from their perceived oppressors.

Such popular perceptions of terrorists are often justified, but we must also face some uncomfortable facts that have become obvious since the events of 11 September (or 9/11). Those whom we call terrorists are not alone in the commission of acts that merit this label (assuming of course, that the essence of terrorism is defined by the methods used by terrorists). States and governments have been responsible for equally and often far more reprehensible acts of violence on scales unreachable by conventional terrorist organizations: this point is blatantly obvious, yet we choose both to derogate and label as terrorism violence that appears to bubble up from 'below', rather than imposed from 'above' (this assertion does not reflect a judgement at this point, but does reflect the reality of how the term is used, and we must be aware of it). This has not only been the case in so-called conventional wars, but applies to the recent extra-legal responses of several states in attempts to quell local terrorist (and non-terrorist) campaigns.

An important and alternative defining feature of terrorism is that for terrorists there is a distinction to be made between the immediate target of *violence and terror* and the overall target of *terror*: between the terrorist's immediate victim (such as the person who has died from a bombing or a shooting) and the terrorist's *opponent* (which for many terrorist movements represents a government). Sometimes, terrorists bypass the symbolic intermediaries to target politicians directly, by assassination for instance, but because of this simple dynamic of terrorism, it might be viewed as one form of *communication* – a violent, immediate, but essentially arbitrary means to a more distant political end. Although the attacks of 9/11 may have resulted in the deaths of almost 3,000 people, the more potent immediate and long-term rewards for those responsible for planning and organizing the attacks were the humiliation of the American government and the subsequent psychological arousal for the greater populace: the victims in this case may be only tenuously related to the terrorists' opponents. When we consider Al Qaeda's additional expectations of political destabilization and galvanization of extreme Islamic sentiment against Western interests, the allure of terrorism as a tactic, strategy and psychopolitical tool to otherwise disenfranchised extremists becomes apparent. It would be easy to explain "Islamic-inspired" terrorism in Eurasia and elsewhere exclusively as a civilization clash, but even this simplifies the strategic considerations underpinning elaborate terrorist attacks, and exaggerates the role of religion many presume to 'inspire' contemporary political terrorism.

The attractiveness of terrorism as a tactical tool is easily appreciable. According to Friedland and Merari,[2] terrorist violence is predicated on the assumptions that apparently random violence can push the agenda of the terrorist group onto an 'otherwise indifferent public's awareness', and that faced with the prospect of a prolonged campaign of terrorist violence, the public will eventually opt for an acceptance of the terrorists' demands (the paradox, of course, is that the use of terrorism against a target does not easily ensure that the target will subsequently be willing to engage in dialogue with, or concede to, the terrorists as a result of what has just happened). The latter is a much mentioned but little understood feature: the ability (or for some, the aspiration) to create levels of heightened arousal and sensitivity disproportionate to the actual or intended future threat posed by the terrorist. Jenkins[3] has often stated that many terrorists simply 'want a lot of people watching, not a lot of people dead', again emphasizing the communicative nature of the terrorist's actions. What follows from this, however, is that to retain a sufficiently prevalent grip of heightened sensitivity, the terrorist group must not only create, but also effectively *maintain* a general climate of uncertainty and psychological arousal. Maintaining this state often becomes a primary concern for terrorist organizations, even during ceasefires or broader peace processes when immediate goals become obscured. Following their bombing of the British Conservative Party conference in 1984 (in an attempt to assassinate the British Prime Minister Margaret Thatcher) the Provisional IRA (or PIRA) issued a statement concluding: 'Remember we have only to be lucky once, you will have to be lucky always'.[4]

In this context, Schmid[5] accurately describes a core feature of terrorism that gives it its potency: a calculated exploitation of people's emotional reactions due to the 'causing of extreme anxiety of becoming a victim of [what appears to be] arbitrary violence'. This is crucial to thinking about the effects (and hence attractiveness to extremists) of terrorism and is developed further by Friedland and Merari[6] who describe what they see as two predominant characteristics of terrorism: (1) a perception of the threatened and actual danger posed by terrorists which is *disproportionate* to the realistic threat posed by the capabilities of terrorists, and (2) that terrorism has the ability to affect a set of 'victims' far greater than those suffering from the immediate results of a violent terrorist act. The immediate aims and results of terrorist violence (intimidation, injury or death, the spreading of a general climate of uncertainty among the terrorists' audience and target pool) are thus often secondary to the terrorists' ultimate aims (and it is hoped, from the terrorists' perspective, political change), which are often espoused in the group's ideology or aspirations.

In this sense, and adding to this list of terrorism 'traits', terrorism is often accurately referred to as a form of sophisticated psychological warfare: outside of the immediate event, terrorism might be thought to reflect enhanced arousal and a sensitivity to environmental events associated with violence. For instance, children's drawings (e.g. of bomb blasts, weapons, soldiers) illustrate this from the child's perceptions but this presumably is equally a reflection of adult concerns. In psychological terms, therefore, it is not terror per se we are dealing with but arousal. Habituation diminishes arousal over time, so there is one sense in which habituation can be a driving force for an escalation of violence where there is explicit use of terrorism to bring forward attainable short-term political agendas. This certainly appears to have typified the situation in Northern Ireland prior to the first peace agreements in 1993 (and sometimes where no short-term goal is attainable, however, we might then expect the emergence of an 'acceptable' level of violence).

Despite our readiness to identify core features of what we feel constitutes terrorism however, and by default, not something else, and furthermore given that terrorism appears to have become what some commentators describe as a necessary feature of contemporary extreme political behaviour, academic and policy-related definitions of what constitutes terrorism vary greatly. It is unfortunate that we are all-too familiar with hearing the frequently overused 'trite and hackneyed phrase[s]'[7] that 'one man's terrorist is another man's patriot'. Indeed, even systematic and exhaustive attempts to define terrorism have not seen much success.[8] Certainly in the context of the general description given above to start the discussion, the use of qualifiers, i.e. by stating what is 'usually' or 'generally' meant by terrorism, permeate discussions of the concept so much so as to question its continued usage.[9] We are already now beginning to validate Richardson's comment in the opening section of this chapter, as well as to convey several implicit assumptions about the potential and actual misuse of the term terrorism. In essence, to begin to say what 'terrorists' do, for many (and not just necessarily in the eyes of the terrorists) carries within it a value judgement even before the actual description itself begins.[10] Certainly by relying solely on the criteria given above (the use or threat of use of violence as a means of achieving political change) as a guide to explaining what it is that we call *terrorism*, working definitions will never even begin to emerge, let alone evolve. Even at a simplistic level, this is because so broad a description of what terrorism 'usually involves' will apply equally to the behaviour of groups whom we generally do not want to refer to as terrorists (e.g. 'conventional' military groupings, such as the army of a state).

An example of the practical ramifications of the definitional ambiguity of the word terrorism is illustrated by examining the number of reported terrorist incidents by different observers using varying definitions. Friedland[11] illustrates the 'wide discrepancies' between estimations of terrorist incidents by noting that the Rand Corporation estimated that 1,022 international terrorist attacks occurred in the ten-year period 1968–1977, while the US Central Intelligence Agency's estimate for the same period was 2,690.

Similar discrepancies and confusion arise when comparing different statistical indices of the frequency of terrorist violence around the globe. Different criteria exist not only for what classifies as terrorism per se, but also in terms of what *kind* of acts should be included in such resources. The Rand-St. Andrews Terrorism Chronology database, for example, mainly includes events of 'international' terrorism, defined as 'incidents in which terrorists go abroad to strike their targets, select victims or targets that have connections with a foreign state (such as diplomats, foreign businessmen, and offices of foreign corporations) or create international incidents by attacking airline passengers, personnel, and equipment'.[12] The database therefore excludes, as its creators themselves admit: 'violence carried out by terrorists within their own country against their own nationals, and terrorism perpetrated by governments against their own citizens. For example, Irish terrorists blowing up other Irishmen in Belfast would not be counted, nor would Italian terrorists kidnapping Italian officials in Italy'.[13] And as the Al Qaeda attacks in the United States illustrated, it can only take one or two large-scale incidents to skew figures substantially and mislead about the apparent extent and direction of terrorism. This issue aside, terrorist events themselves are not the only end result of a series of potentially complex activities (some of which in themselves constitute terrorist events and, therefore, offences), as we shall see in later chapters, but this taken with the inclusion in databases of *successful* terrorist events, presents us with datasets the significance of which is easy to overestimate or misread completely.

Attitudes to terrorism

Embedded in the discourse of definition is one issue that we have not yet fully explored in the literature, let alone understood its importance for developing systematic policy: the degree of willingness to recognize that we are all quite capable of tolerating ambiguous and inconsistent views, something frequently found throughout discussions of the use of violence in the political process more generally. While some of today's terrorism has evolved completely since the early 1990s, the positive image of the traditional 'revolutionaries', perhaps typified by Che Guevara who fuelled the imagination of a generation, or Bobby Sands, the PIRA hunger striker who achieved fame and status in death never attained in life, capture and hold people's impressions, and shape their image of not only the individuals involved in terrorism, but of the process and nature of terrorism and political violence. The reality of death and injury and the legal and moral offences which terrorism necessarily involves rarely impinges on the public image of terrorism, or the terrorist (and as we shall see in Chapter 5, a further complicating issue is that much of the activity that takes place within a broader terrorist 'movement' that both directly and indirectly contributes to specific terrorist attacks is not necessarily illegal in itself). Conversely, in times of media-fuelled crises there is, for a brief time, little to match the public's fascinated reactions to the media's portrayal of the activities of various counter-terrorist groups: notable examples include the SAS's (Special Air Service) actions on the sixth day of the Iranian embassy siege at Princes Gate in London in 1980 (when six Iranian gunmen sought the release of 91 imprisoned opponents of the Ayatollah Khomeini) and the glamorized intervention of the French *GIGN* (Groupe d'Intervention des Gendarmes Nationales) during the 1994 Marseilles airport hostage rescue, foiling an attempt by Algerian terrorists to blow up a hijacked aircraft over Paris. In both scenarios, these counter-terrorist groups shot and killed the hostage takers, and in the case of the SAS, in questionable circumstances.

Some have suggested why we seem so hypocritical in our discerning condemnation of certain violent acts, and terrorism in particular. Taylor and Quayle[14] note that acts of violence committed by small non-state political groups seem to strike out and offend people's sense of fairness and 'universal' justice. This can be illustrated by the apparently random nature of 'no-warning bombs', a tool used by the terrorist to help sustain a general climate of uncertainty (i.e. giving rise to sentiments such as 'will I, or someone I know be next?'). They emphasize that we can understand this inconsistency by drawing on the psychological concept of the 'just-world' phenomenon. This concept is grounded in social psychology and essentially describes our sense of expectation of universal fairness and order in our world. Undoubtedly, the failure to see 'just' and fair outcomes epitomizes the psychological or emotional reactions to both the terrorist and his victim. The fact that the apparently random victim of this kind of violence is arbitrarily selected to die shocks and sickens people, and this unexpectedness leads to considerable personalization of events even at an individual level (e.g. for the television spectator). It is seen as terrible and unjust, the way in which anyone, particularly innocent non-combatant bystanders, can merely be at the wrong place at the wrong time and be killed in the name of some cause that the victim has possibly never even heard of. Terrorist tactics lend themselves preferably to striking the unarmed or the unsuspecting (e.g. the off-duty police officer or soldier), thus provoking responses typically resulting in the denigration of terrorists as 'cowards' – because terrorist victims are killed just to make a point, and are never given a chance to surrender or do something else (e.g. fight back). It has been suggested that perhaps because of this, and certainly facilitated by the personalizing effects of dramatized media coverage, none of us *personally* have any difficulties in deciding what 'should' be classified as terrorism and what 'should not'.[15] Thus, and to draw on an underused analogy: not unlike pornography, terrorism is difficult to 'describe and define' but we all will continue to know it *when we see it*.[16]

Language and labels

Related to the above, *political violence* is a term intermittently used as a synonym of terrorism. As Heskin[17] argues, while 'terrorism is a pejorative term used to describe acts of violence with a political purpose perpetrated by groups without official status', political violence is a 'somewhat euphemistic term for the same phenomenon, with the additional meaning that it may include acts and causes for which there is considerable popular sympathy'. Hoffman,[18] in a discussion tracing the use and evolution of meanings of terrorism, concurs: 'On one point, at least, everyone agrees: terrorism is a pejorative term. It is a word with intrinsically negative connotations that is generally applied to one's enemies and opponents, or to those with whom one disagrees and would otherwise prefer to ignore'. Certainly, this pejorativeness does not apply just to how we label different causes as being terroristic or not, but it also is seen to be applied to judgements about the actors involved in political violence. Hoffman cites Jenkins as writing: 'if one party can successfully attach the label terrorist to its opponents, then it has indirectly persuaded others to adopt its moral viewpoint'. US President Ronald Reagan once described the Nicaraguan Contras as 'the moral equivalents of our founding fathers', yet as Schmid and Jongman[19] quote from a three-year study of verified accounts of activities in which the 'Rebels' engaged, it is difficult to see the morality of acts that included:

> a teacher being assassinated in front of his class, . . . women being gang-raped and disembowelled, . . . a mother having to watch the beheading of her baby, . . . a Contra drinking the blood of victims . . . [which] matches in humanity anything which the elite press's front pages, chronicling anti-Western international terrorism, have presented us in their selective attention to human victimisation.

And herein is another feature, our perceptions of terrorism are limited. According to Heskin,[20] two particular limiting factors determining the nature and extent of people's attitudes towards terrorism and political violence are: our individual subjective perceptions of the righteousness of the particular group or 'cause' in question, and the physical proximity to direct exposure to terrorism. Therefore, unless we, or those close to us are on the receiving end of such apparently random violence (random in the sense that although the terrorist may anticipate civilian casualties, the identity of the individual immediate victim is often truly random), we are often less condemnatory of what we still call terrorist acts. As Taylor and Quayle[21] note, 'how *we* experience the violence of terrorism, how *we* view the rightness of the cause, how much *we* are prepared to see the ends justify the means are critical qualities to how *we* approach the use of violence in the political process'.

Many academic researchers, from the many disciplines seeking to understand the nature of political violence, agree therefore with Heskin's and Hoffman's comments that terrorism remains a deprecatory label, functioning primarily to express condemnation. This blurring of the perceived righteousness of terrorism becomes even more obvious when we examine its complex nature. There is a wide variety of targeting strategies and subsidiary activities to be found across the spectrum of terrorist organizations operating in the world today. An example of this can be seen even in the activities of one of the smaller and lesser-known terrorist movements, the Animal Liberation Front (ALF), an extreme animal rights group based in Great Britain. The ALF has targeted not only hunters (with letter bombs, razor blade traps and other deadly devices) but as Veness[22] describes: intensive farmers, meat traders, circuses, the pharmaceutical industry and animal experimentation practitioners, the fur trade, fast food restaurants, marine conservationists and fishermen. Such tactics have won the ALF very little sympathy, even in the context of a well-known cause, one widely regarded as noble.[23]

In addition, terrorist groups frequently participate in more obviously criminal activities, such as extortion, theft, robbery, counterfeiting and money laundering. That the purpose of raising such funds is said to be primarily for use by the groups to further their politically motivated aims is often the only factor that, from a distance, serves to differentiate such groups from 'ordinary' organized criminal conspiracies (groups such as the Italian Mafia, for instance, open to adopting terrorist tactics for their own ostensible reasons).

What do terrorists do?

Terrorists use violence to achieve political change, and while the motivations vary considerably across the plethora of groups we call terrorists, their principal methods remain remarkably similar. This seems to be the case despite current concerns about the threatened use of weapons of mass destruction (specifically chemical, radiological, biological or nuclear materials) in light of recent technological developments, and changes in the global political world order. While the events of 9/11 signalled a massive shift upwards in the scale of targeting, the group's modus operandi consisted primarily not of using unfamiliar technology or methods, but of exploiting poor security and general complacency, ineffective intelligence sharing, and consequently using the tried and tested method of hijacking aircraft in flight. Indeed, the logic of the event, like most terrorist incidents, as we shall see in Chapter 5, follows a discernable and yet predictable pattern of sub-events, each of which only becomes significant in the context of the final, executed phase of the operation, but each of which from a law enforcement perspective can also be identified and possibly disrupted.

Terrorist violence is conducted with weaponry that mostly includes guns and bombs, the former a traditional yet paradoxical symbol of revolutionary liberation. Although the means of terrorism have remained similar for many years, technological developments have meant that there is an ever-increasing array of modalities through which terrorist violence may be expressed. In particular, terrorism today is complemented with the availability of publicly accessible information on what would previously have been considered military secrets: the phenomenal embedding in modern societies of the Internet has seen a host of material potentially of tactical value to terrorists being transmitted through this medium. This includes information useful as the basis for identifying potential targets, as well as more dramatically, guides to bomb-making. Although results vary in their effectiveness, this information is easily accessible to the point that we might usefully ask why there is not even more terrorism as a result (and as we will see in Chapter 3, the relatively small numbers of actual terrorists is what gives rise to many assumptions of individual abnormality or 'specialness')?

Interestingly, and despite the billions of dollars of investment in defence programmes aimed at countering the terrorist threat, the cost of acquiring the means to commit terrorist violence is becoming cheaper – the Oklahoma City bombing by right-wing American extremists in 1995 and the Manchester bombing by the PIRA in 1996 (both major incidents despite the differences in casualties between them) involved bombs made of fertilizer compounds. The explosives cited in these two examples were those whose primary components can be purchased without any difficulty or major expense. Easily accessible components are the primary ingredients of today's terrorist bombs, just as much as Semtex and other commercial plastic explosives may be. Terrorism is thus not just cost-effective in a commercial sense, but is increasingly referred to as a 'poor man's tactic', a cheaper avenue to political extremism where more conventional avenues have either failed or where a cause lacks popular support. A bomb explosion on board an airliner guarantees the group responsible widespread media coverage, and in the absence of more practical immediate objectives at least the act will ensure a heightened public awareness of the terrorists' aspirations.

The *targets* of terror are central to discussions of terrorism and victim qualities are fundamental to this. Often, our images of terrorist victims include frightened airplane passengers or victims of explosions; as stated earlier, people who simply happen to be in the wrong place at the wrong time. The role of such victims in terrorist violence highlights a major aspect of why we employ such a label of discontent for the terrorist. As indicated earlier, the immediate victims of terrorist violence are in many ways not the actual 'target' of such violence: while the Provisional IRA frequently

killed, tortured and maimed civilians, their rationale for this was that prolonged attacks against 'primary' or 'immediate' targets (mostly security
force targets and the Northern Ireland and Republic of Ireland electorate,
as well as citizens of the Great Britain) can force the 'end' or overall target
(the British and Irish governments) into acceding to the PIRA's demands,
i.e. in facilitating the removal of British troops from Northern Ireland, the
politicization and legalization of the views of the PIRA through their political wing, and eventually the establishment of a 32-county Republic (the
PIRA's campaign having already facilitated the delivery of the first two
objectives).

There are consequently three identifiable actors in terrorist violence,
each having some degree of interaction with the others:[24] the terrorist, the
immediate symbolic target of the terrorist, and the eventual or overall
target. For most politically focused terrorist movements, civilians maimed
or killed by terrorist bombs are not opponents in the terrorists' view (certain
terrorist groups with strong politico-religious aspirations view them differ-
ently, as we will see); they are primarily incidental victims of the conflict
between the terrorists and their enemy (e.g. the targeted regime or source
of political influence), but their 'role' is such that what happens to them
(or what might happen to future potential victims) is rather assumed by
the terrorists to influence the decisions of the political policy-makers.

So far, we have considered chiefly personal issues related to how terrorism
may be conceptualized or defined, and we have identified some very basic
features of terrorism, but before we can arrive at a fuller basis for defining
it, other areas also need brief exploration, not least the issue of how terrorism
might be distinguished from war and other types of conflict.

Terrorism and warfare: useful distinctions?

Thackrah[25] notes that terrorism has also been a synonym for 'rebellion,
street violence, civil strife, insurrection, rural guerrilla war and coup d'état'.
Terrorism can of course be seen as a form of warfare in general terms, but
terrorist campaigns distinguish themselves from what we conceive of as
war-like campaigns through a number of surface dissimilarities. War is
mostly used to refer to conflict between states, whereas terrorists are not
'state' entities in the same sense in that, to give one rudimentary distinction,
they do not have the ability to hold what governments' term a foreign policy.
Terrorist tactics, from the point of view of the terrorist, *must* differ from
those seen in conventional warfare: if terrorists, traditionally small in
number and rarely sophisticated in resources, were to engage in warfare
with reasonably symmetrical boundaries, they would be destroyed. Terrorists
do not have the same level of resources at their disposal, since by the very
illegal nature of terrorism they are semi-clandestine individuals serving clandestine organizations. Instead, terrorists adopt 'guerrilla tactics' in a process

of constant attrition, rather than resembling the victories and defeats of symmetrically-based wars in which levels of technical sophistication and resources are, to a degree, matched. A central aspect of successful terrorist strategy is that by actually determining the 'theatre' of war (and giving their enemies no choice in the matter), terrorists redress this inequality of resources.

Terrorism is distinguished from conventional warfare and other forms of violence used by liberal democratic states and governments in several other basic, but identifiable, ways. Some of these distinctions (even though we might dispute them) will be of benefit later in trying to systematically define terrorism. Hoffman[26] addresses the distinction as follows:

> Even in war there are rules and accepted norms of behaviour that prohibit the use of certain types of weapons (for example, hollow-point or 'dum-dum' bullets, CS 'tear' gas, chemical and biological warfare agents), proscribe various tactics and outlaw attacks on specific categories of targets. Accordingly, in theory, if not always in practice, the rules of war . . . codified in the famous Geneva and Hague Regulations on Warfare of the 1860s, 1899, 1907 and 1949 – not only grant civilian non-combatants immunity from attack, but also: Prohibit taking civilians as hostages; Impose regulations governing the treatment of captured or surrendered soldiers (POWs); Outlaw reprisals against either civilians or POWs; Recognise neutral territory and the rights of citizens of neutral states; and Uphold the inviolability of diplomats and other accredited representatives.

There is no doubt that terrorists' disregard for such boundaries is what contributes to their description as *terrorists*. Groups such as the Basque ETA, the Colombian FARC, Palestine's Hamas or the Sri Lankan Tamil Tigers do not recognize any particular 'guidelines' of war and frequently and purposefully attack non-combatant civilians and military personnel whom at the time of the attack are either unarmed or considered off-duty. Again, the targets of terrorist violence are symbolic ones and terrorism in this way is very impersonal, but not representative of an unambiguous and discriminate form of violence (which in itself may be an unrealistically achievable 'ideal', given the vagaries of conventional warfare). Yet, despite this, there is often a sense of implicit boundaries that may not be breached, especially at a local level.

To reiterate, only democratic state bodies have a mandate by which they are regarded as having legitimacy to develop and engage in war-making strategies. This may of course be a reflection of 'power in numbers': in Ireland the Provisional IRA leadership does not recognize the rights of either the British or Irish governments to pass laws and declare legislation.

Instead the PIRA leadership body, or Army Council, views itself as the direct descendant of the 1918 Dáil Éireann (Irish Government) and as such sees itself as having (although this has not been, and never could be, enforced by the PIRA) the moral right to govern over the island of Ireland as a normal government. At most, the PIRA leadership has simply asserted their entitlement to this right by making reference to higher order revolutionary principles such as 'the rights of the people'. This is a common feature of many terrorist groups.

Linn [27] adds the following to the discussion:

> When compared to terrorism, conventional war has clear norms: there is a neutral territory which is recognised by the fighting forces, the armed forces are identified . . . there is an awareness that the use of armed forces against civilians is exceptional or aberration. In contrast, terrorism is aimed at the destruction of established norms. Unlike guerrilla fighters who are not only breaking the laws of war, who know who is their enemy and attack only the superior combatants, terrorists blur the combatant-non-combatant distinction by saying that 'WAR IS WAR' and that any attempt to define ethical limits to war is futile.

However, as with the distinctions between terrorism and other forms of conflict, including what we term 'guerrilla warfare', there are numerous other 'grey areas' in this debate, not least with regard to defining what properly constitutes a military target. Other obvious questions arise: 'The soldier in the tank is a military target. What about one in a jeep escorting civilian vehicles? Or returning on a bus from leave? A bus that may – and was, when a suicide bomber attacked it in Gaza – be carrying civilians too?'.[28]

And yet further to this, although those seeking to overthrow or destabilize a state or regime may use terrorism, it may also be, and *is*, used by those in control of state power seeking to exercise social control. This may be either over a particular social grouping (a minority), an individual or an element of a foreign power. Terrorism should never be necessarily seen as only violence from 'below', an approach epitomised by early analyses of the phenomenon (state commissioned analyses at that). As a result, describing the differences between legitimate conventional warfare as conducted by a state, and terrorism, may simply be paying lip service to governments. There is no doubt that throughout history, state governments have been responsible for the use of terrorist tactics much more frequently than have the small, anti-state collectives we refer to as the terrorists. It may be a surprising aspect of the discourse on terrorism then that we do not give as much attention to terrorism as employed by states and governments as we do to terrorism by movements such as Islamic Jihad or the Algerian Armed

Islamic Group (GIA). This, however, may be changing and represents a fundamental change in our perception of terrorism, both as a traditionally viewed tool of the underrepresented weak, and as a tool of the strong, and a growing element as a tactic or overall strategy within conventional forms of warfare.

Terrorism defined as psychological warfare?

Thackrah,[29] in attempts to tackle the elusive issue of definition, cites political sociologists as arguing that:

> no definition [of terrorism] in principle can be reached because the very process of definition is in itself part of the wider conflict between ideologies or political objectives . . . The problem is not one of the comprehensiveness or degree of detail of definition, but is one of the framework of the definition.

Thackrah himself argues that the problem of definition is not simply a matter of semantics, but concludes that the 'problem of ascertaining characteristics is vital' both by which 'guidelines are to be established by which social scientists collect and evaluate data on strife incidents' (ibid.) but also by which the problem of terrorism can be tackled by law enforcement. It would seem obvious in light of the White House's discourse throughout the War on Terrorism that a definition of terrorism is for many people now a matter of life or death. Thackrah acknowledges that efforts to combat terrorism based on a *definition* of terrorism will run into difficulty given one characteristic practice of terrorists – that is, to 'produce a terror outcome by threats of violence, *without actual physical injury to any human or non-human target*. Legislative efforts to create a crime of terrorism at the international or state level have to include a definition that *realistically mirrors the terror process*' (ibid., emphasis added).

One way in which terrorism further distinguishes itself from other forms of conflict (and briefly mentioned earlier) is through what we identified earlier as its *psychological* nature. According to Anderson,[30] 'terrorist groups are not living in fear of their host governments. Instead, law-abiding citizens live in fear of terrorists groups'. Anderson cites the example from an American television interview, when a Middle Eastern terrorist leader was quoted as saying, 'we want the people of the United States to feel the terror'. In order to examine this statement further, we must examine yet another aspect of what terrorists do. This is an important theme to explore as the psychological element of terror may begin to help unify those who form increasing numbers of commentators attempting to formulate a definition of terrorism in terms of the *methods* used by the perpetrators of the act as opposed to interpretations of those methods – so often the basis of conflicting views on terrorist ideologies and their 'righteousness', be they small groups of insurgents or large democratic states.

What exactly does it mean that terrorism can be a distinct form of psychological warfare? Again, the wording needs examination because its implications are important. 'Terror' as a clinical term refers to a psychological state of constant dread or fearfulness, associated with an abnormally high level of psycho-physiological arousal. This is central to what terrorists aim to achieve, since after all, while they have some ultimate set of political objectives, it is an immediate goal of most terrorist groups to *cause terror*. In psychological terms, the spread of terror and panic through using violence creates the conditions that may give rise to conditions conducive to political change or upheaval. While we might experience *arousal* from hearing of a terrorist attack (for fear that there may be further attacks, for instance), we will not experience the *terror* that the terrorists seek to achieve unless we are subjected to an attack, and even then, it tends to be of limited duration. Terrorist groups will try to maintain an overall general level of dread, anxiety or uncertainty, all of which amount to *terror* (both in the context of specific events or incidents (by causing an explosion or hostage-taking scenarios), and in the context of protracted *campaigns* of terrorism per se). To do this infrequently is easily possible – bombings, shootings and interpersonal physical attacks all contribute to creating and maintaining a high level of arousal. This can be, and often is, exacerbated by media attention to the event. But to maintain a constant atmosphere of terror is difficult even for the most belligerent of terrorist groups – on reflection, it may be surprising that despite our exposure to terrorist events via the print or television media, our memory of terrorist events appears to recede swiftly.

As argued earlier, that a constant state of dread cannot be maintained forever is illustrated through a slow habituation of the terrorist audience to the situation. For the terrorists, audience 'acclimatization' poses problems, since due to their audience's adaptation to their tactics, their influence diminishes. The question arises for the terrorist therefore as to how this can be countered: how is it possible to maintain this heightened level of anxiety and to *terrorize* effectively?

A small-scale example of the psychological qualities of terrorism and a scheduled pacing of attacks, as adopted by Irish terrorists, was illustrated with a series of shooting attacks in Crossmaglen in Co. Armagh.[31] Ten British soldiers, including Lance Corporal Stephen Restorick, the last British soldier to be killed by the PIRA before the organization's most recent ceasefire (announced in 1997), were killed by what is believed to be a single PIRA sniper. The gunman used a powerful high-velocity rifle, the Barret Light 50, in a traditionally feared area of Northern Ireland, where the PIRA have their strongest support base. Specifically, the area in which the attacks took place has achieved near legendary status in Republican circles, and the actions of the sniper (as well as the sniper himself) have become part of local Republican folklore, with road signs and small murals erected in honour of the sniper to remind any enemy of the Republican movement that they remain uninvited guests. It is a warning that such 'unwelcome visitors' to this area (referred to as 'bandit country' by British security forces) may be shot and killed. As Keane [32] describes:

> Just outside the village of Cullyhanna in South Armagh, IRA sympathisers have erected an extra road sign. With a silhouette of a gunman, the sign declares that there is a sniper at work in the area . . . The South Armagh sniper has become the IRA's most efficient weapon against the security forces and is the basis of a propaganda campaign by the Provos . . . The road sign . . . is one example of the IRA's attempts to undermine the confidence of the security forces. 'A sniper is the worst thing for troops, even worse than mortaring . . . because everybody is wondering if they will be next every time they go out on patrol'.

Taylor and Horgan[33] describe another example by examining events surrounding the war in Bosnia. On one level of course, the Bosnian conflict was never an example of terrorism per se. Certainly from the international community's perspective it was a war, and required the response of large-scale military intervention (e.g. air strikes and the ground deployment of troops). Also, there is no doubt that the governments of states involved saw the conflict in terms of warfare. At another level, however, it seems that the Bosnian example may represent a general example of a form of terrorism, and even a potential future form of terrorism. The citizens of Sarajevo, for example, were subjected by the warring states to what amounts to a series of systematic terrorist attacks which, in its effects, are like those of a sustained terrorist campaign, except on a scale which has never been experienced before. The war in Bosnia was mainly characterized by small-scale individual attacks primarily targeted at civilians. Instead of the familiar car bomb (such as those used by ETA in Spain), the explosions were made through *shelling*, and individual attacks on the civilian population were made through *sniping*. The psychological qualities of this (which in Taylor and Horgan's view makes elements of this conflict examples of terrorism) as it relates to Sarajevo can be illustrated by observations made by aid workers from University College, Cork in Sarajevo. Up to the ceasefire in early 1994, an average of one or two children were killed daily in the city. Of those deaths and injuries sustained by children, 20–25 per cent were the result of bullet wounds, a consequence of sniping. Injury through sniping however, unlike shrapnel injury, is not random. It requires a deliberate act of aiming the weapon. This and other evidence suggest therefore that children were deliberately targeted in this conflict. The reason for this is not because children had some role in the conflict, but presumably because killing them was seen as an effective way of producing fear and despondency amongst the population at large. It could well be argued of course that NATO's intervention in Kosovo in 1999 illustrates the very same point.

The deliberate targeting of children not only illustrates a willingness to broaden the acceptable limits of terrorist violence in order to maintain the overall climate of terror, but also reinforces the message to the audience that *it is worth acceding* to, when faced with either the prolonging of such a campaign of violence, or more chillingly, a possible future escalation of the relentlessness and severity of the violence.

A common belief about why terrorists rarely kill large numbers of people is that either it may be rarely tried, or that attempts at doing so have been foiled by counter-terrorist agencies. Another more potent reason however is that support for the terrorist group may be lost if, and when, the terrorists' objectives seem unreachable, the 'acceptable' or expected limits of the effects of a terrorist campaign are exceeded. A myth about terrorist violence in the popular media is that it is often uncontrolled, frenzied and vicious. While terrorism is often vicious, it is rarely frenzied and uncontrolled, and as Hoffman[34] notes, no terrorist group 'commits actions randomly or senselessly'. The PIRA would have lost substantial support from its own conservative support pool in Ireland and the United Kingdom, its international support from a small number of Irish-Americans, and others, if for example, the organization's rank and file members began shooting the children of British soldiers or members of the British parliament. Certainly it would not have helped its political front, Sinn Fein, to advance Republicanism via the mainstream political process. Circumstances in Bosnia were different in that these same concerns about support did not have the same significance for the individuals involved and their allegiances. Nevertheless, the point remains: adept terrorists will never use terrorism simply as an 'exercise in meaningless horror'.[35] The scale and brutality of a particular attack may obscure political and other dimensions underpinning the strategic considerations of the incident, but they do exist, and we must be aware of them in attempting to make sense of the individual terrorist's behaviour, or the behaviour of the group or movement directly responsible.

The events of 11 September 2001 notwithstanding, similar examples of the escalation of ferocity and the broadening of acceptability of limits come from the Middle East and from a variety of lesser-studied conflicts in Asia. As in the case of the PIRA, specific kinds of tactics used by terror groups are related to the specific kinds of targets the group chooses, their ideology (any reasonably articulated set of beliefs inspiring the group's aims, methods and justifications) and of course their overall strategy. Again, terrorist groups often employ tactics that they are sure of causing terror, if there are no external mitigating factors that might prove detrimental to the sustenance or even survival of the terrorists.

Let us consider one example of a frequently overlooked conflict. In December 1996, a small group of men wearing military uniforms stopped a public bus at a roadblock in Blida province, just south of the Algerian capital Algiers. The apparent leader of the group, a unit of the GIA (the Armed Islamic Group), who was carrying a Kalashnikov assault rifle, boarded the bus and asked the bus driver if there were any 'colleagues' among the passengers. On hearing this, a policeman quickly presented himself by raising his hand and standing up in his seat. The officer approached the uniformed man but was subsequently dragged off the bus by him. To the horror of the bus driver and passengers, the officer had his throat slit, was decapitated, and then, as surviving passengers describe, 'horribly mutilated'.[36] Following the policeman's murder, around forty of the passengers were forced to get out and lie on the ground as their attackers began to kill them one by one. The Algerian newspaper *Liberté* reported that three women, one of whom was pregnant, were also killed. The pregnant woman's 17-year-old daughter also had her throat slit.

In 1992, the first year of Algeria's conflict, rebel attacks were focused on members of the country's security forces, but soon civilians, as in this instance, were increasingly targeted. At first victims usually had relatives among the security forces, but in what diplomats saw as an attempt to defeat 'harsh state censorship', leading Algerian personalities became targets of violence. The killings of these individuals became more difficult to conceal: victims included pop singers, doctors, well-known members of political parties, and nearly sixty journalists or media employees whom the militants accused of 'supporting' the government.[37] The occupants of entire villages have since been massacred.[38] Security forces engaged the 'rebel' group in fighting since the authorities in January 1992 scrapped a general election in which the Islamic Salvation Front (whose military grouping, the GIA, was responsible for attacks such as that described above) had taken a huge lead. Depending on which sources one refers to, at least 60,000 people appear to have since been killed.

Defining terrorism as a type of war and as a tool of war

To advance this discussion, and set the scene for the psychological analysis to follow in later chapters, we urgently need some anchor points. If we agree that terrorism is a label, applied by one group to another, then this poses questions for consideration: what implications does this have for how we might agree on a definition of terrorism? And moreover, for the purposes of a psychology of terrorism, is there any valid purpose in attempting to define a concept whose usage as a derogatory label is often so blatantly recognized? The answer is 'yes'. The confusion surrounding the concept certainly should not be allowed to warrant a discard of it. From the preceding discussions it is clear that terrorism should be seen as an identifiable phenomenon for a number of reasons.

First, and most obviously, the violence committed by groups labelled terrorist is distinguished from 'ordinary' violence because of the political context to the activities and ideology of the perpetrators and (often) to the nature of the victims and the specific victimizing process. Second, there are specific immediate aims of terrorism, such as the psychological aspect of spreading fear. Third, many victims of both state and subversive political terrorism are non-combatant civilians, with no responsibility in any conflict, thereby demonstrating one of the blatant disregards which terrorists have for the stated conventions of conflict. Finally, and a logical next step from these recurring points, can we therefore truly distinguish terrorism from conventional forms of warfare, when as atrocity after atrocity has shown over the years, conventional war and state violence often bears too many similarities to behaviour we label terroristic? This possibly poses most obstacles for conceptual development, but we can address it directly.

Schmid[39] distinguishes between various areas of discourse on the definition of terrorism. The first of these is the academic context, where one would assume we ought to be able to freely discuss terrorism. The second area of discourse is that of the state, whose definitions of terrorism usually appear to be quite vague and deliberately wide to serve the interests of the state if and when necessary: it is easy to argue that this is so because so often this section sees their own sponsored acts of violence as exempt from such judgement. Third, the public arena, which is largely a diluted and focused reflection of media coverage of the event itself, is often susceptible more to the emotional and psychological reactions to the terrorist event as described.

All of these arenas of discourse largely differ from the views expressed by the fourth category, that of the terrorists themselves and their sympathizers, who obviously choose not to be known as terrorists, even in the absence of clearer categories. Schmid reminds us of this last category's constant focus on political ends while their discussions and rhetoric facilitate an avoidance of the particular methods used in terrorism. An example may help to illustrate this. A senior PIRA terrorist gave the present author the following account in an interview conducted in March 1996. When asked: 'what do you think about the word "terrorism"?' he replied:

> I would define terrorism as a mindless act, without any moral conviction or political conviction. Now in a war situation, desperate acts take place, not premeditated, as such right, a bomb going off like Enniskillen and things like that, and innocent people are being killed, a lot of innocent people killed . . . it's . . . the, the Provisional IRA didn't set out . . . I know they didn't set out to kill innocent people, but it happens, like how would, on the other side of

the coin, how would one describe, let's say Dresden, is that, is that legitimate? Whereas if the IRA do a small bomb and kill 8 or 9 people and they, when they kill hundreds of thousands of people, it depends on who presents it, who has the power of the media to present their point of view. Lots of acts that have been put down to the IRA and misrepresented through the media or whatever, portray [it] as if it were a terrorist, a terrorist act. From my own involvement in the Republican movement, I knew that the IRA didn't detonate that bomb in Enniskillen. We can argue the, let's say, whether or not it was right to put the bomb in there in the first place. That is the thing, internally, we would argue, but the intention was to catch the crown forces. That was the intention. Now as it transpired, somebody detonated the bomb, but it wasn't the IRA volunteers. Whether 'twas by a scanner device or somebody else, whatever, the bomb went off anyway. It's, it's irrelevant who detonated it, but the blame was appropriated to the IRA and it was presented as such, d'you know?

This man was a prison inmate during the time of the Enniskillen bombing in 1987, in which 11 old-age pensioners were killed on Remembrance Day. He had been serving a lengthy prison sentence for terrorist offences, and at the time of writing was widely considered to be one of the PIRA's seven-member leadership, the Army Council. He is therefore a member of Schmid's fourth category, and does not appear to hold any qualms about the righteousness of the above act as perpetrated by his colleagues. This man does not, and would never say that he is a 'terrorist', given the negative connotations and expectations that the term conveys. His statement may be seen as arrogant, cold and indifferent to the physical and emotional effects of the bombing on both the survivors of the attack as well as the relatives of the victims. Should what this man terms a mindless act, 'without any moral or political conviction' be referred to as terrorism, and if so what does this suggest to us? Does it mean that such acts of violence he describes are not deserving of the label 'terrorism' (and all the ramifications that it brings with it, in terms of response from law enforcement etc.) when they are *at least* supported by an ideology or issue, however distant from reality they may be? The problem still remains. Who is it that will decide on the *mindlessness* of an act, when this so obviously merely represents yet another subjective evaluation (be it by the President of the United States, the UN Secretary General or somebody else)?

Schmid makes an encouraging step forward here and it is one that enables us to narrow the focus more substantially, while simultaneously allowing us to retain the concept of terrorism as something both valid and useful. He argues that the best definition is one to which most agree and that this should be the starting point: conventional war is so called because, as said above, it is *expected* to employ rules and guidelines during its conduct. The Geneva Conventions and Hague Regulations formally describe these. The exceptions to this in conventional warfare however, as illustrated through probably countless atrocities, sometimes render the concept of terrorism no different, and pedantic distinctions will, upon closer inspection, appear no more than moot points.

Schmid[40] proposes that a narrower definition may help us more than that of a broader one, open to interpretation by many. He recommends that we should seek to always define terrorism in terms of the *methods* used, allowing no room for rhetoric as a measure of legitimacy. By defining terrorism as the 'peacetime equivalent of war crimes', Schmid offers a potential exit from this problem of deciding the righteousness of acts of violence. We can there-fore simultaneously escape the choice between a purely criminal model of terrorism, which highlights the illegal means only, and a war model, which portrays terrorism as the simple (and equally trite) idea of it being a simple continuation of politics by other available means. By suggesting a legal definition as the peacetime equivalent of war crimes, this would in turn move into the arena of discourse, says Schmid, where there is much more international agreement. Although several local and international treaties have been developed in an effort to increase inter-governmental and inter-agency law enforcement responses and resolve against sub-state and state terrorism, there have not been significant successes in the development of truly global legislation on what terrorism is, and who the terrorists are.[41] Nevertheless, such definition of terrorist acts would, according to Schmid,[42] still 'narrow what can rightfully be considered terrorism, but broaden the consensus as to the unpredictability of terrorist methods'.

Thackrah's[43] important essay complements this discussion by restating that the abolition of qualifiers such as 'generally' or 'usually' disallows for the interjection of personal opinion and subjectivity. But if as Schmid advo-cates, we focus on the particular means used by the perpetrators, there may be much more room for international consensus. Even the US Department of State[44] in their Annual Report on terrorism concurred that there has been in modern times (and pre-9/11) a tendency for governments to condemn terrorism absolutely, motive notwithstanding. By focusing on the specific means used in an attack, it will allow us to distinguish between what we now categorize as 'rebels' from 'terrorists', allowing no room for rhetoric of a political or other nature. Thus, when we re-examine the interview segment included above, the PIRA leader's defence of his colleagues with respect to their 'accidental' bombing is left with little strength. Schmid[45] offers the following comprehensive definition of terrorism:

> Terrorism is an anxiety-inspiring method of repeated violent action, employed by (semi) clandestine individual, group, or state actors,

for idiosyncratic, criminal, or political reasons, whereby – in contrast to assassination – the direct targets of violence are not the main targets. The immediate human targets of violence are generally chosen randomly (targets of opportunity) or selectively (representative or symbolic targets) from a target population, and serve as message generators. Threat- and violence-based communication processes between terrorist (organisation), (imperilled) victims, and main targets are used to manipulate the main target (audience(s)), turning it into a target of terror, a target of demands, or a target of attention, depending on whether intimidation, coercion, or propaganda is primarily sought.

This definition encompasses all aspects of the discussion points presented here and taken with the suggestion of terrorism being the peacetime equivalent of war crimes, appears both acceptable and useful as a working dual-sided definition of terrorism, by whomever such acts of violence are committed. We must emphasize that it includes the actions of *states* and *governments* as well as subversive anti-state elements.

However, there is no escaping that Schmid's definition is an academic one, and some would suggest an unpopular one with governments. An important point related to this emerges from the discussion on the use of terror tactics by the warring factions in Bosnia. Taylor and Horgan[46] discussed the probability that terrorist tactics will become increasingly important as an element in the conduct of warfare by states. While to some extent the tactics described in the sniping examples were conditioned by Balkan geography (which for an army, limits the possibility of effective large-scale military interventions), it is because terrorist tactics as a tool are *effective* that the warring factions have adopted them. The second emergent theme, that of the ability to spread fear – a much more diffuse psychological objective – illustrates just how conventional warfare can escalate in its barbarity and produce effects which traditionally have not been explicitly associated with conventional warfare. Taylor and Horgan[47] note:

> The level of violence associated with political conflict seems to be a one-way street, drawing strength from breaching the unacceptable. When violence occurs within a terrorist context [as described in the earlier examples] after a while, what was the unacceptable ceases to be newsworthy, thus ceasing to be effective.

The authors conclude that the attributes of success during such a conflict are not necessarily measured through military objectives, but through *psychological* objectives, and producing anxiety-provoking responses from the conflict audience certainly appears to meet these.

Conclusions

The complex and slippery impression of terrorism is reflected in the substantial problems of definition, the depth of which has only briefly been touched upon in this chapter. A central theme that we will develop in later chapters is the emotional response to the terrorist's actions and how this might shape our view of both the terrorism process itself and those involved in it. It is easy to understand the human nature of the response to terrorism, but this not only affects the process of definition. Moreover, as we shall see later, the emotional response to terrorism is just one of the many problems facing those who wish to study terrorism and terrorist behaviour.

Despite the obvious difficulties, there are grounds for a more positive outlook, especially when a more substantial, meaningful, and above all, *balanced* approach is taken to the process of defining terrorism. While terrorism is an accepted concept, it remains unclear and inconsistent. Depending on where any analysis might start, we might ultimately arrive at very different outcomes, but we must first attempt to work within what frameworks we currently have to the best of our ability. It seems that a useful way of seeing terrorism then is as a conscious, deliberate strategic use of violence against a specific type of target to affect the political climate. By seeing terrorism as a weapon, capable of adoption by a very wide array of both non-state *and* state actors (the latter either as, for instance, part of 'state terrorism', or as a tactic within conventional, 'symmetric' warfare, if such a thing exists any more), we acknowledge that it is not the sole remit of the non-state figure. By acknowledging this we remove part of the mystery surrounding the processes invoked by our thinking about terrorism, and inevitably accept that it is most useful to see terrorism as something that one 'does', as opposed to thinking that the use of terrorism necessarily reflects something (perhaps something 'special') that one 'is'.

Schmid's approach remains the most positive and useful step in this regard, and therefore, we will bear this approach in mind as a good starting point for both the subject area with which the central arguments of this book are concerned, and specifically, the use of the word 'terrorism' in the chapters that are to follow. The next chapter builds on this debate and presents a brief discussion on some further relevant issues aimed at understanding terrorism as a precursor to the psychological analyses to follow.

2

UNDERSTANDING TERRORISM

Introduction

The issue of definition, while in itself able to skew how we subsequently think about the problem of terrorism, is only one of a variety of issues which we need to address. This chapter attempts to broaden the focus on some related issues that affect our understanding of terrorism. Any serious student of terrorism will quickly realize that not only is the labyrinthine issue of definition a major obstacle to broader conceptual development within the area, but that despite this (or perhaps because of it) the extent to which terrorism researchers embrace the perceived need to fully resolve the issue of definition reflects an inefficient use of time and energy. Problems of definition are not exclusive to terrorism, yet the extent to which the issue utterly dominates much of the discourse on terrorism is a strong indictment of theoretical progress in the area and indicates much about our failure to prioritize research issues accordingly.

As briefly touched upon in the previous chapter, whenever we read or hear about a terrorist attack, what is almost always focused on is the *drama* of the event, often at a personal level with emphasis on the scale of destruction and property damage. The total number of people killed or injured, the audacity of the attack, a distant sense of what the perpetrators might be like, and sometimes a sense of personal vulnerability are some of the immediate issues that tend to dominate media coverage, and as a result play a significant role in influencing the broader public perception of both incidents and the conflicts against which they are located. Often, media reports of an event may be coupled with detailed indication of the means by which the attack took place, and perhaps associated with a request from the police or other authorities for help in identifying an individual or vehicle used.

As Xavier Raufer argued in his foreword, we have to look far beyond media accounts of terrorism if we are to attempt to achieve a systematic and informed understanding of it. We know from the previous chapter just how complex the issue of definition can be, but while defining terrorism may be necessary and urgent in a legal sense, attempts to reach an understanding of terrorism, in terms of where it comes from, how it develops, discovering who are 'the terrorists' and so forth, reflect a different set of issues that we often uncritically accept, and sometimes ignore altogether.

Although surveys of the research exist,[1] even within the most dedicated scholarly efforts to understand terrorism, it can be difficult to assess and measure the completeness of our knowledge. This fact is obscured because we rarely appreciate just how much analyses of terrorism tend to mix fact and fiction in various quantities. While terrorism involves callousness, arrogance, barbarity, injury and death, the reality of terrorism in today's world is that political movements around the world that use terrorism, skilfully manipulate events and their media coverage to create for their existing or potential audiences deliberate and often sophisticated impressions and interpretations serving their own particular purposes. The 9/11 attacks and the responses to it illustrate just how the drama and emotion surrounding terrorist violence can affect what should be a systematic, coherent strategy both to prevent future attacks and address the antecedent factors to such operations.

Bizarre as it may seem to the experienced psychologist, the profile of 'the terrorist' as crazed fanatic, hell-bent on mindless destruction for its own sake still exists, with varying degrees of subtlety, within the literature. The normal reality of those who engage in terrorist violence is very different and probably all the more disturbing for it. In fact reality suggests that organized terrorist-directed political violence is usually part of a much more complex set of activities related to the attainment of an identifiable social or political goal, and accordingly what we see or hear about terrorism is always one small (albeit the most public via its dramatic impact) element of a wider and ultimately, more complex array of activities (both in terms of, for instance, a specific incident itself, and its broader political significance). Terrorism may often be well organized, it may be technically adept and it can have sophisticated political ends as many of the larger and well-known movements such as the Palestinian Islamic Jihad, the Provisional IRA and Al Qaeda have, but a major lesson we still fail to grasp is that it is wrong for us to uncritically attribute such qualities to all terrorist groups at all times. This is an important theme in analyses of terrorism that relate both to pure and applied research especially, as well as policy concerns which might relate to some form of threat assessment and the management of the security problems posed by terrorist groups. Particularly since 9/11, amid the paranoia fuelled by confused local, national and international responses to terrorism, the capacity and potency of Al Qaeda have been severely overestimated, and remain misrepresented in the mainstream media. Like all terrorist groups, their behaviour is bound by tactical, strategic and even psychological considerations (despite the scale of its attacks), and like all terrorist groups, they have significant weaknesses and overestimated opinions of their own capacity. The sustained success of any terrorist group can often be, we must acknowledge, a reflection of poor intelligence, uninformed or un-coordinated law enforcement, and poorly directed counter-terrorism policies more broadly.

We can assert then, which may be obvious to some, that the capacities, abilities and presumed intentions of terrorist organizations, as well as what terrorism can and does realistically achieve (indeed what perhaps it should be allowed to achieve) should neither be over- nor underestimated, but examined critically using what intellectual, conceptual and other tools we have at our disposal. Unfortunately, however, while the subject of terrorism continues to be described as a typically 'complex, multidisciplinary issue', arrival at a non-political, objective analysis of this problem was a rare enough phenomenon prior to 9/11, and today seems further from our grasp than ever before. Indeed as two respected commentators on terrorism and political violence have stated in one of the most frequently cited comments from the literature:[2] 'there are probably few areas in the social science literature in which so much is written on the basis of so little research. Perhaps as much as 80 per cent of the literature is not research-based in any rigorous sense; indeed it is often narrative, condemnatory and prescriptive'. Despite the fact that Schmid and Jongman's comment is now over 16 years old, it remains an accurate depiction of the state of terrorism research.

The nature and extent of terrorism research

Before we can develop a sense of where we should be going then, we might usefully consider where we have come from. David Rapoport,[3] one of the foremost scholars in terrorism research, recalled an early teaching experience from his career. He described preparing in 1969 for a series of lectures on terrorism and assassination he would later deliver. Rapoport's efforts were fruitless, with him finding only a handful of items in his search. He then compared this experience with 17 years later discovering a terrorism bibliography that contained over 5,000 items in English alone. In 1992, Cairns and Wilson[4] described an enormous bibliography with a listing of over 3,000 references to work based solely on the Northern Ireland conflict. Rapoport rhetorically asked: 'has any academic enterprise ever grown so much in so short a time?' Thackrah[5] added that the scholarly community itself has been seduced by the violence associated with terrorism, and consequently 'rushed into print almost as fast as the journalists, fashioning typologies, defining, explaining and usually prescribing' (ibid., p. 26). Shortly after, Miller[6] was more direct in his sentiments:

> In an apparent effort to compensate for this intellectual shortfall, the literature of terrorism has exploded. Journalists, social scientists, of every subfield, and historians, of every era, have brought their resources to the subject. Philosophers have seriously entertained

the issue of the morality of terrorism, and psychologists have pondered the terrorist's mindset. Policy specialists have reflected on their 'hands on' experiences dealing with terrorist events. Former hostages, as if anointed by their personal trauma, have become instant experts, undaunted by disciplinary boundaries, on every facet of the subject.

The sheer volume of material being produced, however, did not mask its questionable nature. The results were exposed as ranging from the 'theoretically mindless' to 'arcane intellectual pieces where issues of definition and the press to create theory have driven even the sophisticated reader to despair'.[7] Miller's damning, but accurate, comments were published in the very first issue of the principal academic journal in the field, *Terrorism and Political Violence*, and served as a stern warning to future contributors. In 2004, however, 15 years on from Miller's statement, his sentiments remains equally as relevant and valid today.[8]

Of course, it is easy to agree with Thackrah that the enthusiasm with which this difficult subject has been met is a reflection of the dramatic qualities of terrorism. This seems a fair statement to make, but an exceptional problem with terrorism research is the inability (or perhaps unwillingness) to build on previous research and offer an informed commentary on terrorism that reflects both clear perspective and knowledgeable experience. Calls for interdisciplinary theory-building then appear almost moot. Despite the warnings, terrorism is not the most difficult or threatening problem in our world, yet often the sources from which we might expect the most balanced commentary themselves mirror the intense personalization of the drama surrounding successful terrorist attacks.

Another feature of commentaries on terrorism is that the better analyses are dominated by a small few. This is not only of course a reflection of the enormous and valuable contribution of some scholars, but it is indicative of pressing problems within the terrorism research community. In 1986, at the University of Aberdeen, an international research conference on terrorism produced what is still a cornerstone text within terrorism studies. In co-editing (with Alisdair Stewart) *Contemporary Research on Terrorism*,[9] Paul Wilkinson's foreword to the proceedings addressed a series of 'myths' (Wilkinson's own description) he suggested were typical of perceptions about the progress of terrorism research and those undertaking it. The reality of terrorism research at the time, Wilkinson captures as:

> small-scale, and even peripheral, in most universities and research institutes. Apart from the research groups working in a few well-known major centres . . . most scholars working in this field are working alone, or at most with one or two colleagues in a larger academic institution.

Wilkinson emphasized that much of the important and groundbreaking terrorism research was being financed on 'shoestring' budgets, successfully conducted and finished only due to the interest and perseverance of individual researchers, in tandem with their tendency to 'fund their terrorism research on the back of other projects'.

The situation concerning relevant doctoral research at universities was no more promising. In an analysis of terrorism-related dissertations conducted between 1960 and 1997, Avishag Gordon[10] found that a total of only 278 theses (MA and PhD) on the subject were produced. Over 40 per cent of these were by students of political science, representing the largest single category. At best, the statistics are discouraging, but at worst, they are dismal. Gordon discovered that the number of psychology theses on terrorism produced in that same 37-year period was only *seven*. While Gordon's search included only English language theses, that only seven psychology dissertations have been produced in this period raises serious concerns about how little the area appears to be fostered as a speciality within this particular discipline.

Theoretical issues in the study of terrorism

We have seen in Chapter 1 that terrorism as a tactic can be employed by a variety of actors, operating at various levels and fringes of the political process. The failure to appreciate all but partial aspects of terrorism as a tactic illustrates one of several major theoretical pitfalls inherent in the study of terrorism. Ronald Crelinsten[11] made the case succinctly when he categorized research efforts as focusing on:

> (a) a *truncated object of study*, which reflects (b) a *skewed focus of the researcher*, which stems from (c) a *narrow policy orientation on prevention and control*, which yields (d) *narrow conceptual frameworks* which ignore the political dimension of terrorism, and (e) *ahistorical, linear, causal models* which ignore the historical and comparative aspects of terrorism and focus selectively on individual actors, their characteristics, their tactics, and their stated ideologies.

The skewed focus of researchers reflects not just a definitional issue, but also reflects substantial confusion around the issue of the *identification* of the terrorist – another problem, in other words, is not so much captured by the question 'what is terrorism?' but 'what is a terrorist?' This has been a major stumbling block in psychological analyses. Let us consider some examples to illustrate. If we asked someone what they thought constituted a terrorist act, most would include some reference to violence, but would also offer something more specific, perhaps a reference to bombings, or hostage taking involving the hijacking of aircraft. However, because of a limited focus on only one aspect of what terrorist organizations do, we overlook the impressive variety of activity and function: in some ways it might seem odd to refer to Hamas as a 'terrorist organization', when conducting acts of terrorism is in reality just one (albeit the most public) of many social, political and community-based activities and veritable services the movement engages in and provides. The problem becomes clear in other ways when we look *within* a movement to which we may have already decided to ascribe the label 'terrorist'. Were Provisional IRA hunger-strikers deserving of the label 'terrorist' for instance? In this case, and although the hunger-striker may well have been originally imprisoned for involvement in terrorist activities, the person to die is the hunger-striker him- or herself. Perhaps the label of terrorist is not generic enough to warrant a description of all those people involved in political violence. It is in such a context that the term political violence has been suggested by researchers as a more generic term,[12] however, bearing in mind Heskin's earlier comments (in Chapter 1) about assumptions of sympathy which may be implicit in the term (just as assumptions of condemnation and derogation are implicit in the word 'terrorism'), this might not be so useful as originally thought.

Examples of the problem of identification are abundant. In the United States, in April 1986, the University of South Florida launched an independent investigation of one of its associate professors claiming that he had used a studies group to funnel terrorists into the United States. According to the FBI, the professor had arranged for entry visas for two Palestinian terrorist leaders, Ramadan Abdullah Shallah and Basheer Nafi, to enter the country under the guise of being professors. Shallah became the new leader of the Islamic Jihad movement in Syria in 1995 after its former leader, Fathi Shqaqi, was dramatically assassinated in Malta for his role in the organization of a string of devastating suicidal terrorist attacks on Israeli targets. Should the University of South Florida professor be justifiably referred to as a 'terrorist'? He may not have been involved in any terrorist crimes, but his assistance to the Islamic Jihad organization could have been of great importance to the movement.

An issue related to identification problems concerns how terrorism differs in one of several respects from so-called 'ordinary' crime. Given that publicity is a core objective of terrorist violence, we might expect the perpetrators of terrorist crimes to always claim credit for their actions.[13] This is not always the case, however, and in Northern Ireland for example, various paramilitary groups have not claimed responsibility for some of their acts. The Provisional IRA has used several cover names, not so much in order to distance itself from specific crimes (as the movement generally does claim responsibility for what it does, as Sinn Fein president Gerry Adams pointed out 'when it was in many ways unpopular')[14] but perhaps where strategic benefits arise from the use of such a 'name' (or rather the lack of the name 'Provisional IRA'). An example of this includes the pseudonym 'Direct Action Against

Drugs', who claimed responsibility for killing 13 alleged drug dealers during the PIRA's 1994–1996 ceasefire. There are, upon closer analysis, reasons relating to organizational change and development which illustrate such practices, but it is perhaps worth examining in detail (as we will do later) some activities that while in themselves not constituting 'terrorism' per se (nor would the individuals responsible probably be described as 'terrorists'), whose role and function is central to the effective running of the terrorist organization in question.

The problem of identification can also be extended to one of inadvertent isolation of the subject we are studying. As Crelinsten warned, a sole focus on what we term the 'terrorist' enables us only to see one actor within what is in reality a much larger social grouping (a) not only from which this individual emerges, as has been explained but (b) from which the 'terrorist' claims much of his or her legitimacy for terrorist behaviour. It is in this respect that White[15] encourages researchers to extend more systematically the focus of their research to the opponents of the terrorist, 'especially if they are government actors'. In the context of research in Northern Ireland, and in an attempt to address the question 'why' people engaged in terrorism in Northern Ireland in the early 1970s, the need to combine a variety of methods within the study of terrorism is especially necessary. White[16] asks us to consider the following:

> Following the introduction of internment in 1971 in Northern Ireland, and then Bloody Sunday in Derry in 1972, IRA activity greatly increased. State violence in Northern Ireland produced an increase in anti-state violence by the Provisional Irish Republican Army. This is easily documented with quantitative evidence . . . What the quantitative evidence will not tell us, however, is why the state violence led to more anti-state violence. One possibility, consistent in some respects with traditional explanations of involvement in non-routine political activity, is that in Northern Ireland the advent of large scale state violence brought about a breakdown in the social conditions that typically integrate people into liberal democracy. Cut loose from their moorings, people then engaged in non-routine, non-instrumental, behaviour, i.e. small-group violence by the Provisional IRA . . . Another explanation, and in many ways this is consistent with the breakdown argument, is that state violence made its victims angry and they sought to lash out, or hit back . . . An alternative explanation, from a political process theoretical perspective, is that those who engaged in violence after internment and Bloody Sunday were motivated by political considerations. From this perspective, state violence confirmed for the state's victims the illegitimacy of the state.

The implications associated with each theoretical perspective presented here are important. Are, asks White, these protesters to be seen as 'irrational', 'alienated', 'frustrated' beings acting upon their exclusion from the previously existing liberal democratic conditions which existed in Northern Ireland? Or, he asks, are they to be seen as 'calculating political actors who, with reason, question the assumptions of liberal democracy and respond, understandably, to delegitimated state violence with their own violence'. The implications of these different perspectives are not just as White notes, political, but on a conceptual basis pose many issues for research efforts and the formulation of research agendas (which admittedly, may ultimately inform a political response).

Understanding the nature and heterogeneity of terrorism

An issue raised by White's concern relates to identifying how we should be studying terrorism. By focusing (deliberately or otherwise) only on selective features of terrorism, we might be misled into assuming the dominant relevance of one particular discipline, be it security studies, history, theology, psychology, sociology, political science or something else. Certainly, the diversity of motivation and purpose across those groups who employ terrorist tactics can be overwhelming and confusing, especially when we engage in attempts at categorization. Terrorist groups vary greatly not just in terms of their diverse motivations, but also in size, capacity, resources, as well as in national composition and cultural background.[17] While many of the late twentieth century's terrorist groups ranged in their ideologies from the religious to the overtly political, from the extreme right to the extreme left, terrorist groups also vary in terms of organizational structure, and hence may differ across issues to do with decision-making and targeting (and how influences on these may be brought to bear on the group), weapons used, other tactics, and so on. Understanding Irish terrorism for instance requires an appreciation not only of contemporary politics, but also an appreciation of the real (and mythological) historical dimension to Irish rebellion. Indeed, perhaps no further reminder that to study the history of terrorism should not be anything less than a *requirement* for understanding terrorism can be seen from a statement issued by the PIRA in 1970 in Dublin. In an attempt to prepare the world for the emergence of the PIRA as a fighting force, the statement, entitled 'Where Sinn Fein Stands', had in its opening lines: 'We take our inspiration from the past'.[18]

Indeed, sometimes it is the case that opinions about the relevance of particular academic disciplines to the study of terrorism are rather obviously reflected in the formation of certain typologies and classification systems. Psychologist Ariel Merari,[19] in developing an early typology of terrorist groups based on their target population and bases of operation, writes:

Typological attempts to bring order to this chaos have mostly centred on group ideology (e.g. distinguishing between rightist and leftist organizations), on group purpose or raison d'être (e.g. separation from a mother state, independence from a foreign rule, domestic revolution) and on psychological motives.

From the outset then, and regardless of how we study terrorism, and from whatever perspective, we must acknowledge and accept that it can be an extremely *heterogeneous* phenomenon, ever-changing, and as a *tactic* open to newer types of movements with every passing decade. The US Department of State, in its 1996 Patterns of Global Terrorism Report,[20] in acknowledging this heterogeneity, conceded that identifying clear patterns in terrorism is 'becoming more difficult' (as we shall see in later chapters however, there is much confusion about what 'patterns' we ought to be searching for, a problem that has utterly plagued theoretical progression in psychological analyses of terrorism).

Given this, and often rather implicit in recognizing the heterogeneity, even *within* specific terrorist groups across time, for instance, is the absolute centrality of context. Cooper[21] argues that we can never attempt to treat terrorism as a discrete subject, somehow distinct or outside of the political, social and economic context in which it occurs. It is, he states, a 'creature of its own time and place'. If the Cold War provided us with a readily understood context to 'older', more limited and predictable forms of terrorism (primarily ideological in character), many of today's groups represent exceptionally more complex entities, some of whose tangled and seemingly inconsistent motivations are rooted not only in the changed context to the conflicts which have arisen from the former Soviet Union, but perhaps also from the thorough undermining of traditional political ideologies as a whole as powerful motivating factors in human affairs. In particular, the increase in organized crime and terrorism throughout what Raufer[22] describes as 'deterritorialized' areas has contributed to what he terms 'grey areas', a concept similar to Lacqueur's perspectives of the blurring of boundaries between politically motivated violence and organized criminal groups. That is not to suggest that political terrorism as we have known up to the beginning of what we now term 'the post-Cold War era' is well and truly at an end, but that some forms of political ideologically motivated terrorism clearly cannot be understood with reference to the same political and social context from whence their assumed predecessor came. Indeed, this significantly includes, two movements with the longest running contemporary terrorist campaigns – the PIRA and ETA.

In seeking answers to the problem of terrorism in the post-9/11 era, not only is the sheer number of 'terrorism experts' impressive, but the diversity of their backgrounds has been matched only by the complexity of the subject matter. Psychologists, anthropologists, historians, security analysts, military strategists, journalists, international relations experts, religious experts and others form the entourage. On one level, it must be said, this diversity is not only positive, but we should perhaps encourage efforts to consider it necessary. In Reich's[23] collection of psychological essays on terrorism, he not only stressed the psychological complexity of terrorism, but emphasized the need to consider the diversity and complexity of terrorism from a variety of disciplinary perspectives. Attempts to understand terrorism from one exclusive view, Reich asserted, may press the power of that explanation beyond its valid limits. There may well be a danger in this, and in any study of terrorism we need to draw on knowledge from a range of areas. Equally, however, we need some conceptual anchor points because without intellectual starting points we may find ourselves with other problems, becoming so absorbed by the complexity of conflicting explanations that we fail to see common themes, or more importantly, fail to focus on more practical objectives. The latter has been one obvious casualty of the efforts aimed at resolving the definition issue.

Psychology and terrorism

Given both the heterogeneity and complexity of terrorism, and Reich's cautionary note above, attempts to develop a psychology of terrorism alone might on the one hand therefore seem insurmountable, if not altogether pointless. However, Grant Wardlaw[24] once argued that despite the cross-disciplinary appeal of terrorism, probably the most commonly asked question regarding subversive political violence is 'why do people become terrorists?', a question that would seem to raise obvious psychological issues.

In the weeks following the 9/11 attacks Wardlaw's argument was reflected in particular in the question 'how could they do it?' Few of the experts asked to explain the psychology of the perpetrators were probably completely honest in their replies. Whether Wardlaw was right about it being the most commonly asked question (at least about it being the most *explicitly* asked anyway) is probably open to debate, but the obvious lack of clarity in many responses was embarrassing, indicative of how little psychology has made an impact in answering questions about terrorism. Psychologists and psychiatrists were repeatedly bombarded with the same questions, and rather than admit defeat, tackled their audiences with vague references to terrorist personality traits, obscure psychological processes which are outdated and imprecise within contemporary psychology, as well as equally imprecise references to broad social processes that were so general as to be pointlessly vague. Only a handful of more seasoned scholars were willing to admit the inescapable fact that, to paraphrase Jerrold Post's[25] celebrated comment, we are still 'primitive' in understanding the psychology of terrorism.

One of the core starting points for the analysis that develops later in this book is that any form of behaviour, terrorist or otherwise, exists within a social and political context, but terrorist behaviour (like criminal behaviour) refers to activities that belong to an environmental context which gives rise to, sustains, directs and controls it largely in the same fashion as any other behaviour. We can never separate terrorism from society because it is embedded in it. Given this, its appropriateness, or otherwise, with respect to some political or distant ideological or religious aspiration is not primarily at issue when we try to 'understand' it. This might appear as common sense to a social scientist, but it must be emphasized.

To many, a psychological approach to terrorism might suggest some sort of 'profiling' of terrorists in the same way as fictional representations of offender profiling portray the psychologist as bordering on having some psychic link with the offender which, when tied to some inexplicably accurate interpretation of crime scene evidence, and often coupled with inter-views with the offender's friends or family, eventually leads the police to a portrait of their suspect. The point may appear flippant, but as we will see in Chapter 3, psychological profiles of terrorists have often been based on much less. In any event, most 'profiles' (the word profile is in quotation marks because of the wildly differing views both within and between aca-demia *and* law enforcement as to what profiling actually means to them) are usually led to considering terrorists' individual personalities. This has long been an attractive option for researchers in the 30 years of research so far, and it is easy to understand why. After all, when confronted with the immediate results of terrorist activities, and whether we are psychologists or not, our tendency to focus on the drama surrounding extreme violence inevitably and intuitively leads us into explaining that behaviour with specific attribution to the person responsible. Even at that, we are usually presented with sanitized accounts of the physical destruction of terrorism; if we were to face the reality of a bombing, there is scarcely a person who would not almost certainly be forgiven for assuming that the specific person responsible for it is in some way 'special' or 'abnormal'. This in turn suggests, logically, that the terrorist is perhaps different to the rest of us, and perhaps easier to pick out from the crowd.

Alternatively it might appear relevant to direct the focus to terrorist leaders. After all, terrorist activity requires some leadership function to exist, and within even relatively small size terrorist groups there is diversifi-cation of function to the extent that there are people who are responsible for management functions. These are the people with the wherewithal to identify recruits with potential from the rest, identifying those who can be relied upon for suicide missions or not. If we consider the role of the Provisional IRA leadership in Northern Ireland, we know that despite the numbers of active PIRA members who have come and gone throughout the movement's history, the leadership core has largely remained intact.

It might seem reasonable then to consider if there are special 'leadership' qualities in those individuals.

In addition, a particular feature of terrorism that has implications for psychological theory is that it is undeniably a group process. We might consider what the group dynamics were that bonded the 9/11 hijackers together before and during the air hijackings. It has been widely suggested, and seemingly corroborated by Osama Bin Laden himself, that not all of the hijackers were aware of their impending deaths: we might then need to consider what group dynamics would have been important or necessary for the cell leader to maximize psychological cohesion and mutual solidarity in the face of self-doubt, wavering commitment or a partial lack of focus during the stressful events on the aircraft? It has been suggested that shared rituals (e.g. prayer and other normalizing activity) may have been an important feature of the hijackers' collective behaviour before and during the attacks. Evidence from other terrorist groups suggests that such activity can enhance group solidarity and shield individual members from considering alternative courses of action, at various levels and degrees of both participation in terrorist events, as well as in the terrorist group more generally.

Broader questions we might consider still relating to group processes might encompass what the group dynamics are that encourage people to join, remain in, and perhaps (if still alive), eventually leave terrorist organizations, while a higher-level perspective again would encompass the organizational level of analysis: we might ask what happens to the organization as a whole when the leadership of a movement declares a ceasefire? And to develop this point, we could not truly appreciate the Provisional IRA's decision to decommission some of its weapons (a move posing significant organizational difficulties) without assessing the national and international climate and context that preceded Sinn Fein's announcement. The announcement did not appear to stem from local issues: to many non-Republicans, the decommissioning announcement offered proof that not only did international events overshadow the mighty PIRA's self-importance and unwavering demand for parity of political esteem in the continued absence of decommissioning, it illustrated more obviously that Sinn Fein and the PIRA do respond to international pressures.

While we face obvious challenges relating to what our subject matter is supposed to be and then what level of analysis we might consider appropriate, we face equally challenging questions about how we might go about answering those questions. The type of terrorist or terrorist campaign we think we are able to identify may determine not only what level of analysis we adopt, but also what methods are open to us: how can we gather valid and reliable data to help us understand the psychology of the suicide bomber for instance? We might approach their families for interviews, to try to build a picture of what they were like, and to get a sense of whether any similarities exist across cases through comparative analysis. But difficulties arise when we try to ascertain the reliability of the data collected. In basic psychological terms, we rarely see ourselves as others see us, and so, secondary sources (even family members) may not provide us with the observational data we need to inform our theories. The apparent leader of the 9/11 hijack team, Mohammad Atta, has since had his background extensively investigated. His middle-class parents were interviewed in Egypt, his schoolmates and acquaintances were interviewed, and his German employers in Hamburg were interviewed. None of them suggested signs of depression or any other form of psychopathology. Whereas such findings might well be used to support broader arguments about, say, whether or not terrorists are necessarily psychopathological, there is another type of confusion about what can truly be derived from such statements, and what the nature of the data is that we might extract in an attempt to build some form of process that characterized the development of Atta's commitment to political terrorism. Data collected from families, enemies, diaries and autobiographies are obvious examples of public accounts. 'Private' accounts are more difficult to come by, but ultimately may shed more light on any psychopathological issues of relevance or usefulness to constructing a psychological analysis, despite their obvious incompleteness. We return to this inescapable limitation in a later chapter and offer some solutions.

Methods, sources, avenues

There is a more basic issue to do with not only how we identify terrorism from any particular perspective, but with how we actually collect our data, from which we can subsequently build theories. This is a special problem for psychological analyses because to say that terrorism does not easily lend itself to investigation by traditional methods is a considerable understatement.

For some time, interesting insights into terrorist behaviour have been gained from autobiographical 'terrorist memoirs'.[26] One of the best known of these has been written by Michael Baumann[27] of the West German 2nd June Movement, a Red Army Faction offshoot (the same movement of which Hans Joachin Klein was a member). Sean MacStiofáin,[28] former Chief of Staff of the PIRA, Maria Maguire,[29] another former PIRA member, and Leila Khaled[30] of the Palestine Liberation Organization (PLO) added to the early accounts that were produced. More recent examples of Irish memoirs included books by PIRA double agents Martin McGartland,[31] Eamon Collins,[32] Raymond Gilmour,[33] and Sean O'Callaghan,[34] some of whom have briefly become high profile media figures. One of the most frequently cited primary sources based on the writing of terrorists themselves comes from Carlos Marighella, author of the *Minimanual of the Urban Guerrilla*, for initial use by Brazilian terrorists, but as Mallin[35] noted, its 'instructional contexts [became] valid for guerrillas in any city in the world'.

Pluchinsky[36] was one of the first to identify a similarly important outlet via '[terrorist] communiqués claiming responsibility for a particular attack, strategic pronouncements, and internal circulars', but Rapoport[37] points out that, traditionally, such materials have rather surprisingly not drawn much attention at all. The point has been considered by Crenshaw,[38] who, although corroborating Rapoport's statement on the value of these sources by enthusing that analyses of such accounts (especially autobiographical sources) 'can reveal patterns in individual backgrounds and experiences', argues that the true value of this kind of material will remain questionable. The Sinn Fein President Gerry Adams wrote in the preface of his auto-biography that: 'the participants in any conflict cannot tell the entire story until some time after that conflict is fully resolved'.[39] Indeed Adams received quite a stinging amount of criticism from Irish media sources for producing little more than a book of propaganda material for the PIRA and Sinn Fein. Irish historian and political commentator Fintan O'Toole,[40] in a review of Adams' book, describes it as 'a deliberate blurring of fact and fiction – harsh reality can only be captured in a net of inventions'. Another reviewer tells us: 'The IRA dominates Adams's life, but we learn nothing of his dealings with them'.[41]

Such comments do raise questions about the usefulness of such sources at all, but in any case, books of this kind will remain a limited source of information as few choose to engage in this kind of activity on the whole. Many (including O'Callaghan, McGartland, Gilmour and Baumann) are still in hiding, fearing retribution and/or capture from former comrades and security forces. Eamon Collins, whose memoirs became highly publicized, became known himself as an outspoken PIRA 'dissident' through various print, radio and television media sources. Collins was murdered in February 1999 by former PIRA colleagues based in south Armagh – the PIRA having admitted to a previous attempt on his life.

Some stark exceptions to the much safer path of non-publicity abound however, and perhaps many former terrorists believe that there is some comfort to be taken in self-publicity as a form of protection against possible endangerment. Ali Nejad, the only surviving terrorist from the infamous siege in 1980 of the Iranian Embassy in London, is said to haven given regular 'consultations' to counter-terrorist personnel from his jail cell.[42] Many other former terrorists however, not serving prison sentences, do not appear to share the fears as explained by Kellen, instead participating as, for example, keynote speakers and participants in conferences on terrorism and political violence. Like Collins did before his murder, former PIRA member Sean O'Callaghan speaks regularly to television and newspaper journalists. In any event the true significance of terrorist autobiographies is unrealized by psychology researchers. Far less important is the search for some sort of 'truth' or validation of accounts, than what Crenshaw suggests as the more promising possibility of identifying common themes and structures in the accounts given.

Primary research

One final issue that we need to identify at this point relates to the scarcity of primary, first-hand research on terrorism. Given the attractiveness of such open source material with which one may study terrorism, as Crenshaw[43] warned, there is a worrying tendency for the 'favourite method' of social scientists to come first, when systematically devised research should first identify 'the puzzle'.[44] This has been one of the most significant problems that has bedevilled psychological approaches to understanding why people become terrorists. What psychological theorizing does exist on terrorism is frequently built on unreliable, invalid and unverifiable data, frequently due to a lack of efforts to 'go native'.

Only to an exceptionally limited degree have a small number of social scientists, including psychologists, conducted primary research to gather reliable data on convicted and/or active terrorists (or those suspected of being active). There are numerous reasons for this, and some may seem obvious. For instance, aside altogether from the seemingly impossible access to terrorist organizations, researchers are actually afforded quite little privately held sensitive information by official sources. Governments and their intelligence agencies do not permit access to records and information regarding individuals whose activities have landed them in legally punishable circumstances.[45] Thus, the reliability of what little information is actually made available to the student is highly questionable.

Other reasons for the lack of systematic research by psychologists and other social scientists relate to a lack of field research. This involves speaking to terrorists, and only recently have researchers begun to explore this possibility in a systematic way. If the truth be told, regardless of accessibility to and availability of material including the most excellent of open quantitative resources, and perhaps even regardless of real intelligence data being made available to the terrorism researcher, it remains inevitable that if one is to study terrorism and terrorists effectively from criminological and psychological perspectives, one *must* meet with and speak to individuals who are, or who have been directly involved with a terrorist organization. Unfortunately, research from this approach remains extremely limited. While it is not difficult to understand an academic's reluctance to enter into an area of research in which the possibility of self-endangerment is a real concern, the need for data to be collected in this way is crucial. White[46] produced a list of researchers who have done this:

> J. Bowyer Bell's (e.g. 1979, 1993), Frank Burton's (1978), and Jeffrey Sluka's (1989) work on Irish Republicans, and Steve Bruce's (1992),

and Sarah Nelson's (1984) work on Protestant Paramilitaries. Donatella della Porta's (1992; 1995) work on violence in Italy . . . Each of these authors interviewed current or former active violent activists.

Absent from this list are Jamieson[47] for her work with Italian Red Brigade 'leaders' and 'followers', and Taylor[48] for research on Loyalist terrorist organizations in Northern Ireland, Islamic fundamentalist groups in the Middle East, and Italian terrorist movements. Taylor is the only psychologist in this group that includes political scientists, political sociologists, a journalist and an anthropologist. White is correct in one respect however – the benefits of such interviews are potentially enormous. Furthermore, and in support of another view of White, this is not to suggest that these researchers ever become involved in actual *terrorism* in the advance of their research question – this would clearly exceed the boundaries of what ethical, moral and legal restraints exist to restrain researchers. It may appear redundant to make such a point, but White[49] himself described how respected scholar Joe Bowyer-Bell was present while PIRA bombs were being prepared by the organization. Such activities must surely call into question the moral and legal ethics of those who engage with terrorists in such a way. Bowyer-Bell could be suspected of therefore either (in)directly telling the PIRA that he supports them and their practices, or one might argue that he is not being direct about his (implicit) objectivity.

According to Alex Schmid,[50] universities should 'offer an intellectual forum where scholars can discuss terrorism without being suspected of sympathising with terrorists'. His comment underlines some of the very genuine concerns that arise for academics that participate (or wish to participate) in terrorism research. Kellen[51] emphasizes that to gain a fuller understanding of the terrorist and his actions, it may be necessary to listen to what they are saying, 'no matter how criminal or absurd [these motivations] seem'. If according to Kellen, a psychiatrist, we paid attention to terrorists' communications as carefully as mental health professionals listen to clients, the advantages should become apparent. He outlines several reasons for this reluctance 'to listen'. One is a belief that there is little we can do about the problem of terrorism unless we are in a position to stop such actions through counter-terrorism measures. Kellen also suggests that academics harbour fears of appearing 'too objective' in the face of an issue carrying much emotional and psychological baggage: after all, why should we not condemn terrorists outright?

Lacqueur[52] gives an altogether more critical view of academic terrorism researchers, having once described, among others, psychiatrists as the 'next-best friends' of the terrorist; that they are the 'men and women of goodwill [who] think they know more than others about the mysteries of the human soul and that they have the compassion required for understanding the feelings of "desperate men"'. Kellen's more considerate concerns aside however, a reluctance to study terrorists may instantly appear quite obvious: not only are terrorist organizations illegal and evidently dangerous, they must also be secretive, and protective of that secrecy.

One way in which terrorists recognize the utility of academic work is very insightful into the sometimes elaborate and sophisticated levels of organization and functioning that terrorists can reach. The Official IRA, an IRA splinter group from the late 1960s and early 1970s (and which largely fizzled out in the 1980s) produced one of the most sophisticated training manuals ever developed by any terrorist movement. Entitled *A Reporter's Guide to Ireland*,[53] its opening section instructed regional intelligence officers to read, among others, the books of Professor Richard Clutterbuck:

> While it is true to say that there have been some improvements in the general position of the department, the full information potential of the *entire movement* plus our supporters and contacts, is still not being fully exploited. Every Command I.O. will have to realise that he or she be aware of the identity and occupation of each and every member (and prospective recruit) so that a more scientific approach towards fulfilling our needs can be employed; it will be his duty too to ensure that each I.O. under his command I.O. should read and study the works of the new counter revolutionary strategists, such as Clutterbuck, Carver, and Kitson, to mention but a few.

Richard Clutterbuck, described by the OIRA Director of Intelligence as a counter-revolutionary strategist, was to most students of terrorism research a long time prolific and well-respected author and researcher of terrorist activities. Similarly, on page 21 of the PIRA's Green Book (its internal training manual and general 'guide' for the PIRA's 'Volunteers' or members),[54] the PIRA list Bowyer-Bell's[55] 'The Secret Army' as one of the recommended reading as part of the PIRA recruit's 'frame of reference' (page 11) for learning about Irish Republican history.

There are no conventional procedures in undertaking interviews with terrorists.[56] The reports from what few academics have been involved in this line of research vary considerably. Mallin (cited in Heskin),[57] who interviewed some new PIRA recruits in the 1970s, reported interviews as 'virtually unavailable' while Taylor and Quayle[58] surprisingly state that such activity is 'generally speaking, not too difficult'. Bowyer-Bell,[59] although having been granted access to PIRA members by the PIRA leadership itself (for the purposes of writing the PIRA's 'history'), states that 'access is easier than most assume'. However, unqualified optimism by such authors aside, the consensus emerges that interviews are quite sparse, and it also seems that more often than not, it may be some more 'unconventional' elements such as personal contacts that may facilitate access to such interviews. Brief perusal of the 'Acknowledgements' page in works on terrorism quickly reveals the quantity and quality of the contacts of an author, possibly working in areas including government, law enforcement, journalism, academia and not least members of various paramilitary organizations themselves.[60]

It is highly unlikely that an academic researcher of terrorism, upon deciding to 'go native', will already know members of a paramilitary organization. That is, of course, assuming that a researcher does not come from an area such as west Belfast, or another geographical area in which even rudimentary knowledge of paramilitary figures is difficult to avoid, if only through local gossip and media attention. There is much credibility in the OIRA's *Reporter's Guide to Ireland*, which reminds us that 'even rumour has a basis in fact' (perhaps in some situations more than others). If we assume this however, and for the moment focus on researchers clearly removed from the field, the first important point to make here is that contacts or 'people to go to' can be established through a number of means. Of course, this sometimes highlights the heartbreakingly important role of luck, but otherwise, formally approaching an organization is not as difficult as it may initially seem, and it is possible to agree with Bowyer-Bell at least on this point. Limited experiences from psychologists and other academic 'do-gooders' have shown that within terrorist movements in Northern Ireland such as the PIRA and the Loyalist Ulster Defence Association (UDA), contacts *can* be made and individuals usually tend to be co-operative. However, this is the case only in the light of Taylor and Quayle's[61] encounters 'in so far as you have the capacity to meet some of their objectives of gaining a broader hearing and publicity'. In going some way towards explaining his own success in accessing PIRA members, Joe Bowyer-Bell[62] writes:

> Everyone likes to talk about him or herself, none more than the saved. And talking is much easier when your arrival somehow validates the seriousness of the local armed struggle . . . Such investigation based on access – achieved after an endless vigil in some largely uninhabited hotel at the back of the beyond – often assures that the orthodox assume sympathy with the rebel.

If we take the PIRA as our focus, the means become clearer with some thought. On the one hand written requests can be made, for example, to PIRA paramilitaries serving prison sentences, via prisoner support groups. Conversely one can write directly to the imprisoned person in question. If successful, the interviewer may be allowed to come during prison visiting hours. The result of such a tactic clearly differs across context. In Northern Ireland, where there has traditionally been a great deal of contempt by prisoners towards the prison authorities, it would be unwise and perhaps futile for a researcher to attempt to arrange an interview through the prison authorities. However, in other situations, for example in the case of a single terrorist who may be isolated in a foreign country (such as Islamic extremists imprisoned in British jails), then the full co-operation between the researcher and prison authorities may be essential to facilitate access. In the latter case, the isolated terrorist prisoner is effectively without a support network that for other imprisoned terrorists, as is the case of Northern Ireland's para-militaries, continues to exist inside prison walls. Therefore, practical efforts spent producing carefully drafted letters, fully stating the researcher's intentions, background and motive, and so on can be well worth the time when communicating with either or both prisoner or prison official, as individual cases may warrant.

If, on the other hand, meetings are arranged by a higher, 'legitimate' source within the terrorist group itself, perhaps for example via the movement's political wing, then there is more often than not a set course of procedures to be followed.[63] This is so because the organizations such as Sinn Fein and the PIRA continuously receive many requests, again from journalists and book authors, seeking private interviews either with political figures or with convicted (or active) terrorists. It may be required that detailed lists of questions to be asked be handed over in advance of the proposed interview. Of course, this approach assumes some familiarity with the potential interviewee, even if through media exposure – i.e. the researcher has identified one particular individual whom the researcher feels will be important to his or her work. This of course is not a prerequisite for those researchers who, rather than attempt to approach known individuals, simply 'seek an interview or comment' per se. It is similarly possible to approach the political wing of a terrorist group and ask to speak with, for example 'Republicans', in order to ascertain answers to a particular research question, which might include why people joined the Republican movement (as Bowyer-Bell's work has done), attitudes to crime, drugs or other social problems, etc. This will be returned to in more detail, but for the moment it is important to emphasize that there *are* several avenues of approach.

In a similar vein, the Republican newspaper, *An Phoblacht*, publishes a weekly list of forthcoming commemorations and meetings. There is scarcely a commemoration in the Republic of Ireland at which numbers of former PIRA activists, as well as some suspected presently involved members, do not attend. To attend these as merely an 'innocent bystander' can have worthwhile benefits for a novice researcher.[64] Introductions can be made to a possible interviewee in what is a non-threatening environment, and if successful, the researcher has much potential gain, given the numbers of individuals present and their inter-familiarity.

Another method is to approach individuals informally who have once subscribed to a particular movement but do so no longer: this of course, assumes some familiarity, if only at an intermediary level through a third party. Two broad types of potential interviewee that emerge at this point include the retired terrorist who has renounced his/her involvement (Sean O'Callaghan and Eamon Collins (until his death) are good examples of frequently sought-after interviewees) and the retired terrorist who has not renounced involvement. This is an obvious area of concern for those (including researchers) who are led to believe that 'no-one really leaves' their organizational duties.[65] There does seem to be support from direct interviews, to suppress such fears if a researcher has a preference to seek participation from people who are no longer involved in terrorism (ibid.). The present author asked this question to an early interviewee (in early 1996), a former PIRA prisoner, who rather emphatically stated:

> I've never come across people, in my time in the IRA, and now since then, people being coerced into not leaving. I'll give you an example. One time **** was on the run in ****, and he bumped into an old friend of his from prison who had left the organisation, and **** called him by his prison name and [asked him] if he'd help him. If he'd said no, there would have been no problem, but if he'd gone away and rung up the Brits, well that's different.

A Republican interviewee of Coogan[66] adds: 'Yes, of course a volunteer can leave when he wants to. He's expected not to talk of course'.

To the distant observer, and even more in the context of ethno-nationalist conflicts, the issue of nationality might be regarded as having at least some relevance, but generally speaking it seems that nationality is not a crucial issue in the context of actually being granted an interview by either (former) paramilitaries themselves or from their many supporters. On the morning after Bloody Sunday in 1972, the BBC journalist Peter Taylor walked through a Catholic area of Derry with his camera crew, seeking reactions from people in the aftermath of the previous day's violence. 'To my surprise, I was invited in for a cup of tea', remarked Taylor.[67] This is reiterated by the variety of nationalities of people who have interviewed people from all sides of the Northern Ireland conflict for some years. In the words of one former PIRA member interviewed by the present author (February, 1996) on the subject of further access: 'they'll welcome you with open arms . . . they *want* to say how it is for them'. There is some support for the fact that 'outsiders' might be made more welcome than 'insiders' – Irish-based researchers would, one might assume, appear more suspicious than American, French or Spanish researchers, who come to Northern Ireland (or the Republic of Ireland) in order to learn about the 'Troubles'. As Lee[68] describes more generally, researchers conducting dangerous fieldwork are 'commonly challenged about where their own sympathies lie in the conflict'. He adds:

Particularly when they come from outside the situation, researchers often respond to challenges about where they stand by proclaiming themselves to be neutral, explaining that they are present in the setting as an objective observer rather than an engaged participant . . . Complete neutrality is probably impossible. It is unlikely that all parties to the conflict will engage one's sympathies to an equal degree. However, even claiming to be neutral may be more difficult in some kinds of situation than in others.

Unless the researcher attains an interview at the highest level of a paramilitary organization such as the PIRA, the interviewee (if a currently active member) will, if approached directly by a researcher, and if willing to speak to the researcher, possibly seek approval and/or advice for his participation in the interview from a higher source in the organization.[69] Except for some of the smaller organizations, most have a chain of command – some, such as ETA and the PIRA will have an elaborate, hierarchically organized structure not unlike that of a large business. If the interview has not already been sanctioned or indeed arranged by a 'higher source' on behalf of the researcher, then this will merely follow standard internal security procedures, in which terrorists are fully instructed following recruitment.[70] Much of this will depend on factors such as familiarity and trustworthiness of the interviewer, and common knowledge would dictate that if a researcher appears instantly dislikeable in whatever manner for the interviewee, that a simple 'no' would stop matters very quickly. For many such reasons, it is not difficult to see how, generally speaking, such organizations prefer to deal with very few, but 'key' journalists, with whom some element of familiarity and trust has been established over time.

It is difficult to form conclusions or falsify hypotheses in the literature which might emerge from some of the methodological issues described here, if only for the simple reason that no attempt has been made to identify themes or common experiences between those who have studied terrorism, especially with such a direct perspective. This reflects another large gap in our analyses, and it is one that would do well to be filled. However, there are some avenues for exploration here. Interestingly, within the small circle of 'outsider' people who are able to meet with and talk to paramilitaries in Ireland, a frequent topic for private discussions concerns the 'quality' of subject an investigator encounters or interviews for book or article purposes. In larger organizations, there are a number of very different levels of membership and roles that need to be filled. This includes everyone from sympathizers, supporters and fringe elements, and even the friends of these people, to the leadership core at the very top of the organization. Obviously, there will be an extremely small number of individuals, be they respected and long time journalists or not, who will have access to leadership members.

Bowyer-Bell was granted permission by the PIRA leadership to write his book on the history of the movement. The PIRA leadership facilitated access to personnel for Bowyer-Bell given that an account of the PIRA's history should (from their own perspective) portray them in as best a light as possible. It must be emphasized, however, that this is not to say that rewards are not reaped from speaking to individuals much lower down in the hierarchy, and this is certainly the case for psychological analyses of terrorism. For even though a PIRA active service member (i.e. the individual who pulls the trigger or plants a bomb) may well be unaware of the overall strategy being followed by his/her movement as dictated by the leadership, it is learning about individuals' own involvement and actions we are often interested in, and the decisions made by him or her, before, during and possibly after involvement in terrorism. Crenshaw's earlier comments on the possibility of finding patterns should certainly not be taken lightly. Nevertheless, for more experienced researchers, the 'quality' of subject can change with experience and length of interaction with an organization, the value of this being impressive as it may well be useful to gain access to members at as many levels of the organization as possible.[71]

It is inescapable that such matters raise important ethical issues for this line of enquiry, as they play a central role in any research involving meeting with and talking to individuals directly responsible for injury or death. Remembering Taylor and Quayle's[72] comments about the researcher possibly being regarded as morally obliged to aid the security forces, it is only common sense that no member, at whatever level of a paramilitary organization, or for that matter, no former terrorist (at least those who have not renounced their former colleagues) is likely to co-operate with a researcher if collaboration with security forces is suspected. The grave security risks that this poses for any organization should be obvious, and the seriousness with which this is viewed was illustrated above. Hence, for a 'lone' social scientist, the importance of the development and possible maintenance of some form of trust is paramount in obtaining any form of reliable and valid insights during interviews.

An implication of this is that it is probably wiser not to attempt to engage in discussion on what might be particularly sensitive or dangerous issues. These could be matters, which from the perspective of the terrorist group, might have potential intelligence usage to the security forces. As such it is not the responsibility of the researcher to explore particular lines of enquiry that are not absolutely central to the research question at hand (assuming the soundness of the research question in the first place). In any case, for a researcher to place him or herself in such a compromising position is probably best avoided in the first place rather than mulling over subsequent ethical or moral dilemmas.

Furthermore, for researchers engaging in research with terrorists, as in the case of the journalist, it would be naive to assume that any terrorist organization, regardless of its capabilities (including use of the media), is not aware of the existence of ethical issues and confidentiality clauses. The PIRA are fully aware of codes of journalist conduct and confidentiality and it would be unrealistic to expect most sophisticated terrorist groups such as the PIRA or the Basque ETA not to be aware of such issues in the academic context also.[73] Moreover, if a particular discussion occasionally drifts into revelations of sensitive material, what is always implied by the paramilitaries of course is the threat of violence, a threat of which few interviewers who value their safety will be unaware. A blunt testament to this is that the PIRA shot dead an anthropologist working in Northern Ireland.[74]

Related to this is that any committed member of such an organization, perhaps especially the more 'acceptable faces', i.e. the political wings, may view the prospect of an interview as an opportune moment to voice the objectives or perhaps justification of his/her movement. The media and academic communities are truly the 'oxygen of publicity' for the terrorist. Obviously then, any meetings of this nature may be double-edged. A good example in the context of journalism became evident when in August of 1996, the RUC stopped two cars travelling together at Annahilt in Co. Down in Northern Ireland. In the first car was Alex Kerr, whom the Ulster Volunteer Force (UVF) had earlier threatened to kill as a result of an internal Loyalist dispute. In the second car, being driven by George Milliken, a close associate of Kerr's, were four journalists. The journalists had been brought to a farm in Donaghcloney, Co. Down where they took photographs of nine masked and armed terrorists, one of whom read out a statement defying orders of the paramilitary group's leadership apropos the aforementioned quarrel.[75]

In light of these issues, it is also important that before the interviewer attempts to initiate research that involves interviews, that (a) proper questions and (b) proper interviewing techniques are developed. From a psychological perspective, Crenshaw[76] points out that even if it is possible to interview terrorists that this is still unlikely to produce accurate reconstructions of a person's motives. If such research is to surpass what she terms 'description', Crenshaw notes that 'posing the right questions is as important as finding answers'.[77] In a similar vein, Ferracuti[78] emphasized that interview and autobiographical material 'consists of . . . real motives [which] lie hidden beneath rationalizations and self-serving reinterpretations of reality'. Taylor and Quayle clearly acknowledge this in their development of a psychological understanding of terrorists, underlining the need for interviewers to be able to steer from what might appear to be propaganda to more 'psychologically-based notions'.[79]

A final point worth making here is that in promoting a *psychological* approach to terrorism research (thus making interviews essential), care will always be needed to communicate its vagaries. As Crenshaw[80] implicitly notes, such an approach can misleadingly imply diagnostic attempts on terrorists. Also of course, academics' fears of misuse of their findings are merited (ibid.), highlighting the need for effective communication, not only at an interdisciplinary level but also between academics and policy-makers.[81] Crenshaw[82] described the US Department of State as admitting that expertise on terrorism is 'called into play only during the management of crises. In other words, officials may deny that theory is relevant, but they rely on it constantly, at no time more than during a crisis, when they think they have escaped its influence'.

Conclusions

There are serious problems with the nature, progress and continued direction of terrorism research, but these problems are not insurmountable obstacles, however complex and depressing the lack of progress on some fronts may sometimes seem. That being said, these are issues that students of terrorism must face and overcome if theoretical progress and conceptual development is to realistically be achieved. In particular, for the psychologist, given the importance of psychological issues in understanding terrorism more generally, such issues are of paramount importance. The next chapter presents an introduction to the psychological research on terrorists, and throughout, we can see how the conceptual and methodological issues impinge on not only the kinds of questions that appear to drive our thinking about the terrorist, but often how limited our assumptions about terrorist behaviour can be in the absence of studying terrorism in different ways, and from different perspectives and levels, even within the same discipline.

3

INDIVIDUAL APPROACHES

Introduction

In October 2002, 202 people were killed in the bombing of two popular bars in Bali, Indonesia. Amrozi bin Nurhasyim, a 41-year-old mechanic, who was also a member of the Al Qaeda-affiliated *Jemaah Islamiyah* movement, was the first of several people convicted of the bombing. Upon hearing his sentence, Amrozi swivelled on his chair towards those in the courtroom and with his two thumbs raised in approval, smiled broadly and then raised his fists triumphantly. The press subsequently dubbed him 'the smiling bomber'. While some condemned Amrozi's arrogance, others struggled in shock to comprehend his unusual behaviour. General Made Pastika, the then Chief of Police in Bali, recalled reacting in complete disbelief when he first heard of the bombing: 'I thought, these must be crazy people'.[1] While those responsible for the planning and co-ordination of the bombing remain at large, the image from the Bali courtroom of a smiling Amrozi will remain etched in many people's minds.

Whenever we try to make sense of extreme or unusual behaviour, we face a difficult challenge in recognizing that what we see often only represents the aftermath of a much wider set of activities and events, each of which is linked together in ways that only become significant with hindsight. Although it is often sanitized accounts of political violence that we are exposed to on the television, the amount of destruction caused, and the scale of human suffering, are some of the qualities of a terrorist attack that become dramatized in such a way as to attempt to leave a lasting impression in our minds. Furthermore, when we try to understand anything about those responsible for the attack, our perceptions are more often than not anchored completely in this drama. It is often at this point that we fall foul of what psychologists refer to as the fundamental attribution error. This is an everyday phenomenon and essentially is a way of understanding how we sometimes tend to explain other people's behaviour with reference to dispositional features (e.g. personality, what they are 'like'), while we might attribute situational features to our own (e.g. it was the type of company I was in that night that made me behave in that way).

This simple bias can affect our understanding of the terrorist in several ways. By only focusing on, for instance, the outcome of terrorist events, we achieve a distorted view of both the terrorist and the process of terrorism more broadly. It is at this point that we run the risk of subtly and implicitly (or on rare occasions, as above, explicitly, and not so subtly) regarding the terrorist's behaviour as couched in abnormality. What constitutes abnormality only reflects a normative judgement anyway, but in psychological terms, abnormal behaviour is often consistent with the presence of some psychological disorder or distress, at the very least, suggestive of a debilitating condition adversely affecting the well-being of the sufferer. In trying to make sense of horrific acts of terrorism and those who perpetrate them, however, the tendency towards abnormality-oriented explanations is more closely conveyed by statements including 'they must be sick', or 'they must be mad'. The notion of an illness being present is intuitively understandable because it seems plausible, and makes us feel at the same time more comfortable and capable in understanding extreme behaviour. Of course, this then necessarily blurs the boundary of whether or not the person is deemed to be really responsible for what they have done.

To some analysts, the proposition that a distinct terrorist personality exists is a reflection of these sorts of assumptions. In particular, it reflects a debate that is now probably more of historical interest than contemporary relevance. But this is only partially true – the search for a terrorist personality typified psychological research in the late 1970s and 1980s, while more recently, a productive debate has recommended that we do not uncritically accept the result of a small number of less than rigorous empirical studies of captured terrorists generalized to broader populations. However, the idea of there being a terrorist personality has actually resurfaced with renewed vigour in professional academic journals in the months following 9/11. It is unfortunate that such approaches are not cognizant of previous efforts and appear to selectively ignore the earlier literature, a problem alluded to in the previous chapter.

Many attempts exist to denigrate terrorists and their cause by purposefully regarding them as psychopathic (a label that often brings about the same effects as the decision to use the label 'terrorist'). In the 1970s, the view of the terrorist as psychopathic was popular. Into the 1980s and 1990s, this view was dismissed, but more subtle personality traits were forwarded as possible terrorist traits – narcissism and paranoia in particular. But given the resurgence of the terrorist personality debate since both 9/11 and the intensification of the Palestinian *Intifada* since that time, it is necessary to explore this issue and attempt to arrive at some useful assertions about why such ill-informed and wildly inaccurate characterizations persist in the literature.

Terrorism and psychopathy

Forensic and clinical psychologists regularly come into contact with psychopathic behaviour in professional settings. The psychopathic individual is one whose behaviour is marked by specific and consistently observed trait behaviours, but perhaps typified at the broadest possible level by an unwillingness to conform to social or communal rules. Not all psychopathic individuals engage in violent behaviour, but violence is often an outlet for aggressive tendencies in psychopathic behaviour. Of particular interest to analogies with terrorism are the psychopath's lack of remorse or guilt for his/her activities and a selfish, egotistical world view that precludes any genuine welfare for others.

We can easily make the case for psychopathy as a possible feature of terrorist behaviour. After all, terrorists wilfully engage in destruction, causing suffering and death, and not only that, are generally willing to accept responsibility for such activities, claiming that the behaviour was not only necessary, but important, justifiable and that it will continue unless the terrorists' demands are met. The frequent reinterpretations by terrorists and their political brethren of victims' suffering provokes outrage and subsequent victimization of those caught up in terrorist violence. Gerry Adams, the leader of Sinn Fein, claims to acknowledge the suffering caused to the 'non-combatant' targets of PIRA violence, yet explains such suffering as an inevitable casualty of the war his colleagues engage in. All personal responsibility is removed, and the victim's death is explained as resulting from an 'unfortunate', but external, set of events (with the responsibility for the PIRA's killing of civilians placed squarely on the British government). Such words are not easily accepted by surviving victims, and this unwillingness to express remorse adds further injury.

Conventional wisdom might allow us to conclude that it seems perfectly reasonable to suggest that people who wilfully engage in terrorizing behaviour (at whatever level) reflect a psychological disorder of some sort, and many examples of terrorist violence seem to warrant the psychopathy diagnosis from psychologists outright when we look more closely at the day-to-day behavioural features of terrorist violence. Carroll[2] describes the practice of 'punishment attacks', assaults against those whom the PIRA and their supportive communities deem as engaging in 'anti-social' behaviour. Although the PIRA has recently begun to decommission its weapons, it is clear on closer inspection that it is merely the focus and context of the violence that continues to change in Northern Ireland, and not the traditional methods of terrorists in that region. Carroll gives the example of a 16-year-old boy, 'tied upside down to railings and beaten until his legs were broken . . .' having already been 'deliberately noosed like an animal so that he could not deflect the blows from the clubs'. In explaining why punishment beatings are often more painful than shootings, with wounds taking a lot longer to heal, Carroll describes the perpetrators of such attacks as 'psychopathic'. In another incident, Martin Doherty, a Belfast teenager, was literally crucified, having had steel spikes driven through his hands and knees, nailing him to a post, by a PIRA punishment-gang in February of 1996. For those uninitiated with the sheer scale and ferocity of the level of such continuing violence in Northern Ireland, which has increased since the first ceasefires in 1994, Anderson's[3] description of the punishment assaults is useful:

> the squads have performed with zeal, killing dozens of people and kneecapping at least 1,500 more. No longer content with mere beatings or shootings, they have graduated to more sophisticated forms of cruelty and introduced a whole new glossary of terms to the local language. There is the '50–50' (the victim is forced to touch his toes while a bullet is fired into his spine); 'breeze blocking' (the methodical shattering of bones by dropping flagstones or cinder blocks on joints); and the 'six pack' (shots to the knees, ankles, and elbows). Through long experience, the squads now know how to maximize suffering: injuries can be heightened by forcing a shooting victim to lie on concrete, and the most efficient way to destroy an elbow is by bringing the hand toward the shoulder and firing into the bend.

As a result of what such activities demand of the active member of a terrorist organization required to perform this function, in one of the earliest attempted descriptions of the terrorist from a psychological perspective, Cooper[4] suggested that: 'The true terrorist must steel himself against tender-heartedness through a fierce faith in his credo or by a blessed retreat into a comforting, individual madness'. Cooper concludes that as a result, it is a simple inevitability that 'the political terrorist needs either a highly-insulated conscience or a certain detachment from reality'. This theme has long been reflected in the literature. In a 1981 review of approaches to terrorism that emphasize the presence of distinct psychological abnormalities in terrorists (specifically, 'that terrorism is driven by mental disorders'), Corrado[5] concluded that *psychopathy* was then the feature most prominently associated with terrorists.

By and large, however (and despite suggestions to the contrary), the psychopathy argument will remain limited. There remains little to support the argument that terrorists (from whatever background or context) can or should be thought of as psychopathic in the main. To illustrate this argument, it is useful to draw on some examples of the reality of terrorist lives. Cooper[6] was correct when he argued that: 'The life of the true, political terrorist is a hard and lonely one'. Without necessarily commenting otherwise on the personal motivation of terrorists, it is difficult to argue with the assertion that the social and personal lives of some terrorists do suffer psychologically and there are many other accounts of terrorist lives, and again, from different contexts, that can testify to this.[7] Membership of a terrorist organization involves the formation of focused and lasting relationships which themselves are important in facilitating greater movement towards more extreme commitment towards the group and its ideals. A senior Sinn Fein member, who is an alleged PIRA leader, described to the present author in great detail in August 1997 (not all of which is presented below) how his involvement in the PIRA affected him, his family and Republican colleagues:

> It was . . . it was very hard. And it still is, often. Actually, I'm very lucky in the sense that my wife *shared* my [political] convictions, and the fact that she realised the depth of my involvement without knowing what I was *actually* doing, she had an understanding of what it was about, and like the fact that she had been arrested herself and she had been strip-searched in the house at one stage she had a full understanding of what the pressures [were] that could come on her and for her own benefit, it was better not to know, y'know? And . . . I'm very lucky in that sense.

The presence of pathological egocentricity commonly found in psychopathic individuals seems to conflict with some of the required characteristics sought after by terrorist leaders of their members – high motivation, discipline and an ability to remain reliable and task-focused in the face of stress, possible capture and imprisonment. Taylor and Quayle,[8] in a study of Loyalist terrorists in Northern Ireland, gleaned the following remark from a terrorist leader: 'there are very few obvious what do you call them . . . psychopaths . . . they'd stand out like a sore thumb and everyone would know them'. His comment reflects an organizational concern across terrorist movements and its underlying sentiment has been the basis of a logical argument used by several other authors in dismissing the presence of an 'obvious' psychopathology in terrorists. Loyalty in the face of continuing hardship and unrelenting commitment to the greater ideological cause and movement are qualities that go hand in hand with being a member of an illegal, underground organization. Let us remember an important point that may shed light on terrorist dynamics – the terrorist's victims are often incidental, chosen on a purely symbolic basis (e.g. American citizens, passengers on a 'Western' airliner). The nature of terrorist victims contrasts significantly when we compare how victims are chosen by psychopathic murderers, in that, rather than aspiring to 'a broader ideological context'[9] (as in the case of the terrorist), the psychopathic killer's reasons are personal, fuelled and sustained by elaborate personal fantasies. Frequently, the terrorist's actions are independent of his particular victim – given the use of bombing by proxy, for example, that distances the terrorist from the victim, and the terrorist may actually have, as Taylor[10] cautioned, 'no direct personal experience of the damage and mutilation caused'.

Of course, few terrorists succeed in attaining a completely thorough sense of insulation described by Cooper from the effects of their violence, at least at the beginning of their involvement in terrorism. Similarly, Cooper[11] argued that '[f]ew terrorists seem to derive a real satisfaction from the harm they cause'. Kellen[12] criticizes analysts in this respect in that they 'never postulate that terrorists feel sorry for what they do. But some terrorists do experience remorse, and we have proof of it'.[13] The view of terrorists as *necessarily* abnormal in this regard ignores the processes whereby members become brutalized and more committed as a *result* of membership and increased psychological commitment to the group, with individual responsibility for terrorist activity subsumed within a shared sense of communal identity, as we shall see in Chapter 5.

Heskin[14] argues that the dispute about whether the concept of psychopathy is applicable to terrorist psychology may be dealt a blow through our inability to form a rational distinction between terrorist behaviour and that of other conflict-oriented groups. For the reasons which we sometimes pejoratively use the term 'psychopath' in looking at terrorist violence (especially in the context of emotional media and political responses to terrorist atrocities) it seems that the term 'psychopath' or 'psycho' (as in the term 'terrorist') would be more widely applicable to other forms of violence as well – notably that of many combat soldiers in most wars. Yet in such contexts, as with the inconsistent and euphemistic labelling in our usage of the words 'terrorism' and 'terrorist', we prefer to employ altogether different terminology.

Another inconsistency, somewhat different in character but very revelatory of a tendency in psychological analyses of terrorism, relates to how our judgement tends to be inconsistent in what merits diagnoses of psychopathy in the absence of any clinical diagnosis. For instance, Konrad Kellen's[15] arguments that Carlos the Jackal was a psychopath were purely based on 'what he says about himself and from the exploits he stresses in his interviews'. Furthermore, according to Silke,[16] Pearce's emphasis on psychopathy appears to be based on 'secondary sources such as terrorist autobiographies, biographies and media interviews. In one case, Pearce made a diagnosis of psychopathy based mainly on an individual having tattoos on his torso'. If then, to agree with a point often made by political scientists that we already know enough about terrorist behaviour so as not to warrant keeping the rather naive expectation of there being a 'terrorist personality' (or 'phenotype' in Paul Wilkinson's words), we might be forgiven for wishing to explore further the basis on which such claims are made in the first place, given the nature of such claims as made by Pearce and Kellen.

Perhaps if the opportunity ever arose to examine terrorists in clinical settings (and within the rigours of proper psychological investigation and analyses), there might be some evidence to link at least a few of the 'sore thumbs' with pathological disorders. This seems likely given the nature of some activities for which we have evidence that people with violent dispositions appear to be selected for specific tasks (e.g. punishment assaults by the PIRA), and more likely again given the sheer numbers of people involved in some of the larger organizations. In the meantime, however, poor evidence exists for the principle that psychopathy is an element of the psychology of terrorist organizations. Despite the *attractiveness* of the theme (and the subtlety by which this attractiveness permeates common assumptions in aspects of the behavioural literature as will become increasingly obvious in the following sections), terrorist movements should therefore be seen neither as organizations of *necessarily* psychopathic individuals *because* of the brutality of behaviour involved, nor should terrorist groups be seen in the main as likely to recruit people with psychopathic tendencies.

A terrorist personality?

As with behaviours associated with psychopathy, many researchers have focused their efforts on the similarities between terrorist behaviour and the predominant traits of those who might be characterized as one or more of a number of personality types, or characterized by a set of finite traits, supposedly similar in degree across terrorist groups. A distinct body of research exists and is used in support of the argument that the terrorist is, at the very least, psychologically 'different' from the non-terrorist. Such a view has its origins in a major school of nineteenth-century criminology known as 'positivism', which was initially proposed as a counter-argument to the notion that criminals have free will: the perspective that offenders have free will and determine their own behaviour implied that their decisions to engage in criminal activities are largely informed by a rational process of judging whether the expected results of engagement in crime outweigh the consequences of the punishment that would follow if apprehended. On the other hand, the deterministic 'positivism' suggested that influences *outside* the realm of free will offer a more sensible approach to viewing the criminal. These influences were to be found, positivists argued, by looking at biological, sociological and psychological factors (e.g. genetics, environment and personality, respectively) or any combination of two or more of these. One might argue, of course, that most psychological approaches to crime and criminality could be seen as positivist in nature, and this certainly applies to the vast majority of contributions from psychology to understanding those who engage in terrorism. Although some of this particular form of psychological research on terrorists is dated (much of it considerably), that it persists as apparently valid research (in both its nature and stated findings) *and* that its conclusions are developed upon within similar kinds of analyses in the contemporary literature, warrants that it be addressed in some detail so that we may conclude with much-needed assertions about its veracity and overall worthiness.

In 1981, by far the largest ever study conducted on terrorists to date was produced by several researchers working under the auspices of the West German Ministry of the Interior, who commissioned the team 'to examine the cases of over 227 German terrorists.[17] Some terrorist leaders were typified by an extremely extraverted personality, characterized by a tendency for their behaviour to be 'unstable, uninhibited, inconsiderate, self-interested and unemotional'.[18] The second type of terrorist leader, according to the team, is the neurotically hostile, who 'rejects criticism, and is intolerant, suspicious, aggressive and defensive'.[19] According to Crenshaw's[20] analysis of the research:

> Bollinger . . . a member of the West German study team, also found that some of the terrorists he interviewed were attracted to violence – which he attributed to unconscious aggressive motives . . . the terrorist group represents an outlet for archaic aggressive tendencies, frequently rooted in youthful conflicts with stepfathers. The attraction to violence may also be a result of identification with the violent acts of father figures (a violence several individuals had actually experienced); that is, an identification with the aggressor . . . Jäger, however, found no common pattern in attitudes towards violence, neither ambivalence nor attraction . . . some individuals reported a strong prior aversion to aggression. They were conscious of a need to justify their behaviour and felt a sense of limitation.

Any results that involve such different findings by members of the same team have particular importance for a conceptual debate about the reliability and validity of analyses, especially in this case given the implications that the role of the heterogeneity of terrorists and terrorism might have within it. For the moment however, this lack of consensus between researchers is all the more significant since, despite the variety of results, the detailed case analyses revealed that 'the communal life from which [the West German terrorists] emerged was extraordinarily homogenous'.[21]

To reiterate, Sullwold's (another team member) initial findings were associated with traits illustrative of *narcissism*, as later elaborated upon by his colleague Bollinger, and later again in the 1980s and 1990s by other authors.[22] Crenshaw[23] develops a discussion on the results of the German research, and states that certain emotional deficiencies blind narcissists to the negative consequences of their actions. According to Crenshaw's analysis of the research findings, those displaying narcissistic tendencies might 'also possess a high tolerance for stress'.[24] Post[25] also supports the German researchers' claims and argues that in general:

> individuals with particular personality dispositions are drawn to terrorism. A feature in common among many terrorists is a tendency to externalise, to seek outside sources of blame for personal inadequacies . . . Bollinger found psychological dynamics resembling those found in narcissistic borderlines. He was particularly struck by the history of narcissistic wounds, which led to a deficient sense of self-esteem and inadequately integrated personalities. The terrorists he interviewed demonstrated a feature characteristic of individuals with narcissistic and borderline personalities – splitting. He found that they had split off the de-valued parts of themselves and projected them onto the establishment which then became the target of their violent aggression.

Unfortunately, methodological issues reduced the strength of the assertions from much of the original research. Not only were most of the terrorists unwilling to meet with the researchers (since the study had been commissioned by the state), but researchers reported receiving a lack of local co-operation from 'local government authorities'.[26] As if not problematic enough, Crenshaw reminds us that the researchers were in fact interviewing *suspected* terrorists 'under arrest or undergoing trial, but [who] had not yet been convicted. Since interviews with social science researchers did not have the status of privileged communications, the researchers could have been subpoenaed to give evidence in the cases'. The implications of these problems should be borne in mind when examining subsequent discussions that attempt to build on and develop the conclusions made in the earlier attempts.

Meanwhile, in the Irish context, Heskin[27] was to argue that terrorists might be characterized with reference to a different type of personality construct. He asserted that conflict-oriented groups that tend to be conservative in their ideology and organizational structure (be it a police force or terrorist organization) will tend to attract certain types of people. Heskin draws on evidence that authoritarian individuals tend to be somewhat more aggressive towards outgroups than others, and this, he asserts, helps us understand why particular types of people are drawn to terrorism while others are not. Heskin suggests that authoritarianism is a common trait of PIRA terrorists since, he argues, it may be reasonable to assume that Irish people in general (both North and South) are somewhat more authoritarian than normal, given the country's traditionally conservative political and religious attitudes and behaviours. Heskin's hypothesis has, however, not been corroborated in subsequent empirical studies.[28]

In a 1992 review, Friedland[29] presented an overview of personality-centred explanations of terrorism which refer to processes supporting the existence of some degree of 'abnormality' in the terrorist:

> Such explanations hold, for example, that the turning to terrorism may be attributed to abusive child-rearing. Gustav Morf, on the other hand, maintained that the rejection of the father and his values plays a dominant role in the making of terrorists. Robert Frank noted that terrorism is prevalent in societies where fantasies of cleanliness are prevalent. Peter Berger attributed terrorist behaviour to the sense of fulfillment and power that individuals presumably derive from absolute dedication, commitment and self-sacrifice, and from the infliction of pain and death.

Reich[30] also describes several similar reductionist accounts, some of historical significance including Lombroso's attributions of explanations in terms of vitamin deficiencies to explain 'bomb-throwing' (*pellagra* in particular); psychiatrist David Hubbard who forwarded the idea that faulty ear functioning may be common among terrorists; while perhaps most impressively of all 'Paul Mandel, a biochemist . . . having studied the inhibitory effects of gamma-aminobutyric acid (GABA) and serotonin on violence in rats, extrapolated his findings to terrorism'. Friedland[31] provided an ideal summary of such approaches:

> These theories promote the notion that political terrorists are psychologically deviant or abnormal. As for empirical support, to date there is no compelling evidence that terrorists are abnormal, insane, or match a unique personality type. The validity of such theories may be questioned on both a-priori and empirical grounds. Some of the theories, for example Berger's, are logically circular. In addition, most of them are predicated on single, core proposition and their predictive power is thereby curtailed. For instance, many reject their fathers' values at a certain age, yet only a negligible few turn to terrorism.

Overall, as attempts to assert the presence of psychological abnormality in terrorists, such accounts are, in the context of a scientific study of behaviour (which implies at least a *sense* of rigour), exceptionally weak. This being said, if such obviously limited accounts may be dismissed more readily from the outset, three very specific characterizations of the terrorist as psychologically 'special' persist in the literature. They certainly have not been chastised as readily as some of the more simplistic characterizations of terrorists as above, although there are many grounds for arguing that they be relegated to the same basket. These approaches emphasize the processes of (a) frustration–aggression, (b) narcissism (and narcissism–aggression), and (c) psychodynamic influences.

The frustration–aggression hypothesis

Friedland, who makes it clear he is critical of reductionist accounts pointing to psychological characteristics of terrorists, outlines and examines factors that purport to explain first, what dictates the conditions leading to movements turning towards wishing to exert social change; second, how and why such movements then turn to violence; and third, why such violence often subsequently escalates. Friedland characterizes the movement of minority groups towards social and political conflict, and their ensuing (although not necessarily consequential) turn to violence as a result of a (real or imagined) underprivileged, disadvantaged status and aggressive response from a failure to have their grievances resolved. This model has been popular in one form or another with a multitude of commentators.[32]

According to Tittmar,[33] who in 1992 presented quite a forceful argument, terrorism may be explained by resorting to one of the most popular psychological interpretations of aggression, the frustration–aggression hypothesis (FAH). The FAH, originally developed by Berkowitz[34] describes the response to frustration, or blockage of attainment of one's personal or environmental goals. The response to this denial or blockage may emerge as a 'fight or flight' situation – as either an aggressive, defensive reaction, or none at all (i.e. either physically or psychologically running away, or by attempting to ignore the problem, or at least attempting to reduce its perceived importance through *dissonance*, for example). Although Friedland[35] finds this type of explanation 'quite compelling', several criticisms may be directed at this type of model. Ferracuti[36] criticized this psychological approach, as well as derivatives of the FAH[37] as potential explanations of terrorist and other political violence on the grounds that: 'this moves the problem from the social universe to the idioverse, and motives and countermotives are superficially handled. Also the theory is at least partially tautological and does not account for those who abstain from terrorism, although frustrated, or "repented" terrorists'.[38]

The adaptation of the FAH in understanding terrorism (essentially, we must remember, a hypothesis used to explain individual violence) was, it seems, 'done by various authors with little apparent regard for modifications that the transition from the individual to the group might necessitate'.[39] Merari and Friedland[40] subsequently argue that even if one has identified 'correlates of [social] destabilization', that this can only go so far in actually explaining terrorism, noting: 'the process whereby destabilization generates terrorism remains undetermined'. As Friedland himself also notes, several authors criticized the practice of applying the FAH explanation not only on the grounds of questionable validity in the first place (in the individual context) apart at all from the 'transferring' of the FAH across to group and collective contexts, as also noted by Ferracuti. According to Friedland, one particular social scientist claims that the persistent popularity of the FAH may be due to its inherent simplicity. Unusually, Tittmar's attempt to validate the theory's applicability to terrorist motivation rested on generalizing from an examination of a case history of one (unsuccessful) terrorist.

The FAH and its derivatives (e.g. the relative deprivation hypothesis – initially proposed by Gurr)[41] will remain limited analytical tools in the context of explaining terrorism, both on individual and collective bases. Even Friedland's own attempt to direct a discussion of the FAH and relative deprivation theories is forced to arrive at the same question that led to the discussion in the first place – given the supposed influence which the 'frustrating' conditions give to particular 'privileged members of society' (the exception to the 'terrorists as deprived citizens' rule, as indicated earlier), 'why is it [still] that so very few undertake terrorism?'[42]

Kampf[43] has offered similar hypotheses emphasizing the attractiveness of terrorism and extreme violence to 'intellectuals', and 'affluent youth' and their 'drive' to change their societies, based on the frustrating conditions of conflicting social climates which, according to Kampf, give rise to terrorism and extremism.[44] Again, although the explanation appears an attractive one (certainly at least in the context of revolutionary notions and the kinds of ideological fervour influencing many ideological groups), the level of integration in this approach is weak, not only from being rather too context-specific, but also with notions about ideological attractions not considered within a process of involvement that is more appropriately considered, as we shall see in Chapter 4, within a process of underlying supportive qualities that shape initial and sustained involvement for the terrorist.

In conclusion, amid the persistence of ill-informed discussion and second-hand analyses and interpretations of (what amounts to unsystematic and unreliable findings from) psychological research on individual terrorists, it is fair to say that it is not good enough to be satisfied that, when explaining groups' movement to terrorism (and the individual's move to the terrorist group, and once a member, *then* to terrorist violence), that an explanation such as the FAH might suffice for a *certain* proportion of terrorists, i.e. the 'have-nots' (e.g. which might broadly capture the spirit of the re-emergence of terrorism in Northern Ireland in the late 1960s). Not only that, but if for the *exceptions* to this rule, the 'have-a-lots' (e.g. West German students (some of whom came from wealthy backgrounds) who joined the RAF etc.) or the 'intellectuals', we are simply forced at some stage to revert to *internal* predispositions, as is implied, then such an inconclusive theoretical framework as this does not pose great optimism for our discussions. Furthermore, even if the purpose of such research is not to generalize with psychologically-based concepts, it is clear that the limits of individual research are being pressed beyond their explanatory power and fall foul of the trap Reich[45] warned of. The boundaries of explanation need to be made much more explicit if that is ever to be the case, and moreover, secondary discussions and attempts to develop and extrapolate findings to broader contexts should not be uncritically encouraged.

Narcissism and narcissism–aggression

Although many of the most influential psychological studies of terrorism, as those described above, are old, there have been some relatively newer attempts at reviving many of the themes they supported for establishing a terrorist personality. Attempts to portray 'narcissism' as central to terrorist motivation have been popular since the original West German study that suggested it.[46] According to Richard Pearlstein,[47] a major contemporary proponent of this assertion:

> narcissism may be viewed as a range of psychoanalytic orientations, impulses, or behavioral patterns either wholly or overwhelmingly subject to ego concern, as opposed to object concern. Narcissism also might be seen as the manner in which an individual relates to the external, object world, either wholly or overwhelmingly upon the latter's potential capacity to provide that individual with sufficient ego reinforcement, satisfaction, or compensation . . . narcissism should be defined as an internal, intrapsychic, regulatory 'tool' that enables the individual to defend the self from damage and harm.

Pearlstein sees a theory of narcissism–aggression as a worthy successor to the FAH, and cites 15 references to narcissism as a supportive theme in explaining why people turn to terrorism (p. 28). Although several of Pearlstein's citations (e.g. three articles by Post) are in *themselves* simply reiterating others' previous work (i.e. the research of Jäger, Schmidtchen and Sullwold), Pearlstein relies on data he later concedes as containing only 'cursory suggestions of this interrelationship'.[48] Furthermore, in Pearlstein's analysis of the studies apparently indicating the existence of narcissism, he does not refer to any of the works (empirical or otherwise) firmly indicating the *lack* of traits such as narcissism (e.g. even when established clinically from a much earlier timeframe),[49] or the conceptual and other critiques of studies that suggest narcissism,[50] nor does Pearlstein seek to address, for instance, Post's apparent unwillingness to commit to the idea that terrorists *are* narcissistic, and not that their behaviour simply displays 'similarities' as Post stated. Pearlstein is clearer in his own conclusions: 'the external psychological determinants or sources of political terrorism appear to lie in what are termed narcissistic injury and narcissistic disappointment'.[51] He claims: 'in 90 percent of political terrorist case studies, narcissistic disappointment plays a critical psychobiographical role'.[52] In support of this, Pearlstein presents an analysis of 'nine case studies of individuals who dealt with the decision to become a political terrorist'.[53] The challenges in relying on such case studies, however, are obvious. By only relying on a select sample of sources to give us the terrorists' own explanation of their decisions, the difficulties with the validity of interpretations of autobiographical memoirs, one of which, according to Pearlstein (Susan Stern's account of her involvement in the 'Weathermen', a US-based terror group), involves the terrorist intimating to us her 'personal life and the nature of her psychological and psychopolitical evolution', are obvious. Pearlstein argues that Stern '*honestly* and *successfully* attempts to unify her personal life and political beliefs' (emphasis added). Pearlstein's other cases are based on similar sources, including letters sent by terrorists to judges, government reports, journalistic stories and similar secondary and tertiary sources. Although Pearlstein argues that his choice to select nine terrorists from different contexts and situations is illustrative of the need to recognize this heterogeneity, he does not acknowledge the pitfalls of uncritically accepting data generated from a group of terrorists who have received a substantial amount of attention from authors and journalists (especially Carlos, Ulrike Meinhof (of the Baader-Meinhof group) and the leader of the Symbionese Liberation Army).

Psychodynamic accounts

Although, as Taylor[54] argues, psychodynamic theories of human behaviour appear to have somewhat of 'a waning role in psychology, and generally speaking, have been supplanted by more empirically-orientated approaches', this is not the case within psychological analyses of terrorism. The origins of psychodynamic psychology lie in the work of Sigmund Freud, and essentially posit a view of human behaviour heavily influenced (if not completely) by a range of latent, unconscious desires, the origins of which are argued to have developed as a result of real or imagined unresolved childhood conflicts. In his 1988 review, Taylor strongly criticized a variety of psychodynamic-orientated theories of what implicitly amounts to explanations based on terrorist Oedipal and Electra complexes. He therefore criticizes what has been, and continues to be, a long-standing and possibly (certainly as far as numbers are concerned) the most popular approach to understanding the 'terrorist personality'.[55]

Kellen[56] was one of the first to emphasize the applicability of explicit psychodynamic theory, and in examining the case of former West German terrorist Hans-Joachim Klein, asserts:

> unbeknownst to himself, he was engaging in a struggle with authority because unconsciously he was struggling against his father. Klein quite consciously hated his father (he says, 'I would never talk about that man as "father"'), but he may not have been

aware of the fact that his rampage against the established order and those defending it may have been a continuum and extension of that struggle.

In support of his argument, Kellen points to Klein's later disillusionment and subsequent renunciation of the brutality of the group's violence and his exit from the movement. Kellen argues that Klein is probably not a good example of a 'true terrorist', echoing Cooper's earlier discussion about what being a 'good' terrorist *apparently* seems to involve (a ruthless dedication to 'merciless' destruction and so on). Klein is described as not 'profoundly fanatical in a political sense. He seems like a man who acted all along from the unconscious motives of merely inflicting pain and destruction on the hated enemy – in his case, persons of the establishment, i.e. "father figures"'.[57] Kellen argues the same with respect to Carlos the Jackal, although, as Kellen admits at the outset, it is not 'apparent from [Carlos'] words' that a similar sense of 'unconscious patricidal impulses' (ascribed to Klein) exists.[58] Carlos had once, it appears, described his father as 'cruel and powerful'.

Other researchers have incorporated one or more elements of psychodynamic theory in other ways,[59] some subtle, others not, but another attractive focus for several researchers has been on the process of 'identification' or 'identity', which is still rooted in psychodynamic theory (although with much less emphasis placed on stricter Freudian notions). In mainstream psychology, Erik Erikson[60] developed a personality theory that suggested that the formation of an 'identity' (and soon after, 'negative' identity) is crucial to personality development. Erikson argued that child development is characterized by a series of crises, each to be overcome in succession so that the child's personality can become wholly integrated. Failure to resolve these early childhood conflicts manifests itself in later life, according to Erikson, via various psychological problems. In this respect, Post, like Kaplan, argues that terrorist motivation is overwhelmingly and inseparably linked to a need to 'belong' to the group (any group will do it seems, and if the opportunity arises, the terrorist group will do) and 'hence' the group becomes central to identity formation in the terrorist.[61] This, according to Post's hypothesis, is then further developed by interpersonal relations within the structure, as well as the ideology and strategies used by the terrorists. Crenshaw[62] and Taylor[63] both consider the process of identification as it might apply to terrorism. Crenshaw[64] in interpreting Erikson's theory with special regard for terrorist motivation, describes the process:

At the stage of identity formation, individuals seek both meaning and a sense of wholeness or completeness as well as what Erikson . . . terms 'fidelity', a need to have faith in something or someone outside oneself as well as to be trustworthy in its service.

Ideologies then are guardians of identity. Erikson further suggests that political undergrounds utilize youth's need for fidelity as well as the 'store of wrath' held by those deprived of something in which to have faith. A crisis of identity (when the individual who finds self-definition difficult is suffering from ambiguity, fragmentation, and contradiction) makes some adolescents susceptible to 'totalism' or to totalistic collective identities that promise certainty. In such collectivities the troubled young finds not only an identity but an explanation for their difficulties and a promise for the future.

This type of explanation squarely rests within a psychodynamic framework. It has also been applied by the West German research team's analysis of the German terrorists, and further by Knutson[65] in a study of American terrorists. However, the process of identification (in its *present* incarnations) will probably remain a limited tool in understanding terrorist motivation for several reasons, not least due to accounts of terrorists' involvement that easily contradict suggestions about generalizing from such an approach. A more sophisticated model of identity, and one aware of the need to integrate levels of analysis, might prove beneficial particularly in terms of efforts to understand how terrorists' own sense of identity forms and develops in response to not only their 'own' world but to external change (e.g. globalization trends for instance). The more practical issues of relevance to any critique of psychodynamic perspectives however, relate to the unfalsifiability and circular logic of psychodynamic theories, their claim to 'special' knowledge, and characteristic reluctance to share in the rigorous scientific demands of contemporary psychology as far as theoretical development and hypothesis testing is concerned. Undeniably, there are some cases that in retrospect (e.g. through looking at autobiographical sources especially) quite easily seem to fit the identity model in which family influence serves as a factor for involvement in many cases, and although this approach might draw greater attention to the role of the family, its limited applicability to understanding terrorists in general, and the equally limited conceptual utility of psychodynamic explanations altogether only serves to confuse the clarity of our knowledge of terrorist psychology. Psychodynamic attempts to push forward explanations purporting special 'psycho-logic' of terrorist behaviour is so conveniently vague and broad in equal measure as to offer little or no predictive value.

The 'normality' of terrorist behaviour

In a detailed review, Silke[66] argued that 'most serious researchers in the field at least *nominally* agree with the position that terrorists are essentially normal individuals' (emphasis added). In general, his assertion can be strengthened by looking at research supporting evidence for lack of abnormality; research supporting evidence *for* normality (not exactly the same as the first point), and developments in the context of alternative explanations for abnormal (including violent) behaviour. This last point refers to an increasingly prevalent tendency in criminology and forensic psychology to refer to the findings of well-established research in social psychology in explaining the influence of situational factors upon violent behaviour,[67] and particularly, how involvement in extreme behaviour (e.g. involving the increasing adoption of extreme attitudes and values as much as supporting and possibly eventually engaging in extreme violence) need not necessarily be discussed within positivist theorizing and assumptions about psychological 'specialness' or an overreliance on the roles assumed to be played by distinct psychological traits or personalities.

First, one can identify a body of evidence in support of the position that terrorists are not necessarily characterized by types of distinct personality traits suggested by other psychological research in the area. Gustav Morf,[68] with one of the very first studies to inform terrorist psychology, in an analysis of the FLQ (the *Front de Liberation du Quebec*, in Canada) neither observed nor recorded distinct personality traits. A similar claim emerged from a study by Rasch,[69] a German psychiatrist, who studied 11 male and female members of the Baader-Meinhof group. Rasch's conclusions point to a complete absence of any indications of paranoia, psychopathy, fanaticism or any other psychotic or neurotic illness. Significantly, Rasch also emphasized the need to illustrate the presence of such 'illnesses' (if they were indicated) within the *rigours* of academic research and analysis: not only should research be methodologically sound, but statistical significance and careful interpretation with the issue of generalization need to be evident. As psychologist McCauley[70] emphasizes in a more precise manner, 'that is not to say that there is no pathology among terrorists, but the rate of diagnosable pathology, at least, does not differ significantly from control groups of the same age and background'. While such a sentiment might ultimately seem to support the notion that we continue to search for 'the terrorist personality' (i.e. in theory anyway, and that we should strive to improve our methods in order to make conclusions more concrete), the nature of this search might seem to be much more susceptible to questioning in its own right, as the discussion below will suggest.

Corrado[71] reviewed several approaches to terrorists that had emphasised a reliance on explanations referring to psychological abnormalities and personality deficiencies, but also could find no reliable, systematic evidence in support of such claims. The Italian Red Brigades were also unlikely candidates for psychological abnormality. On the contrary, as Jamieson[72] wrote, even 'those who have confronted Italian terrorism directly are the first who discredit the notion of the bloodthirsty desperado'. Jamieson described the typical Italian terrorist as 'a person whose ideas are meticulously worked out through careful analysis and serious reflection, for whom everything is seen in terms of politics, someone who above all is "well-prepared"', characterized furthermore by 'great intelligence, great openness and great generosity, with sometimes a bit of exhibitionism'. Jamieson notes that there has been a pronounced failure to fit the Italian terrorist into a discrete psychological or sociological profile, and especially given her repeated interactions across time with members of the group, Jamieson's observations are more noteworthy again.

Psychiatrists Lyons and Harbinson[73] found that in a study to compare 47 'political murderers' with 59 'non-political murderers' in Northern Ireland, the politically motivated killers generally came from more stable backgrounds and suffered from much less incidence of psychological disturbance than the 'ordinary criminals'. Indeed Lyons[74] argued:

> These are not people who are psychiatrically abnormal . . . The political killers tended to be normal in intelligence and mental stability, didn't have significant psychiatric problems or mental illness and didn't abuse alcohol. They didn't show remorse because they rationalised it very successfully, believing that they were fighting for a cause. The politicals, generally speaking, did not want to be seen by a psychiatrist; they feel there is nothing wrong with them, but they did co-operate.

Philip McGarry, a consultant psychiatrist, is described by Ryder[75] as arriving at a similar conclusion having also worked with terrorist prisoners in Northern Ireland: 'The evidence is that in the main they are quite ordinary people . . . most paramilitary killers are not mentally ill'.

Elliott and Lockhart[76] demonstrated in their own study that 'despite remarkably matching socio-economic backgrounds, juvenile scheduled offenders (broadly, those found guilty of terrorist-related offences) . . . were more intelligent, had higher educational attainments, showed less evidence of early developmental problems and had fewer court appearances than "ordinary" juvenile delinquents'. Although Taylor[77] did identify methodological concerns about the rigour of Lyons and Harbinson's methodology, it appears that such comparative work, as with Elliott and Lockhart's, is conceptually useful in supporting an overall argument of normality, and/or lack of individual pathology as a necessary feature of terrorist psychology.

Heskin[78] concluded on the basis of interpreting several instances of others' limited contact with Irish terrorists, and on the basis of the prevalence of alternative explanations from (social) psychology to explain both the involvement in and the conduct of extreme violence, that there were few grounds for attributing explanations of both psychopathy, or hints of 'abnormality' more generally, to Irish terrorists.

Finally, although Crenshaw is not a psychologist, her analyses of psychological issues often puts psychologists' efforts to shame in the context of assessing and commenting on psychological research on terrorists. In one of several reviews offered by researchers on the early efforts to examine terrorists, she has also concluded that terrorism does not appear to result from 'mental pathologies', and cites several findings in support of this.[79]

To conclude this section, if the elements of psychopathy and other psychological abnormalities can be dismissed as rather simplistic explanations of complex phenomena, and often through some rudimentary logic (as in the case of the psychopathy model), the reader may well wonder why such explanations have proved to be so remarkably persistent in the terrorism literature,[80] *and* why such apparently 'simplistic' characterizations of terrorists have proceeded largely unchallenged (despite the ready availability of detailed research agendas to fuel psychological investigation). This is a necessary discussion given that one of the original suggestions that it be discussed in more detail[81] has not yet been considered in the literature, despite consistent reminders of its neglect.[82]

Persistence through inconsistency: a closer look at the literature

Despite the persistence of evidence to suggest terrorist normality (as well as the poor quality of research indicating the contrary, *and* the availability of an alternative range and type of explanations), a general claim of psychological 'normality' does not permeate the individual psychological literature and current analyses as much as one would expect having not only reviewed the above literature, but especially having assessed its quality. Despite the types of concerns expressed so far in this review of the literature, explanations in terms of blatant psychological abnormality clearly persist in some of the relatively modern accounts.[83] It is useful to draw on some brief examples to illustrate the conceptual confusion in the interpretation of many of the results of the work on the psychology of terrorists.

Ferracuti,[84] in an attempt to develop a sociopsychiatric view of terrorism and terrorists, noted that predominant explanations of terrorist motivation related to the 'generally accepted characteristics . . . [of] violence and death wishes', but based on the observations made by him in studying Italian left and right-wing terrorists, they:

> rarely suffer from *serious* personality abnormalities. Generally, they demonstrate a good capacity to stand stress, both in clandestinity and in long term imprisonment, and an ability to organize themselves in groups, to sustain each other and to carry out adequate actions aimed at propaganda and dissemination of their principles [emphasis added].

Although Ferracuti's findings are frequently used (and particularly the above quotation) as support for the normality of terrorists, they need closer examination with respect to their internal inconsistency. Kellen,[85] who himself does not appear to address the inconsistency, cited Ferracuti as describing the psychology of right-wing terrorists thus: 'Even when they do not suffer from a clear psychopathological condition, their basic psychological traits reflect an authoritarian-extremist personality', characterized by behaviours such as an 'ambivalence towards authority', 'poor and defective insight', 'emotional detachment from the consequences of their actions', 'destructiveness' and 'adherence to violent subcultural values', among others (p. 15). Ferracuti himself argued that the implications of his findings were apparently 'self-evident' in that 'right-wing terrorism can be very dangerous not only mainly because of its ideology, but because of its general unpredictability and because of its destructiveness often resulting from psychopathology'.[86] Therefore while terrorists are not suffering with a 'clear psychopathological condition', they are still certainly 'not normal' – they are distinct in psychological terms from non-terrorists by being characterized by a specific, finite set of trait behaviours. Ferracuti's ideas about the psychology of the terrorist appear befuddled with an unclear conceptual argument, and there are several factors that illustrate how and why.

First there is an obvious reluctance by Ferracuti to describe the terrorists as either wholly 'normal' (i.e. as not being distinctly characterized by several marked traits) or wholly 'abnormal', possibly a reflection of the kind of unhelpful language being used. So as far as being psychologically characterized in terms of personality attribution, the Italian terrorist thus apparently lies in some grey area between the two – there is something slightly less than the stated 'serious' personality disorder. Ferracuti then says that their behavioural pattern 'reflects' a personality type, but not that the terrorists *have* 'authoritarian-extremist' personalities. This is not a pedantic criticism, although bearing in mind the point above about language, it reflects conceptual confusion within the theoretical parameters that Ferracuti has adopted. The issue that emerges appears to be that such research is all too willing to ascribe positivist explanations of behaviour, yet it argues that this still does not either characterize 'abnormality' or set the terrorist aside from the non-terrorist. The terrorist is simply quite 'different', therefore, and not 'abnormal'. Furthermore, for Ferracuti to argue that the implications of his results were 'self-evident' on the basis of the 'ideology', 'unpredictability' and 'destructiveness' associated with terrorism, he seems to be suggesting that the existence of some 'psychopathology' is an inevitable consequence of becoming a right-wing terrorist per se. Again, this needs to be very carefully qualified with respect to what he appears to be hinting at as a form of increasing brutalization occurring as membership is prolonged and commitment to the group ideals increases. This obviously then calls into question the predictive utility of measuring terrorist personalities after the event, particularly when the measured 'traits' (when they are actually *measured*, and not implied, as Pearlstein, Post and others suggest) are used in arguments about why people become involved in terrorism in the first place.

Ferracuti later admitted that attempts to explain terrorism on certain levels were still, even by then (1982), scarce: 'attempts to explain . . . terrorism . . . at a group phenomenon level, or the process of becoming a terrorist, are less common'.[87] Although Ferracuti was himself responsible for earlier research concluding with suggestions that terrorists *are* psychologically different from non-terrorists, he argued that 'although mentally imbalanced individuals, in the psychiatric range, can be used by terrorist groups, what is of greater interest is, of course, the 'normal' terrorist, that is the individual who is mentally sane'.[88] Despite this implicit recognition of an apparent absence of convincing evidence to suggest terrorist abnormality, Ferracuti did not let go of the argument that 'the terrorist' was still at least 'only slightly altered, at most in the psychoneurotic or psychopathic range'.

Given the relatively tiny amount of detailed psychological studies on terrorists altogether, the lack of conceptual clarity in what research does exist is still astounding. Using such conclusions then as a basis for supporting and building on these assertions can be dangerously misleading. Certainly it makes subsequent discussion quite difficult, and allows for much flexibility in the interpretation of the conclusions of studies like these (which, in this context, is not necessarily helpful).

Ferracuti, Kellen and Cooper together represent some of the earliest but confusing foundations of modern day assumptions about terrorist psychology. At best, they conclude the terrorist is either completely mad (e.g. Carlos, as Kellen argued) or 'half mad' (or mad some of the time) (e.g. the Italian terrorists in Ferracuti's study). Kellen's arguments, like Cooper's and Ferracuti's, do not appear to embrace their implications fully, but it is only from direct analyses of their original works (and not second-hand reviews which skim over the details) that this trend emerges – indeed it should be clear that the second-hand interpretations open up a variety of problems that are symptomatic of something altogether different. Sometimes the inconsistencies in the original research are quite blatant – while Kellen is satisfied to describe terrorists such as Carlos as psychopathic, Kellen still criticizes other 'observers' in that, as described earlier, they 'never postulate that terrorists feel sorry for what they do'.[89] Again, this is not an unnecessarily critical point but illustrates the conceptual confusion by what appears to be an unwillingness to characterize terrorists firmly within the given framework adopted by the researchers.

A final point to make here is that Kellen often emphasized the lures associated with some terrorists' lives, quoting Carlos as saying both that 'revolution is the strongest of tonics'[90] as well as Kellen particularly emphasizing that Carlos reported: 'I like women'. While the idea that people join terrorist groups because of some (usually not apparent) 'lures' is well described in several contexts (as we will see in the next chapter), to interpret them as necessarily feeding some personality disorder is misleading.

Inconsistency appears to tarnish much of the individual psychological research on terrorists, and again this side to the research has not been a theme which has emerged clearly enough from the literature. As if the question of 'who or what is a terrorist?' was not problematic enough, there are now clearly differing views between researchers on what constitutes 'abnormality' and what does not, as well as whether positivist explanations constitute valid means of exploration in this field given both the absence of common identifiable personality characteristics, and even the presence of *similarities* between terrorists and non-terrorists (aside at all from the issues of generalization of findings or theoretical extrapolation).

As also argued in Chapter 2, the methodological issue is very important as it is possibly the only one with which total agreement between conflicting views of researchers might be found; for example, even though the present author might disagree with some theoretical positions of others (and/or vice versa), the fact that some of the attributions of abnormality and positivist theorizing described above are *not* based on first-hand analysis is an unavoidable and real problem. While some may attempt to develop the West German team's original findings based on those traits subsequent researchers *assume* as 'characteristic' of terrorists, there can be little progression beyond the same type of attractive logic, inconsistent and wholly flawed as it is, beyond the use of psychopathological models as described in the opening sections of this chapter – this might help clarify why it was necessary to present and follow the simple logic of the 'psychopathy' discussion earlier in this chapter, even though we tend to dismiss the idea so very quickly even now. In particular, Andrew Silke[91] has vociferously opposed Jerrold Post and others for this: 'So while on the one hand freely acknowledging the lack of "major" psychopathology, Post . . . [has] been quick to switch the search towards finding some form of *minor* psychopathology'.

The unchecked tendency to reinterpret and re-circulate the conclusions of earlier findings based on renewed data 'usage' pays far too little credence to the original context in which it was used. Although a clear conclusion from the present review (to this point) suggests the need for systematic, analytical (and not just descriptive) reviews of this literature to be produced, reviews of the literature that examine evidence for 'abnormality' and 'normality' might seem almost pointless then, because some reviews (e.g. Crenshaw's 1986 review) would easily be able to use arguments from the *same* studies to support *either* perspective (subtle as this may be).

Silke describes such interpretations as 'dangerously misleading. It encourages the notion that terrorists are in some respects psychologically abnormal, but it balks at going so far as to advocate clinical personalities. In the end the trend has done little except taint terrorism with a pathology aura'.[92] Silke surmises that such approaches have 'left the psychology of the individual [terrorist] corrupted in their wake. Blatant abnormality is rejected by most commentators (though ... there is a steady stream of speculators who return to this notion). Instead, a pervasive perception exists that terrorists are abnormal in more subtle ways' (p. 67).

The difficulties of the 'terrorist personality' research

In his highly critical review, on conceptual, theoretical and empirical grounds, of psychological research suggesting terrorist abnormality and positivist-inclined research in terrorist psychology more generally, Taylor[93] highlighted the attractiveness of such explanations and points to what might be seen as an expression of simple logic that such explanations are used: 'Indeed, it might be argued that the *nature* of terrorist acts offers excellent vehicles for the expression of paranoia and other abnormalities' (emphasis added). Silke,[94] in a later review of the same evidence, also emphasizes the attractiveness of using terms such as 'antisocial, narcissistic and paranoid personality types', which portray the terrorist's behaviour as characteristic of an abnormal personality since there is the obvious conclusion that 'observers cannot but fail to notice the striking parallels between the two'. Again, a significant danger in such analyses is that some exceptions to the rule of terrorists as 'normal' can be (and are) pointed to as a means of supporting a more significant position.

Taylor has warned that these types of psychological explanations of terrorism are attractive because they allow for what appears to be a simple categorization of complex situations. It is possible to argue, however, that the key emergent issue from discussions of psychological work on terrorists does not relate to the potential use of psychological traits as explanatory causes for becoming terrorists. Rather the relevance of the issue would become clearer by examining the *interpretation* of the *usefulness* of those traits, if and when they do exist at all, and presumably if they are rigorously recorded and verified – this is one major pitfall of current attempts at 'profiling' terrorists: there is little or no sense of how the identification of presumed common traits might actually be harnessed for practical purposes.

The purpose of such a critique is to question the nature and direction of this research in the hope that it might encourage researchers to focus efforts onto more fruitful areas, or at the very least be explicit about the uses and limitations of the concepts described. In contemporary psychological investigation, psychometric evaluation formally and systematically identifies and assesses personality characteristics through putting questions to an individual – thereby, according to Blackburn,[95] reducing the intricacies of behavioural observations into more easily categorical 'classes of behaviour', i.e. traits. Of course, access to groups of terrorists would be necessary in attempting to establish trends and thus would be needed to render any conclusions based on psychometrically measurable traits valid (whether *between* certain kinds of terrorist groups or *within* them). An important issue here (recognition of which is sorely lacking in the context of terrorism research in general), and one that Blackburn reminds us of, relates to the *predictive utility* of trait measures as used by psychologists – particularly here in the context of research suggesting that certain types of people are more likely to become terrorists than others. It is clear within contemporary psychology that traits are weak predictors of behaviour in specific situations, and responses that are, as Blackburn suggests, 'supposedly indicative of the same trait' do not inter-correlate at a significant level.[96] One cannot, of course, expect trait measures to predict single occurrences. Personality traits cannot be inferred from single behavioural responses – instead it is generally assumed that some *stability* exists for a wide range of social and emotional personality traits over time and situation (ibid). This simple assumption does not translate well into psychological analyses of terrorism however. Merari and Friedland[97] raise an important conceptual point in relation to this issue. They summarize the nature of the personality-based research in terrorism as continuing to reflect:

> clinically oriented analyses [which] have typically been carried out on a small number of cases, and their conclusions are frequently overgeneralized . . . moreover even if it were possible to identify some common attributes of the terrorist personality, transformation of such information into an explanation would be hindered by its predictive irreversibility. That is, the fact that terrorists share certain characteristics or traits by no means implies that any person who has these traits is bound to become a terrorist.

The authors argue that hence, this automatically limits the usefulness of terrorist profiles.

Many attempts have also been made to develop individual or broader taxonomies or typologies of terrorists. Broader attempts have included categorization systems based on their 'commonly held motivations that seem to move individuals and groups to use terrorist techniques for political change',[98] and socio-economic profiles of specific groups. Handler, in arguing for the development of improved terrorist 'profiles' of American left- and right-wing terrorists, notes that while 'evidence is available . . . [and] comes from a variety of sources . . . none of these efforts has brought together conclusively a definitive sense of how membership in these two extremist political groups differed'.[99] In 1990, Handler offered a now well-known socio-economic profile of American left- and right-wing terrorists, arguing that the West German study of 1981–1982 had been previously the most significant. According to Handler, efforts at developing such a profile would eventually allow for greater insights into understanding how 'these groups were organized', as well as 'differences between leadership qualities

and rank-and-file characteristics, and even the importance of gender . . .'
Handler's analysis indicated 'clear socioeconomic differences between right-
wing and left-wing terrorists'. How useful this type of research is as far as
trying to establish explanations of why people turn to terrorism might be
better served by taking the discussion further however.

Attempts to produce an *individual* terrorist profile include Russell and
Miller, who described the 'typical' terrorist as: 'likely to be single, male,
aged between twenty-two and twenty-four with some university experience,
probably in the humanities. He is likely to come from a middle- or upper-
class family, and was probably recruited to terrorism at University, where
he was first exposed to Marxist or other revolutionary ideas'.[100] Strentz[101]
gives a very detailed demographic profile of 1960s and 1970s left-wing
'American and international terrorist groups', and gives profiles of Middle
Eastern terrorists, and right-wing terrorists. He is quick to remind us however that the (very detailed) data presented in his analysis should be seen
rather as of historical benefit 'which presents what terrorists groups *were*'
(emphasis added). Rather this statement (and indeed other attempts at demographic profiles) could be rephrased to: 'which presents how *specific* members
of *specific* groups were at *specific* times of *specific* stages in their own *specific*
types of terrorist campaign'. As asserted in Chapter 2, we cannot hope to
examine terrorism outside the context in which it takes place.[102]

Taylor[103] agrees in reflecting on the usefulness of such composite pictures
of terrorists: 'its utility depends largely upon assumptions of uniformity
amongst terrorist groups, and the acceptance of uniform characteristics in
the data base from which the summaries are drawn'. Of course, there are
innumerable examples of terrorist groups (not least the Irish ones, which
Taylor uses as his example to contrast with Russell and Miller's profile)
that contrast vividly to those characteristics drawn from their sample (of
18 terrorist groups). This clearly suggested a limited scope and the usefulness of this should be apparent from much of the discussion in this chapter.
Blackburn reminds us also that the issues surrounding the utility of traits for
understanding behaviour are 'as much conceptual as they are empirical'[104]
but Friedland,[105] otherwise dismissing the utility of personality traits in the
context of understanding terrorism, concludes: 'The critique of the attribution of terrorist behaviour to individual idiosyncrasy or pathology is not
meant to imply that individual predispositions play no role whatsoever
in the emergence of terrorist groups and in eruptions of terrorist action'
(McCauley expressing the same sentiment, as described earlier). This in
turn might lend support to the idea, for example, that psychological motives
may influence the particular *form* that terrorist campaign tactics take (for
example, the seizure of hostages as opposed to assassination) as opposed
to relating to some supposed conscious decision to become a terrorist,[106]
which in fact is yet another misnomer. As Drake[107] ably demonstrated, we
have only just begun to delve deeper into much-needed research on terrorist

target selection. Many terrorist movements, especially those larger ones such as Al Qaeda which rely on support networks from their wider communities, plan their attacks carefully as we shall see in detail in Chapter 5. Trying to instil fear without assuming 'responsibility' then for deaths can be a strong concern, particularly for ethno-nationalist terror movements.

Terrorists are not always necessarily 'psychologically' compelled to conduct terrorism, or even specific *types* of terrorism, and the strategic logic (sometimes relatively sophisticated) needs close attention in attempting to discern which factors (e.g. psychological or strategic) appear to determine terrorism more, if either. The debate need not necessarily be a polar one between psychological and 'rational choice' or strategic explanations of terrorism – terrorism, from both a psychological, personal *and* group/ organizational strategic perspective, often appears to follow a rational choice process. Attempting to polarize the two might represent a misunderstanding about the nature of how psychological perspectives might only *complement* views from other disciplines (and vice versa). The psychological and strategic dimensions are easily observable from much of what terrorists say about themselves. Consider the following comments from a PIRA Army Council member, who discussed with the author the breakdown of the first PIRA ceasefire (in 1996), as a good illustration of the tactical and strategic considerations of the movement:[108]

> I would say that since the breakdown of the first ceasefire, the campaign has been very . . . restrained, I would imagine. I think it was inevitable it [the 1994–1996 ceasefire] was going to break down, because there was no movement from the Brits. You see, and this is what a lot of people didn't do, you had to look behind the print and look at the tactical, the strategy . . . being pursued by both the British, by the Republicans and by nationalists in general. But you can see now that the British strategy in our mind was to prolong the ceasefire without giving a thing for as long as possible, in the eventuality that it would create disunity or fragment the republican movement in general. Now the republican movement has to look at it in such a way as saying that our priority here, or our objective here, is to get into negotiations as soon as possible, so that we can negotiate constitutional political change. Now to do that, we need to have a nationalist consensus . . . like a strong nationalist consensus involving the Dublin Government, the SDLP, and various nationalist political parties, which would in reality be far stronger than anything the IRA can afford to deliver, militarily. Now if the British [saw] that, they were in a no-win situation. I say in a sense, that if the IRA ceasefire broke down, automatically the nationalist consensus was completely weakened right? On the other hand if they can prolong the IRA ceasefire, then they thought that the

IRA was going to fragment, and therefore, Irish nationalism had no 'teeth', I think it was the only option open to us. We certainly thought that we were going to be lulled into a sense, a false sense of promises that was never going to be delivered. And with regard resuming military operations like, to maintain the, the pressure, as well as the unity and the strength of Irish nationalism, which in a positive way has always been effective, but like, at that particular point in time, with the Brits openly not delivering, it was the right course of action for us to take. I would hope that we would be in a position to be able to, which I have no doubt that we will be, that we will be able to a maintain the pressure on the British, with, ah, *quality* operations rather than quantity. I would *hope* that that would be the case, know what I mean? To try and make it more surgical, ok? But, ah, well, I mean, it's always difficult to form even a proper judgement, d'you know like? From here, like, the leadership at the moment, are on the pulse of everything, and they have things available to them, information available to them, that they ah, determines whatever actions they're going to take. And of course, we are still concerned with intelligence. It's the people behind the scenes that we would be more aware of now. Ah, back to the days of pre-ceasefire, let's say, I mean, for example, John McMichael would have been targeted, and all those others involved in the UDA action squads, the death squads, whatever you want to call them. All of those people who *behind* the scenes would have been promoting their activities would have been targeted, and McMichael would have been one of those. He would have been one of them obviously because for us, he organized them in the sense, not just to be proactive, but to be *effective*. So that would be the reason, why people like David Ervine and Billy Hutchinson, these people, that have previously been very effective as military leaders, if you know what I mean, ah, and I can tell you this straight away. Right up to the very day of the ceasefire, they would have been tops on our list. And as far as the ceasefire goes, if things did break down, in a crisis, they would probably be the first to go.

The 'non-psychological' elements of terrorism may not always be so obvious then, not just for how individual and group behaviour is shaped and determined within an existing terrorist context (which has implications, for example, for how we might understand escalation and de-escalation of individual commitment, violence and even entire campaigns of violence) but for analyses attempting to understanding why people become terrorists in the first place.

A key theme to emerge at this point, however, is the concern raised by Crenshaw, mentioned at the beginning of this chapter. It is the integration of levels of analysis that has proven difficult, and especially in discussions that attempt to highlight the potential for thinking about the role of personality in analyses – yet most researchers continue to ignore this issue. While the example above from the PIRA member illustrates just how there is a strong strategic dimension to internal decision-making (related to organizational conduct, targeting, etc.), it must be emphasized that this does not necessarily resemble either the nature of, or types of, reasons why people join terrorist groups in the first place, or why terrorists subsequently behave (or are constricted to behave) in the ways that they do once membership of a group has been attained. This is a crucial point, and is one that has been long recognized in the criminological literature, as we shall see in the next chapter.

Taylor,[109] and Taylor and Quayle[110] are altogether more blunt in their critique of the accounts attempting to explain terrorism on the whole. These attempts in Taylor's view aim to provide overall encompassing theories of terrorism, and perhaps it is by this dimension that they do not succeed. Taylor argues that all in all, existing psychological accounts of terrorism continue to offer little more than 'common-sense accounts', replete with 'broad concepts, which on examination are not readily translatable into more detailed psychological concepts'.[111] As he notes, such explanations suffer from a 'lack of specificity' and a failure to address why so few people exposed to the presumed generating conditions of terrorism will actually become terrorists. One solution to this is offered in the next chapter.

A further important issue about the validity of existing individual psychological approaches to understanding terrorists is that there is little appreciation of the immense heterogeneity of terrorism. While there remains such an emphasis on reductionist thinking about terrorist behaviour, our focus will probably remain on the *individual* rather than encourage us to a consideration of his overall strategy or aspiration. This highlights the need to incorporate more detailed analyses of the issues and complications posed by the heterogeneity of terrorism and it is an assertion which validates the need for context-specific and detailed case studies of individual terrorists and terrorist organizations (in my view, before comparative studies – in a psychological sense – are even suggested). Arguments about heterogeneity are also supported when cultural factors are considered. It is clear that Western analysts have very little understanding or knowledge of the basic social, cultural and other relevant differences that exist between Western Europe, the Middle East or Asia that are significant to a wide variety of issues and even types of explanations found in Western research (and particularly the assumptions that guide such research to the degree that we do not even think of them, let alone question them).

An important conceptual implication of this, according to Merari and Friedland,[112] is that because of the heterogeneity of terrorism, there is, again: 'no sound, a priori reason to assume much in common between different terrorist groups'. This may also be responsible for the failure of attempts to arrive at a 'coherent, well-grounded' psychological theory of the causes of 'terrorism' per se.[113] The conceptual problems of definition do not help either in this light, but efforts to arrive at formulating a theory of terrorist behaviour (in whatever shape) must account for and accommodate the heterogeneity of the phenomenon as well as the wide heterogeneity of individual motivations that terrorist members might themselves push as explanatory factors. Researchers must recognize that heterogeneity is a very pervasive emergent theme, not only across the spectrum of terrorist groups, but even *within* certain groups. This is perhaps another potentially most useful reason to study historical and biographical accounts of terrorism within psychological contexts.

Conclusions

Some of the more technical yet necessary arguments presented in this chapter have suggested that the quality and rigour of the research pointing to abnormality is such that its propositions are built on very shaky empirical, theoretical and conceptual foundations. Nevertheless, for many in the research and analytic community this still does not mitigate against the possibility that terrorists (and, in some cases, even the *supporters* of terrorists) are still psychologically 'different' or special, and unfortunately it will probably continue to be difficult to challenge this view forthrightly in the absence of basic and pure research on terrorist activities from psychologists in particular. It is indeed pessimistic that one of the few certainties about this issue is probably the lack of conceptual and practical clarity with which the term 'abnormality' is understood and used (even solely within the academic world), possibly a reflection of the multidisciplinary nature of the spread of terrorism research and researchers. However, it is equally significant that contributors from psychology have not even addressed systematically the conceptual issues surrounding the utility of trait measures. The psychological research on terrorism would do well to be cognizant of the concerns raised by forensic psychologist Blackburn for example, if psychologists were to outline and describe the relevance and utility of personality traits and more generally the role of any 'individual psychology of terrorism', that might seriously have something to offer the study of terrorism and the complex process whereby people 'become' terrorists.

At this point, it may be worth summarizing some basic assertions:

(1) Explanations of terrorism (particularly at the level of the individual) in terms of personality traits are insufficient in trying to understand why

people become involved in terrorism. At the risk of making a very obvious point, this is still a necessary assertion to make in light of the direction of some of the contemporary literature. This is not exactly the same as saying that psychological explanations alone are insufficient in accounting for people turning to terrorism (true as this may be) because the 'personality concept' issue needs to be temporarily isolated as far as its explicit and implicit purported importance is concerned, in this context. Although the frustration–aggression hypothesis (and its implications about the actors whose behaviour it purports to explain) and its derivatives have found their way into several political science theories of terrorism, the lack of acknowledgement of the conceptual problems involved (as viewed by contemporary psychology) persists and we need not only to recognize this, but strive to address its utility at all; this assertion is also a reflection of the need to heed Crenshaw's caution about integrating levels of analysis.

(2) Explanations of terrorism in terms of personality traits are insufficient alone in trying to understand why some people become terrorists and others do not, or more generally why people join terrorist groups. This is not exactly the same as the first point. This assertion also relates to the inherent attractiveness yet danger in placing too much emphasis on the 'needs-fulfilment' and psychodynamic stance, and for the same conceptual reasons as we might criticize other trait-based approaches (and the interpretations of personality types and traits in this context altogether), such hypotheses are susceptible to the same concerns; in mainstream contemporary psychology, trait theories do not attempt to be all-encompassing and to explain all behaviour – therefore the same mistakes should not be made in applying such models to explain terrorism (which to an outsider might seem to involve discrete and non-complex behaviour) and future attempts at developing individual terrorist profiles ought to bear this in mind; the nature of the terrorist personality research is such that some of it does suffer from this simplicity while more of it simply equates itself (intentionally or not) with the crudely simplistic idea of 'nature' vs. 'nurture' in *both* explaining terrorism *and* explaining why people become terrorists; terrorism research using personality concepts needs to be explicit in its aspirations, stated utility and boundaries.

(3) *Existing* explanations of terrorism in terms of personality traits that try to suggest reasons as to why some people become terrorists and others do not (all other situational factors presumed more or less similar) suffer from so many conceptual, theoretical and methodological problems that they are not only weakened as asserted (and testable) hypotheses but are flawed internally, inconsistent and demonstrate a lack of understanding of basic psychological concepts. As the next chapter will illustrate, it might be the case that we have to distinguish questions relating to why people become terrorists as opposed to how they become terrorists. Questions of any occu-

pational choice (be it the movement into becoming a terrorist, an accountant, or something else) are in truth essentially impossible to answer, and more often than not relate to a variety of idiosyncratic and often accidental factors. How questions describe the process that unfolds, however, can be developed and understood in terms of developmental processes, and not theories that suggest the possession of 'traits' or state qualities.

(4) Related to this is a more explicit caution about attempts to profile terrorists, even in a broad sense. Much improvement is needed if researchers are to continue to seriously forward such views about the role that personality plays in explaining terrorist behaviour, whether the present author might conceptually disagree or not with the approach in the first place. Again if we might make an inference from contemporary psychology – psychologists do not attempt to make inferences about personality from single behavioural occurrences, single meetings with individuals, or other equally casual observations about people's behaviour. Personality assessment is something that derives from tried and tested methods (e.g. psychometric testing), and even then, this is only the first step towards offering some kind of explanation for behaviour. A next step is for psychological approaches to acknowledge the instrumental nature of terrorism, thereby encompassing emotional and instrumental dimensions.

The purpose of these assertions is not necessarily to attempt to comment on the nature of psychological theories of personality or motivation, but to shed some conceptual and theoretical light on the overall utility of the 'individual' psychological research on terrorists and the subsequent policy directions in which further research is currently being directed (terrorist profiling exercises to name but one). The most positive conclusion we might arrive at by this point is that research on terrorist personalities, if it is to continue (and again, it probably will), would at least do well to be aware of the kinds of limitations which have marred the conclusions of much of the existing work of this nature.

On a more practical note, there are still not enough detailed case studies of terrorists to inform psychological analyses and perhaps even comprehensive reviews of the literature. Even attempts to assess literature by supporting some general points (e.g. this chapter also) might be accused of over-generalizing in support of a point that has its roots in conventional wisdom (e.g. stating that because PIRA members appear 'normal', and because Palestinian Islamic Jihad members also appear 'normal', then terrorists seem to be normal people). Generalizing with cross-sectional comparisons (let alone generalizing across what we think constitutes 'membership') such as this is a dangerous trap to those unfamiliar with the logic behind the need to conduct longitudinal analyses (e.g. those that examine single cases across a period of time to see if any important changes happen, and if so, how and why these changes occur). The need to have longitudinal studies in terrorism research is highlighted with the simple problems seen from social psychological research efforts, with *primacy effects* for instance. Getting to know someone takes time and requires many interactions of course, and also it is first impressions that generally have the most impact and are the most enduring. Hence sparse meetings in the field have impact in many more subtle ways that field researchers might not always be aware of. When terrorism researchers meet 'normal' terrorists for the first time, they may then be 'primed' to form more positive views about other terrorists they meet and interact with.

This is a significant assertion to make as the importance and depth of attention paid towards locating personality factors (i.e. generally positivist approaches) in understanding, and moreover *explaining* terrorism per se, becomes undermined. At the very least, it raises questions relating to the utility of such efforts. A large part of the conceptual confusion surrounding the early (but still very prominent) accounts of terrorist 'psychology' relates to conceptual confusion, and particularly the scope of such theories remains very unclear. It does not clearly emerge whether the approaches described earlier are discriminate regarding their explanatory power. It does appear that they attempt to be over-encompassing in their projected capacity, by attempting to provide explanations for involvement in terrorism which simultaneously also explain the occurrence of terrorist violence. Indeed, it may well be that a failure to adequately understand and appreciate the complexity of the nature of terrorism may well play a part in this. As the discussion in this section illustrates, there are specific processes that may characterize both parts of the terrorist's 'life' (i.e. becoming involved, and remaining involved). Unfortunately, the terrorist literature still does not reflect this, few exceptions aside.

Finally, despite its slightly increasing prevalence, a characteristic of much of the individual psychological literature examined in this chapter that continues to be cited by terrorism researchers is its *age*. If psychology is to play an effective part in the multidisciplinary grouping of research efforts in an area which is not only complemented by, but *demands*, a multi-disciplinary approach, it would do well to approach the complexity of terrorism (and the implied complexity of its own 'kinds' of questions) in a much clearer manner on several fronts, and to begin to explore more system-atically some of the pressing issues that concern policy-makers and ultimately the general public. If not, we not only run the risk of doing a dis-service to efforts at understanding terrorism, but also do a disservice to how a psychological contribution to this complex problem (from the perspec-tives described in this chapter) might ultimately be perceived. That much (but, fortunately, not all) of the psychological literature that has emerged since 9/11 has once again attempted to revise the notion of terrorists as necessarily abnormal is not encouraging, but such approaches must continue to be challenged.

The next three chapters represent a challenge to these approaches by attempting to shift the focus onto the problem from different perspectives, by asking different questions, and thereby suggesting a search for different outcomes.

4

BECOMING A TERRORIST

Introduction

One of the implications of the analyses discussed in Chapter 3 is that there not only is confusion about what a psychology of terrorism implies, but that even in some of the simplest critical analyses of the concept of the terrorist or terrorism, a multiplicity of inconsistent and confusing uses of psychological findings emerge. Because of this confusion, it might appear already that an attempt to develop a psychology of terrorism is an unattainable objective. It might also be the case that perhaps we ought to consider instead, the exploration of ways in which our knowledge of psychological processes can inform and improve our understanding of terrorism (and all that that implies). At any rate, it would obviously suggest that we attempt to develop a more sophisticated way of understanding involvement in terrorism. With this in mind, this chapter, and the two chapters that follow it, present a different approach to understanding the terrorist by not just acknowledging that involvement and engagement in terrorism is best thought of as a *process*, but offering a fresh perspective on the benefits of exploring the outcomes such an approach might bring. By making several critical distinctions throughout, not only should we have a way of seeing the reality of involvement in terrorism for what it is, but we have a conceptual base from which we might develop other types of analysis, as well as on a more practical note, offer an identification of more obvious intervention points from which counter-terrorist and anti-terrorist efforts may emerge (in the broadest possible sense).

This and the following chapters present then the bases for a possible *process model* of terrorism that may, in addition, begin to move the debate away from complex but essentially sterile discussions about definitions of terrorism as some sort of abstract event, to identifiable behaviours and their antecedents, expected consequences and outcomes that are associated with terrorism. Furthermore, and perhaps with particular significance at this stage of our analysis, the process model of these three chapters attempts to capture a meaning for psychological approaches that does not depend upon narrow definitions derived from elsewhere, or from definitions that have to be so general as to be meaningless and of no real utility to anyone.

On another level, this approach represents a very different approach to traditional analyses of the terrorist in that there is an explicit effort made to consider involvement in terrorism as a process comprising discrete phases to 'becoming' a terrorist, 'being' a terrorist (or what might be construed as both (a) remaining involved and (b) engaging in terrorist offences) and disengaging from terrorism. In light of some of the conclusions from Chapter 1 and the dangers of pathologizing terrorist activity for its own sake, perhaps the term 'becoming a terrorist' might be more usefully reinterpreted as 'initially becoming engaged and/or involved in doing terrorism'. To those familiar with theoretical criminology, these kinds of distinctions are not new. In particular such distinctions have proved useful in understanding what factors influence and limit involvement and engagement in juvenile delinquency,[1] involvement in gangs[2] and other criminal activity. Its application to terrorism, however, has so far been notably underdeveloped.[3]

Clarke and Cornish[4] developed the rational choice theory (RCT) of criminal behaviour, which, although deriving from economic concepts, essentially attempts to integrate distinct phases of decision-making as it applies to crime.[5] Rational choice theory is deceptively simple in its features, but powerful in its clarity of integrating what might otherwise seem exceptionally complex. Clarke and Cornish argue that offenders, like the rest of us, seek to benefit themselves by making decisions that are to some degree 'rational', or shaped by supportive qualities. Furthermore, the focus of the theory is not on offenders themselves in terms of presumed individual differences from non-offenders, but on the offences themselves, and their features. Finally, a core distinction is made between involvement in crime and engagement in specific criminal events (or offences).[6] Clarke and Cornish argue essentially that different kinds of decisions are made between how and why a person becomes 'involved' in crime (or perhaps is 'open' to criminal behaviour) and why a person decides to commit a specific offence. In the criminological literature such notions are well developed, although their true conceptual potential has not yet been realized (attempts to anchor RCT in crude crime control and planning issues have largely hindered this development). Outside contemporary criminology however, they have not translated well across to efforts at understanding terrorism.

Critical distinctions

Using criminology-centred notions as a starting point, we have at our disposal some interesting and useful ways of driving the psychological analyses of terrorism forward. As we have seen, one of the most potent traps from the lack of conceptual clarity in the individual psychological literature is that there remains the risk that when we talk of why someone becomes a terrorist, we might still consider involvement as indicative of some individual 'state' or 'condition', rather than something (i.e. 'being involved and doing things') that someone seeks out, and strives to sustain for whatever reasons. The principal features of this and the next two chapters are not to demonstrate how individual factors in themselves are useful or predictive, but serve to highlight that a clearer way forward is to identify the factors that maintain involvement and sustain behaviour, and eventually contribute to the commission of acts of terrorism. Indeed, the critical importance of such distinctions cannot be over-emphasized. We can easily see how asking what we believe to be valid questions can mislead and confuse our understanding. Although such questions may be posed with the noblest and most willingly objective of intentions, vague and unhelpful questions about becoming a terrorist (e.g. 'what makes a terrorist?') may in fact be implicitly attempting to answer any or all of the following questions at the same time.

1 Why do people want to become involved in a group that engages in terrorist violence (for which we will have to rely on individual accounts from terrorists themselves, via interviews or autobiographical accounts, to supplement our own efforts to develop plausible and *verifiable* explanations)?

2 *How* do people become involved (the distinction between this and the above point will be of critical importance in terms of attempting to drive this research forward)?

3 What roles or tasks do they fulfil once a member (although there may be a hidden assumption here that it is possibly to identify the criteria for membership as having reached some clear 'state' or position)?

4 How *and* why does a person move within and through the terrorist organization?

5 How *and* why does the individual both 'assimilate' the shared values and norms of the group, and how *and* why he then 'accommodates' to engagement qualities not previously considered or expected prior to membership (*and* how and why different members 'assimilate' and 'accommodate' at varying rates, as well as whether or not this relates to some individual qualities as opposed to post-recruitment processes experienced at individual levels)?

6 How *and* why do the members commit specific acts of violence (e.g. do people become 'hardened' through experience?).

7 How *and* why they affect other members (and are themselves influenced by others) at various stages of their own and others' involvement?

8 How *and* why do they ultimately want to, or have to, disengage from terrorist activities, move into other non-violent but relevant support activities, or leave the organization altogether?

A critical conceptual point we can make at this point, and one that would be important in informing response strategies (at whatever stage they may be focused) as far as some sort of prevention or control is concerned, is that the issues that *each* of these individual questions address may (a) not be necessarily related to each other, and (b) answering one may not necessarily reflect upon another. This logic is not only consistent with the rational choice approach but arises from the same kinds of issues that have hindered criminological theory for so long – all of the above can equally capture the confusion around, for instance, the question 'what makes a criminal', or 'what makes a delinquent' etc.

Answering questions about why people may wish to become involved in terrorism then may have little bearing on the answers that explain what they do (or are allowed to do, as we shall see) as terrorists, or how they actually become and remain involved in specific terrorist operations. Similarly, answering questions about what keeps people involved with a terrorist organization may have surprisingly little if any bearing on what subsequently sees them disengaging from terrorist operations or from the organization (and/or broader movement) altogether (as we will see in Chapter 7, we have yet still to achieve some sense of prioritization even of efforts that would already seem focused and well-structured within narrow counter-terrorism strategies).

Similar issues were addressed at the 'Root Causes of Terrorism' conference in Oslo, in June 2003.[7] While terrorists are adept at identifying and publicizing what they perceive to be legitimate grievances, little attempt had been made to try to ascertain the links between apparent root causes and the emergence of terrorism. The following 'root causes' are routinely associated with leading to the emergence of terrorism:[8]

- Lack of democracy, civil liberties and the rule of law
- Failed or weak states
- Rapid modernization
- Extremist ideologies of a secular or religious nature
- Historical antecedents of political violence, civil wars, revolutions, dictatorships or occupation
- Hegemony and inequality of power
- Illegitimate or corrupt governments
- Powerful external actors upholding illegitimate governments
- Repression by foreign occupation or by colonial powers
- The experience of discrimination on the basis of ethnic or religious origins
- Failure or unwillingness by the state to integrate dissident groups or emerging social classes
- The experience of social injustice
- The presence of charismatic ideological leaders
- Triggering events

The history of terrorism is not going to be described here, as this is something that has been done numerous times elsewhere, and in substantial detail. For our purposes, however, and for the nature of the discussion being developed, there are some important issues we need to attend to. A popular belief is that by addressing the 'root causes' of terrorism we substantially reduce the threat of terrorism, an apparently plausible effort to contribute towards addressing the problem. Terrorist organizations often claim to represent legitimate grievances of a broader community, and often when the state is seen to react to the terrorist threat with a heavy-handed provocation, sympathy can become generated. This assumes a rather naive and simplistic cause and effect relationship, which, in reality, just does not exist. We must not assume that the identification of such root causes allows us to assume terrorists as passive actors. We know terrorism can be, and often is, based on imagined or 'virtual grievances', and whatever perceived 'real' grievances are identified as having existed at one time or another, terrorist organizations can be remarkably adept at changing the identity and nature of such grievances, all the while presenting them in a positive light when frequently attached to other publicized plights. If we were to attempt to produce a representative list of the grievances of terrorist groups then we would have a list with thousands of items. Those present at the Oslo conference agreed that we might best view such factors as preconditions that, according to Björgo,[9] 'set the stage for terrorism in the long run . . . producing a wide range of social outcomes of which terrorism is only one. Preconditions alone are not sufficient to cause the outbreak of terrorism'.

By attempting to critically assess the utility and relevance of identifying root causes of terrorism in this way, that is not to minimize the seriousness of such issues, but they naturally are problems that need solving in their own right, and not as a consequence of being associated with terrorism. Discussions that attempt to root terrorism in poverty alone or civil strife alone miss the fundamental attributes of terrorism identified in Chapter 1, that it is primarily a strategy and tactic open to any group from any background and for any politically related reason. Terrorism can technically come from anywhere and anyone. What the existence and identification of such preconditions does, as well as the failure to address them, is to heighten the likely risk and direction of the emergence of terrorism, which, when combined with triggering events such as police brutality, massacres or some other significantly provocative event, increase the likelihood substantially that terrorism might develop as a strategy for influencing, or stopping, such activities while simultaneously bringing about more of terrorism's effects. A more appropriate way then of seeing such root causes might be as both preconditions and potential triggering factors for terrorism. Notions of causality are unhelpful and imply a sense of predictive value that belies the complexity of terrorism as well as the strategic factors underpinning decisions to adopt terrorism either as a specific tactic or as (or part of, via the former) a broader strategy of violent protest. An underappreciated feature of terrorist campaigns that we shall explore in Chapter 6 in the context of disengagement is that terrorist campaigns are frequently sustained for reasons that differ significantly from those reasons that gave rise to the formation of the group in the first instance.

These critical points are important to make, but for the purpose of moving our present discussion forward, root cause issues primarily emerge whenever we try to answer the 'why' questions – e.g. *why* does someone become a terrorist? This is opposed to the 'how' questions that in reality may give us a clearer sense of what factors influence individuals to become involved with and engage in terrorism.

Unless we make these distinctions explicit, it is possible that when we ask 'what are the root causes of terrorism?' we may in fact be trying to force the answer to all of these 'routes to, through, and away from terrorism' and other questions through some singular explanation (and even at that, we may need to distinguish between how and why an individual becomes part of an *existing* terrorist group from that person who becomes part of an effort aimed at creating a *new* terrorist group altogether, or at least a group which eventually comes to embrace terrorism as a tactic within that group's broader strategy). In other words, if we do not ask the right questions, we will not arrive at meaningful answers. Similarly, the question 'how do we prevent terrorism?' may be as complex as 'what causes it?'

The relevance of making these distinctions also represents the need to move away from attempts to answer the 'why' and 'how' questions in the same ways that the individual psychology literature has proposed, as described in the previous chapter. Again, such approaches tend to assume that terrorism reflects some sort of unique or atypical social movement, or a homogeneous threat deriving from some homogeneous origin. Rather we might begin to think of involvement in terrorism as a process that is susceptible to, and limited by, among other things, strategic and psychological factors at whatever stage or degree of involvement we are examining. Thinking about terrorism as a process of course reflects its complexity, but thinking in this way can also help us to prioritize the questions we need to answer, and better focus policy decisions and resource allocation, which after all, reflect the reality of any response.

Answering questions about 'why' people become terrorists

Although it is apparent from Chapter 3 that too little is paid to terrorists' own accounts of their activities as a means of constructing a sense of their involvement in terrorism (whilst avoiding the kinds of diagnoses found in early accounts), it is useful to examine individual case histories for reasons that have little to do with inferring personality traits and more to do with attempts at identifying similarities across processes that may indicate a sense of development via engagement in a terrorist group. Perhaps an obvious point to begin with, but in answering questions about why people become involved in terrorism, we should first consider, if possible, posing questions to those who have been or are involved with terrorist organizations. The point may appear frivolous, but given some of the points developed in Chapter 2, we know that it is possible to meet with and speak to terrorists (indeed, increasingly so, as is becoming apparent from the literature). A member of the Provisional IRA who held a senior position in the movement agreed to be interviewed by the author, and to elaborate on his involvement, an excerpt from which is given below. The question posed to him was simple – 'why did you join the IRA?'

> I grew up in a non-political family. My mother would vote republican but that was it. My father was non-political and he seldom ever voted, at least it wasn't consistent I suppose. I think probably my first introduction to it was actually when I was going to primary school. I always had a tremendous interest in Irish history, and that continued on for a few years until secondary school. The history they taught us at that time was fascinating. Learning about Brian Boru, the Flight of the Earls, right up to the 1916 Rising, of course. I always had this tremendous interest in the history of the whole thing, but it wasn't until when the trouble broke out in the six counties that I . . . found myself . . . I think in conscience anyway, becoming more and more . . . committed. Well, I suppose really, our understanding of conflict, or our politicisation, is something that grows and it continues to grow throughout our lives. And I know it varies of course, but for me anyway, the sight of the B Specials [a paramilitary reserve police force in Northern Ireland] and the RUC [Royal Ulster Constabulary, the police service of Northern Ireland] beating nationalist people off the street in Derry was a big factor in joining the Republican movement. When I started going to Republican marches, things like that sort of, awakened some kinds of a commitment I think, within my conscience. It certainly was later a commitment I would be prepared to pursue at that stage. So it took a while, but yes, I became involved then as a republican, ah, activist. To me, *terrorist* is a dirty word, and I certainly don't . . . nor have I ever considered myself to be one, but ah, I remain an activist to this day. But that said, I always felt that the initial emotional thing, sort of developed into a greater understanding of what struggle is all about. And also, the fact, that I wouldn't be as emotionally responsive now as I would have been back then . . . it's deepened now, if you know

wh-, if you understand me. I think it's something that's still developing I'd say even today.

This man was charged with several attempted murders, attempted kidnapping, arms possession, as well as membership of an illegal organization,
and was released from prison in 1994 as part of the British Government's
early release scheme for prisoners. By the time he was interviewed by the
author, he had already served two lengthy prison sentences (yet, he still
regards himself and his involvement in the PIRA as part of an ongoing
'process' of politicization, a theme we will return to later). A number of
features of this account suggest the following tentative qualities:

1   The events vicariously experienced viewed by him were deemed signifi-
    cant enough to be perceived as as catalyst for his involvement with the
    PIRA. This appears, however, to gain significance only in the context
    of his already existing activities (i.e. his participation on Republican
    marches in Northern Ireland) coupled with some prior learning experi-
    ences (i.e. his exposure to and perceptions of Irish history) as well as
    what he identifies as an emotional state (an emotional 'responsiveness')
    that might suggest a greater openness to involvement when combined
    with the above factors.
2   There appears to be a deep sense of personal morality and identification
    with those victimized.
3   The circumstances and references to the broad socio-political conditions
    are described in a very basic, simplistic way.
4   In relation to (2) in particular, there seems to be an associated sense
    of urgency for action as well as a sense of inevitability for subsequent
    action.

Catalysts as primary involvement features

A frequent assumption about those who engage in terrorism relates to the
existence of a 'catalyst' event for involvement – the event suggested above
was the sight of civil rights abuses against the nationalist population in
Northern Ireland. This is another way of talking about possible triggering
factors more generally and reflects efforts to point to singular events that
helped 'push' the individual towards an existing terrorist group. A well-
known example from Northern Ireland was the events of what became
known as Bloody Sunday. On 30 January 1972, the Parachute Regiment of
the British Army shot dead 13 unarmed civilians during a civil rights
march that had been designated illegal by government authorities of the
time. The ensuing outrage spurred many Irish republicans to seek out
involvement in the Provisional IRA.

When recalled from memory, such events are deemed to hold great personal significance for individuals, but while some might have had personal experience of such victimization, either in terms of personal victimization through assault or some form of abuse, for others that victimization may not necessarily be proximal or real (as in the case of the man above, where the exposure to the victimization of others was more distant). What is real, however, appears to be something that might be characterized as a sense of communal identification with those victimized, and often an unwavering, confident dedication to the preservation and importance of the memory of the particular event itself. It can be misleading to attempt to identify the presence of unifying catalyst events as unambiguous 'push' factors, however. It might be more useful to attempt to examine how and why specific people are individually affected and experience those events in ways that act as a catalyst towards increased involvement (the notion that there might be certain 'predispositional' socialization or learning experiences that explain this will be explored later).

In relying only on unsubstantiated personal accounts (whether from interviews or other sources, such as autobiographies), there is a real risk in analyses of overstating the significance of particular aspects of the terrorist's life, or the significance of presumed catalyst events when such accounts of involvement are recalled. In terrorist autobiographies especially, particular events are usually recalled with more clarity and vivid detail than are the stages of gradual movement and socialization towards initial involvement and increased involvement in terrorist-related activities. It is perhaps a tendency of individuals themselves to push particular events as contributory factors and with the benefit of hindsight attribute as high a degree of causal responsibility as possible to external forces. The resulting reduction of personal responsibility can serve a vital purpose for the individual by minimizing any discomfort that may arise even when confronted with the direct knowledge of the consequences of their subsequent activities. The tendency to place the blame for personal behaviour on one's enemies reflects a simple attribution bias that can serve as a powerful control mechanism in conveying a sense of legitimacy for past behaviour and righteousness for further engagement.

To appreciate the relevance of this point further, Cordes,[10] and Taylor and Quayle[11] successfully identified common themes in terrorists' self-perception which have relevance to understanding the development of involvement in terrorism, and this appears to be a reflection of the importance of both the language terrorists use in general as well as how they use it.[12] Taylor and Quayle[13] reported that terrorists view their involvement in violence as a *provoked reaction* requiring *defence* against an *enemy*. Whatever the exact nature of the group, this is a common reason put forward for becoming involved. It is immensely difficult to ascertain of course, whether these types of verbal explanations would have existed without the acquired effects and qualities of membership, and life as part of a terrorist movement more generally. It is well known (and illustrated by the interview segment earlier) that many active terrorists became increasingly politicized the more time they spend in the movement, and perhaps especially so in prison.

However, while terrorists quickly become adept at justifying involvement and engagement in terrorism as a defensive reaction, they are rarely so articulate when asked to elaborate on the attractions and perceived benefits associated with the decision to join a terrorist movement (e.g. status, power, a sense of identity and camaraderie, the personal 'buzz' of excitement that accompanies the new role, the adoration by the broader supportive community, and even the lull of financial gain, in isolated cases).

The terrorist interviewed above refers to 'conscience' and a moral and political awakening – he sees it almost as a duty to take up arms in defence of his people and what is invoked in such accounts is a sense of legitimacy which many terrorists firmly ground in a sense of collective identity and collective responsibility. Legitimacy does not appear to be invoked or raised as an individual matter, but always at the level of the group, or wider victimized community. That is not to say that it is necessarily a criticism of the 'truthfulness' of individual accounts per se, but a reminder that it may reflect another quality of engagement with the terrorist group or even at a more basic level, another self-serving bias invoked when asked to explain past behaviour.

At another level, a person's stated motivation for involvement and justification for violence, Cordes[14] argues, can sometimes tell us more about the organization's internal use of propaganda and ideological control than anything conclusive about the completeness or otherwise of any personal account. The implication of this being that sometimes it can be difficult, if not completely impossible, to tell when self-accounts of involvement in terrorism derive from the individual's own sense of truth or some sort of commonly shared or acquired 'truth' that might develop from being involved in terrorism over time. While it may be plausible, certainly given what might appear to be bona fide personal accounts, to assume that such 'fraternalistic over egoistic' goals exist from the outset,[15] it is more likely that this reflects a learning quality incurred from continued involvement. This helps understand the importance that the frequently repeated rhetoric from terrorists can hold (which we so often dismiss as being unimportant or irrelevant). Terrorists reveal knowledge about themselves, according to Cordes, through propaganda (in an effort to persuade others – usually expressed at a group or organizational level, through statements or communiqués, etc.), but also through the less frequently identified 'auto-propaganda' efforts, in an effort to persuasively convince and remind themselves of the righteousness of their activities. Clearly then, identifying fraternalistic sentiments as motivating factors behind involvement can be fraught with difficulty unless considered within the context of broader issues.

A frequent feature of accounts displaying elements of a sense of being 'pushed' into terrorism by external forces is the significant lack, or reduction in significance, of the supportive qualities that influence individuals' movement into terrorism. Members of terrorist movements interviewed by Burgess, Ferguson and Hollywood[16] displayed this quality clearly – none of the interviewees 'indicated personal beliefs as a motive for their participation in violent or peaceful demonstrations'. Such features only become apparent when we examine accounts more closely or conduct interviews more critically. The degree of acquired ideological control and auto-propaganda that might exist for a person might be measured in one way as a function of how little the individual terrorist is prone to acknowledging the existence of a variety of real and imagined rewards available for joining the terrorist group, and being part of something that brings with it a whole variety of benefits, as described above. The true significance of particular assumed or self-identified catalyst events must thus be considered with caution: it may well be the case that their true significance is likely to be more potent to those already progressing through some already existing 'borderline' activity, such as expressing support via peaceful protest or something else. In fact, the overall significance of pushing catalyst events as triggering factors can only be appreciated in the context of other qualities of the descriptions given by activists. Particularly in those terrorists interviewed by Taylor and Quayle, the notion that there was simply 'no other choice' was a commonly offered explanation of initial involvement in a terrorist movement. Frequent references to violence being an inevitable response, a form of self-defence in fact, to broader conditions are common in all terrorist groups, and such explanations reflect heavily conspiratorial dimensions (legitimized usually with clear references to the victimized 'group' or community) in fundamentalist groups in particular. These issues will be described further in Chapter 5, but for the moment we must acknowledge that in terrorists themselves identifying particular events as especially significant, such events often tend to be recalled with a sense of importance and purpose that may obscure a host of other personal reasons that played a direct influence at the time of the initial move towards engagement with the terrorist group.

Identification as an attraction and byproduct of other positive features of involvement

Some authors refer to the positive attractions of membership of a terrorist group as *lures*. These reflect supportive qualities which the terrorist him or herself may be either reluctant or unintentionally forgetful to mention either in an interview situation or in an autobiographical account. We might consider lures as essentially positive features of increased engagement. They can be numerous, but the significance of each will vary for the individual concerned as well as the particular subjective importance they attach to each feature.

An appreciation of the community context is important in terms of trying to identify the source of what both creates and sustains such legitimacy. In this context, Post[17] draws a useful distinction in an attempt to classify terrorist groups. Rather than attempt to develop a typology based on methods or motivations, he identifies two major types on the basis of the distinct relationships such groups have with their environments: Post argues that each type may exert psychological influences on those members in dissimilar ways and accordingly may differentially attract members on the basis of different kinds of expected rewards. The first of these is the 'anarchic-ideologue' group. These were often relatively small, 'revolution'-based groups, committed to the overthrow of current political or social regime, largely for ideological reasons. The old left-wing European terrorist movements such as the German Red Army Faction and the Italian Red Brigades would have typified this type of group in the past. What Post describes as 'alienation' from the member's family or immediate community is characteristically found in members.

The second type of terrorist group is the 'nationalist-separatist' group. The Provisional IRA, with its long historical tradition of resistance against England and British rule, is a good example of this type of group and family involvement (whether father, uncles, cousins, etc.) has certainly been a pervasive element. The important point made here is that the members of such organizations are certainly not estranged from their families or communities, whose interests they claim to represent. An important point that Post develops here, however, is that the legitimization of one's decision to engage in violent protest, as well as involvement in a more general way, may, within the context of local circumstances, be seen as a rite of passage, a movement towards consolidation of one's identity within the broader community. This has been well described in the West Bank and Gaza strip where martyrs from Hamas, the Islamic Resistance Movement and other movements are held in high esteem within the community. Hassan,[18] who interviewed many militants in the region, describes how in Palestinian neighbourhoods:

> the suicide bombers' green birds appear on posters, and in graffiti – the language of the street. Calendars are illustrated with the 'martyr of the month'. Paintings glorify the dead bombers in Paradise, triumphant beneath a flock of green birds. This symbol is based on a saying of the Prophet Muhammad that the soul of a martyr is carried to Allah in the bosom of the green birds of Paradise.

Post and Denny[19] engaged in interviews with 35 incarcerated members of various Palestinian-affiliated groups, in particular Hamas and its armed wing Izz a-Din al Qassan, Hizbollah, the Islamic Jihad and others from secular movements. They were surprised at the similarities between individual 'pathways' into terrorism, a point made all the more salient for the researchers given the wide variety in their participants' backgrounds and histories:

> The boyhood heroes for the Islamist terrorists were religious figures, such as the Prophet, or the radical Wahabi Islamist, Abdullah Azzam; for the secular terrorists, revolutionary heroes such as Che Guevara or Fidel Castro were identified. Most had some high school, and some had education beyond high school. The majority of the subjects reported that their families were respected in the community. The families were experienced as being uniformly supportive of their commitment to the cause.

Such role models serve to both offer a source of authoritative legitimacy as far as the justification of violent reaction is concerned (as we will see in the next chapter, what the individual terrorist perceives to be as the *authority* inherent in such roles plays an exceptionally important role in sustaining the commitment of the individual) as well as to facilitate movement into the violent group more generally to the point of actually engaging in violent acts. In Post and Denny's analysis, the social setting appeared to be the source with the greatest apparent positive factor for joining (via implicit or explicit approval from peers and family), but the supportive qualities of engagement became clear via the researchers' interviews with imprisoned activists:

> Perpetrators of armed attacks were seen as heroes, their families got a great deal of material assistance including the construction of new homes to replace those destroyed by the Israeli authorities as punishment for terrorist acts.

And

> The entire family did all it could for the Palestinian people, and won great respect for doing so. All my brothers are in jail. One is serving a life sentence for his activities in the Izz a-Din Al Qassam battalions.

As Post and Denny describe, joining Fatah or Hamas increased 'social standing' among would-be recruits:

> Recruits were treated with great respect. A youngster who belonged

to Hamas or Fatah was regarded more highly than one who didn't belong to a group, and got better treatment than unaffiliated kids.

Similar data emerge from interviewees with activists in Northern Ireland. Burgess, Ferguson and Hollywood[20] interviewed one activist who pointed to his awareness of the importance associated with becoming involved in active resistance:

> The idols among our community shot up because they stood for something . . . As soon as your parents, and the priest at the altar, and your teacher are saying 'These men are good men. They are fighting a just thing here', it filters down quickly that these people are important and whatever they say must be right. So all of a sudden, you are bordering on supporting something that is against the government.

As briefly mentioned earlier, an additional expected benefit associated with attaining such a role, and most probably a factor in sustaining and keeping that role, is the realization that the role carries status not only within the immediate circle of activists, but also within the broader supportive community. Not only then is there a perceived value of being accepted within the group in its own right, but there is also an accompanying sense of status and excitement for the individual faced with the knowledge of the significance of the role within the broader community. This can be equally powerful not only for sustaining involvement but as a partial lure for onlookers.

The community context to involvement can vary substantially, however, depending on the nature of the terrorist group and the relationship it has with the community it claims to represent. Occasionally, unusual situations develop whereby involvement displays qualities that are at odds with any sense of voluntary movement into the group. Silke[21] describes how in some cases, particularly in Loyalist communities in Northern Ireland, it was not only unusual for certain young men not to be involved in the local paramilitary groupings, but in fact that a conscription-type scenario was not uncommon:

> The UDA press-gangs seventeen-year-olds into their organisation. If you get into trouble, they tell you to join the UDA. Last year one of my son's mates, who was seventeen, joined. Now he can't get out. He daren't speak out about it. Mostly you know that if you don't join, you're history.

This would be unusual, and typically would reflect specific local conditions or specific climates under which what might constitute 'membership' might have to be broadened for operational reasons (it is unlikely that duties central to the running of the organization in achieving its stated aims are conducted by those press-ganged into membership), but the example used by Silke is important, indirectly raising questions of what involvement might imply in a broader sense.

Even on a more personal level, a sense of approval from a significant other person can catalyse socialization into more extreme behaviour. We may recall the PIRA member cited in Chapter 3 who recalled: 'Actually, I'm very lucky in the sense that my wife *shared* my [political] convictions', and depending on the specific history and cultural influences on the group in question, injury (be it real or imagined) can be considered not as negative, but a positive feature of involvement. Atran[22] argues that Palestinians regularly 'invoke religion to invest personal trauma with proactive social meaning' to result in injury being seen not as burden but as a 'badge of honour'.

The following excerpt is from a former member of the UDA, interviewed by Crawford,[23] which reflects a willingness to engage in an initial degree of activity as a result of reinforcement or support from the UDA member's wife:

> My wife and I went for a walk down Agnes Street, and on down to the bottom of the [ultra-Protestant] Shankill Road. The atmosphere at the bottom of the Shankill was eerie, very tense. We could see that something was wrong. There were women standing outside their front doors and huddling in small groups but no children or men were about. I asked one of the women what was wrong and she said 'the Catholics were here last night throwing stones and petrol bombs, to burn us out' . . . There had been a lot of sectarian tensions in the area and everybody had known for a long time that there was going to be trouble. Then she [the lady in the doorway] said, rather proudly, 'our men are down there [Bombay Street] now, they're going to sort them [the Catholics] out'. I turned to my wife and said, 'Listen, I have to go down there.' I half expected her to say no but she didn't. She just nodded. The lady of the house said, 'You go on love, don't you worry about her, she'll be fine here with me.' 'Just you go on and do what you have to do, she'll be here when you get back'.

Although, on subsequent recall, the events that followed this man's initial decision may be perceived as the catalyst event towards involvement in specific activity, it may be the case that his wife's implicit approval, coupled with the second woman's comments may have served as the catalyst for involvement at that particular moment, and given those particular circumstances. Without access to fuller, and more comprehensive accounts, we will not know if such discrete influences shape increased involvement and engagement in different ways at different times, but we may be in a position to identify supportive qualities of initial steps towards what may subsequently prove to be extensive activity and involvement with the group.

Another relevant social quality here of personal accounts is a sense of gradual progression towards increased involvement with terrorist activities. For the most part, the ways in which people 'become' terrorists reflect a gradual process of incremental involvement. This is a common thread (although not always explicit) for many people involved in terrorism and, from examining accounts closely, we do get a sense of a process of involvement characterized by a slow, but real, marginalization away from conventional society (conventional relative to what the individual is moving towards) and towards extremism. In the case of Kellen[24] who examined the histories of German terrorists, and Taylor[25] who interviewed Loyalist terrorists in Northern Ireland, an emergent pattern was that the individual involvement in terrorism featured not only a gradual socialization into increasingly committed involvement, but a sense of increasing disillusionment with alternative avenues developing in conjunction with an increasing involvement in activities that culminate in having eventually become a terrorist. What constitutes an alternative avenue may vary considerably, and may not necessarily be really identifiable, but the perception of the person involved is real and tangible, and allows for this relative judgement to be made.

This sense that initial involvement in terrorism may develop from a series of incremental steps (each of which if taken in isolation would rapidly diminish in overall significance) is powerful. As we saw in Chapter 3, our tendency for our thinking about the development of involvement in terrorism to be determined by the drama of particular terrorist events obscures this process.

Timing, opportunity, pacing and progression

A limiting factor for the pace of increased movement into terrorism is revealed by examining some of the organizational features of terrorist movements. In particular, interesting data from Northern Ireland reveals features of the role played by the terrorist leadership in shaping the aperture through which recruits may enter. In the case of the Provisional IRA, some individuals made known their intentions to join the group, but it was reported to take some weeks before the would-be recruit is actually accepted into the organization.[26] When he or she is finally accepted, the recruit then does not necessarily embark upon the activities of *active service* for some time either. While there are a number of roles to be filled within the organization, active service is but one, which entails some degree of military-style disciplined training in 'army'-style matters, weapons and explosives training and the like. While expectations to occupy such a role may play a part in influencing a potential recruit to seek out opportunities for increased engagement, the recruit may find him or herself having to occupy roles that carry much less observable premium attached to them, and seem less significant or important overall, i.e. there is evidence for a process of gradual progression even once a member of the PIRA – the individual who joins with the intention of becoming an active service volunteer may serve his time moving weapons for example. He may be forced to establish his worth to the group in apparently more menial (although indirectly relevant and important) tasks before what is perceived to be a more prestigious position may be obtained, if at all, since these issues are primarily determined by a leadership function. To develop this further, it is worth recalling the words of the PIRA interviewee earlier who described his development as an Irish Republican to be still developing. Clearly while this man is apparently not engaging in dangerous active service operations any more, his role in Sinn Fein increased substantially since his release from prison.

An interesting if rare insight into a sense of 'role allocation' comes from terrorist documentation itself. The following excerpt is from *The Reporter's Guide to Ireland*[27] described previously, and written by the Official IRA Director of Intelligence for distribution only to his regional Intelligence Officers.

INTERNAL SECURITY AND ORGANISATION:

A.   1. Recruitment: This is a vital stage for the movement and the new recruit, the importance of which is not sufficiently understood and appreciated by Recruit's Officers and others responsible for the intake of new members into all branches of the movement. The age, address, and any other easily available statistics about the recruit should be made known to the Command I.O. in each and every case; he should then assess the relative value of the applicant to the movement – present and future – by virtue of occupation, family circumstances, hobby, relations with other groups and associations, or any particular ability or skill which would place him (or her) in a position to be of greater potential value as a secret member than otherwise. The categories of employment we have in mind hardly need elaboration.

2. Security: A thorough screening of each recruit should be undertaken to establish if they are suitable for membership, not just from the security standpoint, but just as importantly, to establish their political/military suitability (i.e. an acceptance of our policies/or a willingness to learn to understand and accept such policies).

And in a later section:

> A full dossier on each member, detailing his occupation, contacts in vital services both privately and government controlled and owned, should be prepared by each command I.O. and should be available to the Director of Intelligence if so required. Such information is vital to the building of an efficient and comprehensive network of the maximum employment of the information potential of each and every branch of the Movement.

What we see through these examples is a sense in which individual qualities and levels of experience in new recruits are identified to the extent that they may determine, or at least heavily influence the subsequent role assigned to them.

Autobiographical descriptions of terrorists' lives[28] also reveal characteristics such as those described above. Again we get a sense of slow, but gradually increasing, involvement in terrorism, primarily characterized by increased personal commitment towards activities related to the group at each subsequent stage. In fact, support for the existence of a process of gradual socialization and progression of involvement appears to be found not just between members of the same group, but *across* various different terrorist movements. McCauley and Segal[29] illustrate that well before they became the Red Army Faction leaders, Ulrike Meinhof and Horst Mahler were involved respectively in community activism opposing nuclear proliferation and the 'moderate Socialist German Student Society'. Many PIRA members in Northern Ireland come from the ranks of Sinn Fein (and some move back into Sinn Fein roles at some later point), while in Spain, Clark[30] in his study of ETA notes that not only does a picture of gradual socialization towards increased involvement exist, but what revealed this were ambiguities associated with attempting to define what being an 'etarra' (ETA member) means:

> the process by which new members are recruited is usually a slow and gradual one, and it is difficult to say exactly when a young man crosses the threshold of ETA membership . . . the process by which a Basque youth is transformed into a member of ETA is a long one full of detours and the exploration of competing alternatives. Even the actual recruiting process is a gradual one which many potential etarras resist for months or even years before yielding to the call to join.

In Italy, Alison Jamieson's[31] interviews with former Red Brigades (RB) member, Adriana Faranda, are exceptionally revealing, providing us with unusually lucid accounts of involvement. Jamieson tells us that Faranda became engaged in politics around 1968 as a student in Rome. When Jamieson said to Faranda that she once heard her describe her involvement as almost 'necessary', Faranda replied:

> Things are never quite as clear as that. Countless others lived in Rome at the same time as me: kids of my age who weren't as involved as me, either in the political struggles or in the choices of the successive years. I suppose really it was the way I experienced the events of that time, my own personal stand-point on the problems, the crises, the hopes and the expectation that we had as well as what was happening outside which determined that particular path . . . there were lots of little steps which led to where I ended up . . . it wasn't a major leap in the true sense of the word. It was just another stage . . . it was a choice.

Faranda's comment is especially important in that it reveals why, on one level, asking questions about motivation (or the 'why' questions) in terms of understanding involvement in terrorism are essentially unanswerable (e.g. 'I suppose really it was the way I experienced the events of that time'), but also epitomizes the way in which any such career path is shaped by what she describes as 'lots of little steps'. She also added later in the interview that although she saw her involvement as characterized by taking 'lots of little steps', she acknowledges that she saw herself as later having reached a 'point of no return'. This we will see becomes the reality of incremental progression towards increased involvement and will be explored in the next two chapters. For the moment, however, it is worth noting again that reaching a point of 'no return', or reaching 'membership' does not appear to be clear-cut in any specific way, but might be characterized ritually, through perhaps engagement in a specific operation, where the previously virtual line between supportive activity and 'direct action' is no longer unambiguous.

Again in Northern Ireland, White and Falkenberg White[32] interviewed a PIRA veteran who pointed to a process of 'nurturing' upon his initial progression into the movement:

> well it – there's progression, you know? When you would go in you wouldn't be, you would be given less difficult tasks initially. And then just as you become more experienced you would move along and somebody would come in behind you. And you know, and then somebody – people were probably getting arrested or interned or whatever, so there was that kind of progression along with military training until you were actively involved in operations . . . I suppose it took maybe six or seven months.

Billig[33] describes Red Army Faction member 'Rolfe', who marked his involvement in the RAF initially as a courier, but some years later had progressed to active duty within the RAF and was involved in the kidnap and murder of German businessman Hans Martin Schleyer, while Jamieson[34] discovered similar (although more formalized) processes within the Red Brigades. The Red Brigades' attempts to infiltrate and provoke left-wing factory-based movement in the early 1970s saw a process whereby a gradual move into illegality was fostered. Jamieson describes the situation in the Milan factories whereby:

> a sympathizer would be given the task of distributing BR propaganda documents around his factory department, or store material, money, or even weapons in his home. Later he might be asked to spray graffiti on the factory walls, leave intimidatory messages in offices or at homes of factory management. These were known as 'individual illegal actions'.

The 'real qualitative leap', she describes, came with the individual's participation in armed action, with the individual member having been monitored through a series of prior 'prove' or tests.

Another positive feature for the individual's commitment to taking successive 'little steps' sometimes is the acquisition of certain skills, often even if only for the member to acquire the verbal and intellectual ability to defend and legitimize the use of violence, and the inevitability of the circumstances in which the individual has found himself with no other choice in attempting to react against impending external threats. The significance of this cannot be underestimated, as it is a powerful sustaining factor often leading to prolonged engagement in terrorist activities. With this, an increased sense of control and power may emerge, both through informal supportive behaviour shown to the recruit by older or more experienced members, and through formal training and education. Clark[35] found that a common feature of recruitment and increased movement into involvement with ETA was increased social support. Often an existing member, usually older, would be the sole source of social support for the recruit, offering something akin to a buddy-system.

Again, it is important that we do not interpret these supportive qualities as indicative of some sort of pre-existing deficiencies in personality or indicative of some disorder but of behaviour reinforcers that illustrate the attractiveness of pursuing particular avenues of activity that become accessible or obvious for the individual at any stage of the process. They may not be entirely obvious or accessible to the *potential* recruit, but to the newly embraced recruit, become obvious over time; and indeed in general, some potential recruits will have a clearer sense of what positive features of involvement and increased involvement may become apparent to them, but increased investment over time may be required to realize those expectations and experience their relevance and potency. This theme we will explore in the context of disengagement in particular (for some, expectations prior to increased involvement may prove to have been either unrealistic, idealistic or unattainable altogether).

Given all of this then within the terrorist movement and its fringes, we get a sense of constant change and vastly differing levels of activity, commitment and overall 'involvement'. As McCauley and Segal[36] describe, some members are 'beginning to find out . . . others are becoming committed, others are firmly committed, others becoming less committed, and still others are in the process of leaving entirely'. We can see at this point how the profiling of terrorists (based on attempts to identify individual qualities of those filling certain specific roles) will be quite limited without a sense of the varied factors influencing how and why that role became attractive, open and attainable for a specific individual moving through the terrorist group. What might determine the total extent of active *terrorists* at any one time might relate to a whole host of local internal and external group, organizational, leadership and other 'management' or response issues. What is clearly necessary from a counter-terrorism perspective is a way of assessing capacity and threat or risk without having to revert to limited notions of counting membership based on what might be restrictive and unrelated criteria anyway.

A final feature of increased engagement for the individual that we will identify here is the realization that the steps into involvement have different levels of 'currency' attached to them. As we have already seen, the variety of roles and functions within terrorist groups is impressive even in the smaller groups where this diversification exists, but there is also a sense of the psychological baggage that is attached to each particular role and/or function. While *active service* roles within the Provisional IRA (that is, the role that results in individuals directly planting bombs, or engaging in a shooting) or the role of martyr in Hamas or Islamic Jihad may be limited as a result of security concerns (i.e. to minimize the risk of sections of the organization being compromised via security breaches by counter-terrorist agencies), there is also a strong sense of psychological value by keeping opportunities for access to such a role limited. Interviews conducted by Hassan[37] with members of Al Qassam revealed that by limiting those accepted for martyrdom operations, 'others are disappointed. They must learn patience and wait until Allah calls them'. To reiterate an earlier point about how the actual numbers of terrorists (i.e. those directly involved in violent activity) are minimal relative to the overall movement, the leadership of terrorist groups will often place a psychological premium on certain high profile roles, aside from the 'reward' of granting membership more generally in the first instance. This plays an important function in terms of sustaining a sense of attractiveness – after all, and barring internal security issues and organizational management concerns for the moment, if such roles were open to everybody then the currency value would diminish significantly in the context of the perceived attractiveness of attaining and fulfilling such a role. Any more general problems of 'inflated' membership, Zawodny[38] pointed out, can (apart from security concerns) have the detrimental effect of creating a 'credibility gap' when viewed by 'friends and foes alike'.

Openness to socialization into terrorism: from personality to predisposition

One other major issue must be addressed here. Given the widespread exposure of a group or community of individuals, each of whom is exposed to the presumed generating conditions and triggering factors, and each of whom may be at least tentatively aware of the perceived rewards associated with involvement and subsequent associated lures, why is it that only very few of those will actually proceed towards and along increased engagement and subsequently become and remain terrorists by crossing the boundaries between merely being supportive and being engaged in activity as a result of engagement with the group?

This question has not only driven the research of the type described in Chapter 3, but persists in some of the most valuable empirical accounts recently produced. For instance, Barber[39] surveyed 900 Palestinian male Muslim adolescents and found that during the first Intifada (1987–1993), participation in violence was high, with stone throwing in particular high for males (81 per cent), while over two-thirds experienced both physical assault and were shot at. Over 80 per cent of those interviewed by Barber admitted to supplying deliveries to activists, while a similar amount went to visit the families of dead martyrs. Yet from all of these youths, very few are likely to become operational activists for one of the main terrorist groups. In Northern Ireland, and even on the marches described earlier, the numbers of people who became involved in a direct way with the PIRA was minimal. The obvious question then is why?

Given the examples taken from some of the interview data above, it might be useful for us to identify factors that point to some people having a greater *openness* to *increased* engagement than others. The temptation here of course is to explain the difference in terms of some sort of personality trait, but the reality is more closely related to individual, idiosyncratic (and essentially unpredictable) learning experiences as much as anything else.

In the absence of systematic empirical research, these questions are not fully answerable in any reliable or complete sense, and there is the danger of engaging in circular logic in an effort to provide some sort of satisfactory answer. However, we do have ways of developing possible answers from a collective consideration of the following factors. These might be usefully thought of as 'predisposing events' based on individual perceptions and experiences.

(1) The individual's experience, degree and nature of some sort of previous relevant engagement (e.g. perhaps through throwing stones against the security services, going out on a protest and experiencing its consequences at an emotional level (via excitement, or fear etc.), the extent of prior knowledge and understanding of the group or conflict situation and background, the extent and prior exposure to the accompanying lures of increased engagement more broadly, etc.).

(2) More specifically, the nature and extent of the individual's relevant *early* experiences (e.g. victimization at the hands of security services, or vicariously experiencing victimization perceived as located against the social grouping with which the individual identifies, be it 'Muslim', 'Palestinian', 'Irish Republican', etc.).

(3) The nature of the community context and its significance for the individual particularly in light of the expected value of involvement (e.g. we might recall the accounts elicited by Post and Denny in their interviews with militants who appeared to attach significance to the status afforded to militants in their community).

(4) The nature and extent of adult socialization, which may affect both the individual's openness to increased involvement as well as the willingness of the group to accept him or her. For instance, many suicidal terrorists appear to be unmarried males aged in their late teenage years or early twenties – the significance of these demographics at this point might reveal more about the increased range of opportunities for increased engagement open to consideration for those who do not have clear and explicit duties and responsibilities to families, a husband or wife, etc. Hamas and Islamic Jihad do not apparently favour married young men as potential martyrs, but rather appear more open to selecting and 'preparing' unmarried men, with no families to support[40] – it is likely that the group is aware of the emotional responsiveness of people at a younger age and the increased susceptibility towards greater involvement this might bring, when combined with the other factors. On the other hand, it does not appear to have been an issue for the PIRA leadership: 'I've never found wives a hindrance, you know? I found it a big help. That you have the support of your wife and family, you know? I'd say that being married could be a hindrance in some cases, depending on what type of support you'd get from your wife and family'.[41] The significance or nature of the recruit's personal attachments may be differentially perceived depending on whether or not that attachment exists at recruitment, or develops during prolonged membership (while it initially may be a perceived barrier on the part of the leadership, i.e. from the perspective of security and suspicion issues being less problematic for an individual without ties, the leadership may be more amenable to an

existing committed member who subsequently engages in a relationship, having at least provided a return on the leadership's initial 'investment'). Naturally too, whether or not the leadership has a particular role in mind for a specific recruit at the time of recruitment will be relevant.

(5) A sense of dissatisfaction or disillusionment with the individual's current persona or activity. This may be a factor in helping understand the reasons that contribute to some peaceful activists progressing to more violent action in the first place, but also helps us understand the possible basis for a movement between roles once a member. A sense of dissatisfaction is often interpreted in analyses as a possible personality defect or *vulnerability*, but it might be more appropriate if not useful to consider the latter more in terms of how the individual may be more *open to influence* at any juncture, particularly in terms of recruitment concerns for a terrorist leadership, the role of point 3 above is a real consideration. We saw earlier how terrorist leaders are adept at placing a psychological premium on membership so as to have ostensibly positive features associated with attainment of that role (e.g. status in the community, importance to the group, high regard by a significant influence within the group, e.g. the terrorist leader or significant religious or political figure, etc.).

(6) The nature and range of competing alternatives and opportunities. For example, the extent and nature of membership, we must realize, will always be determined by some leadership function, which at any moment functions as a result of internal and external climate factors; on the other hand, and from the perspective of the potential recruit, fear of recrimination from the security services might prevent some from moving into illegal activities and may limit their involvement to a certain point. This might be influenced by any number of factors, including prior experiences and socialization as 1 and 2 above illustrate, which can more obviously translate into fear of losing one's job, given particular family and financial commitments, etc.

Although some or all of these might be relevant to any one potential terrorist, we ought to consider their identification as feeding into working hypotheses. These factors may help us understand why what might appear to be a homogeneous pool of 'potential members', exposed to similar internal and external influences, still only produces a relatively small amount of people who are open to increased engagement. Indeed, in this sense, they might be perhaps considered as potential 'risk' factors, which might inform individual or group profiling efforts much more appropriately than those currently being extended beyond what they can actually explain (or intend to).

One clear assertion here, however, is that it is again impossible to understand the factors that influence the decision to move into terrorism outside of the social and organizational context in which the individual exists and moves. We must remember, however, that these factors can be considered relevant at whatever stage we consider the individual along a possible continuum of junctures for what might be considered 'involvement' (i.e. ranging from the clearly legal, e.g. expressing support via a public protest, to the illegal).

Critical assertions

In attempting to develop a 'process model' of involvement in terrorism, identifying issues relating to 'how' people become involved may be more valuable than attempting to arrive at answers 'why' people become involved. Essentially then we need to shift our expectations about arriving at a simple, and probably naive, answer about terrorist motivation. This complexity is captured well by Taylor and Quayle[42] who describe involvement in terrorism as:

> in this respect no different from any of the other things that people do. In one sense, embarking on a life of terrorism is like any other life choice . . . To ask why an individual occupies a particular social, career or even family role is probably a deceptively easy but essentially unanswerable question. What we can do, however, is to identify factors in any particular situation that helps us understand why particular life choices have been made. This same analysis applies to the development of the terrorist.

The common personal, situational and cultural factors across accounts that reveal issues relating to why and how people become involved are usually quite broad and seem unrelated in a practical sense, in that very often there is no clear, and certainly no singular, involvement catalyst (and when an individual him or herself suggests this catalyst, we ought to interpret its significance with great caution since it often obscures the expected positive features of involvement, and generally forms an incomplete picture of the factors seen to influence involvement), let alone suggest it in the absence of it being driven by individual accounts by terrorists themselves. It is clear that when we are in a position to consider accounts from activists around the world that different qualities emerge, with different degrees of ideological control, commitment, etc. found between members. Sometimes this can reflect simply the degree to which an individual activist is articulate or not, whether he or she has verbalized openly the rationale or morality of his or her activities, or as is frequently the case, we are able to access accounts from terrorists who have placed their behaviour into such an elaborate, spiritually or ideologically dogmatic framework that we receive very little (if any) notion of the terrorist having had any apparent conscious role in their movement into terrorism.[43]

In addition, a sense of gradual socialization into terrorism appears to be a common theme, with an initial sense of involvement seemingly characterized by gradual increases in commitment. Combined with this, group factors are centrally important in attempting to identify supportive qualities of initial engagement, and overall we get a sense of the boundaries between apparent *degrees* of involvement sometimes often appearing more psychological than physical (although as we will see in the next chapter, actual terrorist operations can bring with them a sense of ritual aimed at ensuring commitment to the group and its activities), with a sense of premium attached not only to membership, but moreover to certain, specific roles.

Furthermore, there are frequently overlooked and misinterpreted positive features of increased engagement for the individual terrorist, and these include the rapid acquisition of some sort of skill or skills, an increased sense of empowerment, purpose and self-importance, an increased sense of control, which appears to reflect the common effects of ideological control and auto-propaganda, the use of particular involvement steps as currency, as above, mirroring the point above about distinctions between degrees of involvement, a tangible sense of acceptance within the group, and in combination with this, the acquisition of real status within the broader community, often expressed subsequently via identification with the broader supportive community. Again, we must note that each and every one of these factors can be brought to influence the individual at any stage of his or her involvement (as will become evident over the next two chapters).

Although, as we have considered at the outset of this chapter, it is not difficult to identify broad preconditions for the development of a climate that supports terrorist activity, it remains the case that very few people will still engage in terrorism altogether, let alone specific violent terrorist activity. Factors that might help us understand why this sense of *openness to engagement* is more readily found in some people rather than others (even within the same group of people, all of whom may have been clearly exposed to the same assumed generating conditions for terrorism) have been outlined, although the predictive ability of these remains untested in the absence of more fully developed research.

The complex reality of what 'becoming a terrorist' implies justifies an approach to understanding this process by considering it as such. Although the complexity of life histories, the problems associated with relying on the truthfulness of such accounts, etc. can be overwhelming, we can identify core psychological features of what becoming a terrorist appears to involve. Involvement is perhaps best characterized by development based on initial supportive qualities that vary in their significance for the individual, the individual group, and the relationship which both of these have with each other and their surrounding environment. The reality is that there are many factors (often so complex in their combination that it can be difficult to delineate them) that can come to bear on an individual's intentional or unintentional socialization into involvement with terrorism.

The next chapter extends the analysis to consider the group and organizational influences on the member that become readily apparent upon increased involvement and particularly upon engagement in terrorist operations.

5

BEING A TERRORIST

Introduction

In some ways, there is no unambiguous distinction between what might be seen as the process of *becoming a terrorist* and that of *being a terrorist* except to perhaps define the latter either by way of perhaps some notion of prolonged involvement, or in a more tangible way through identifying engagement in specific terrorist activity as a point of delineation: while involvement in terrorism is something that can at once be either abstract and vague, it can also be tangible and identifiable, when the individual engages in a specific, clearly understood offence. In the context of ordinary crime, while legal systems currently require for a person to have committed a criminal act, the problem in the context of terrorism arises when we move from questions to do with what a person has done, to a more general notion of membership or association or affiliation. Since 9/11, the problem of the identification of the terrorist has become difficult and extremely confused, with individual qualities moving inadvertently to the forefront of political debates. Donald Rumsfeld, the US Defense Secretary suggested that a 'new vocabulary' would emerge from the War on Terrorism and the Bush administration's doctrine of pre-emption.[1] It would be dangerous to over-look how the use of language impacts on the identification of terrorism and the terrorist, as this is an enormously important issue that has the poten-tial to both singularly skew, and improve, our understanding of the processes involved.

In fact, the point is worth considering further. The relationship between the terrorist and his/her environment is central to understanding the rele-vance of agreeing in our analysis on 'who or what a terrorist is', and this has been repeatedly exposed since 9/11. Again this is not so much a question about the legitimacy of the label 'terrorist' per se, but has more to do with an issue of both the scope and management of the problem. In the days after the Al Qaeda atrocities, President Bush made a series of then significant speeches in preparation for the Administration's attempts at solidifying American and world opinion towards their impending campaign. A critical warning, repeated in several speeches within the same week by the President, was that: 'anybody who houses a terrorist, encourages terrorism will be held account- able', 'we're talking about those who fed them, those who house them, those who harbor terrorists', 'it is a different type of battle . . . a different type of battlefield', 'if you harbor a terrorist, if you aid a terrorist, if you hide terrorists, you're just as guilty as the terrorists'.[2] Given the intense public fallout from political negotiations at the time, both in the United States and Great Britain, one might argue that at the heart of such sentiments is the assumption that there is no legitimacy to some kinds of protest or dissent. Equally, however, it reveals a change in what might be thought of as 'terrorist behaviour', broadening our perceptions of who the terrorists are and what it is they do. In ways perhaps unintended from the expected consequences of the Bush speeches, the question 'what is a terrorist?' became very focused and clarified, and the goals of counter-terrorism suddenly became much more pointed, both in the time leading up to and beyond the War on Terrorism and the war on Iraq.

This shifting away from notions of 'doing something' to one of associa- tion, or a more indirect form of aiding and abetting, makes for definition confusion on the one hand, but also makes for conceptual confusion in terms of trying to understand involvement in terrorism. The recent experi- ences with the events at Guantanamo Bay illustrate this perfectly well. These distinctions, if we can call them that, are perhaps an artefact of the ways in which we think about possible legal responses to identifiable events. The law tends to see itself as an absolute, and it might be this quality that exaggerates the definition confusion, which leads to further confusion when we move towards issues to do with trying to answer when a person 'is' a terrorist or not.

Sustained, increased, focused involvement

It might be useful at this point to recall the direction of the process model being developed throughout these chapters. Consistent with the rational choice perspective is the assertion that will be developed at this point that the factors influencing why people remain involved in terrorist organizations can be identified as possibly distinct from the reasons that contributed towards initial involvement as well as distinct from both reasons why people leave or disengage, as well as what factors influence the commission of specific terrorist acts.

From a cursory identification of the initial supportive qualities of involve- ment in a terrorist group, what is obvious from the outset is that terrorism is a group process. The group plays a significant role in shaping the behavioural processes inherent in becoming a terrorist, but plays perhaps an even more obvious role in terms of sustaining involvement and promoting engagement in violence. Engaging in terrorist acts, however, as well as the decision-making process that both underpins and arises from such acts, is determined (or at least heavily influenced) by the immediate and proximal context to the individual's involvement. Furthermore, however, engaging in terrorist acts can have a signficant bearing on how involvement develops and changes for the individual (and how the individual reacts accordingly to meet such change). We might then consider how the complexity of terrorist events, in particular, can help us understand the fulfilment of roles and duties of those involved either indirectly or directly in terrorist behaviour.

This chapter will examine two important dimensions to increased involvement in a terrorist movement. First, we will consider terrorist behaviour in and of itself and the influences that can come to bear on engagement in terrorist activity. Second, we will attempt to identify the relevant factors that give rise to some of the social and psychological qualties or consequences of both engagement in terrorist activity as well as continued involvement more generally.

The cycle of a terrorist event: an initial examination of terrorist behaviour

A core theme of the analysis presented in this book so far has been, as highlighted already above once more, that terrorism is a complex activity. It follows then that if we are to try to understand it, we need to have some appreciation of that complexity. Regardless of what specific terrorist incident we examine, each is in a sense unique, having a dynamic, context and logic of its own. Equally, however, we can think of terrorist incidents in general as those involved in a terrorist group progressing through a series of stages, almost with a natural history from inception to completion. Thinking of 'events' in this way may help us once more gain some sense of the different issues involved. Terrorist incidents similarly do not occur in a vacuum, but within a social, political and organizational framework, all of which may influence the nature, direction and extent of a particular target activity. What follows here then is an attempt to characterize the natural history of a terrorist event in terms of a process or series of stages. In doing this we will informally introduce the major features of terrorist events before continuing to develop the more formal analytical framework considered to date through an identification of the accompanying and consequential social and psychological relationship processes that emerge from 'being' a terrorist.

From the outset we can probably say that only in a very limited sense does an *individual terrorist* carry out an attack. Except in the very smallest of dissident groups, terrorism tends to be an organized activity involving a number of different people, occupying different roles, each of which performs a specific function, some operationally relevant, others supportive. In some of the larger movements, such as Al Qaeda, Hamas or ETA there is considerable specialization of function, both in the sense of co-ordinating, organizing and executing a particular event, but also in the sense of using that event within the broader political and organizational objectives of the terrorist organization (e.g. Al Qaeda demonstrated this quite dramatically with the train bombings at the Atocha station in Madrid on 11 March 2004). One way we can begin to develop some understanding of this is to consider the natural history of terrorist incidents as a process, with various stages that are worked through.

We can identify four specific stages:

(A) Decision and search acvitity – targeting and 'pre-terrorism'
(B) Preparation or 'pre-terrorist' activity
(C) Event execution
(D) Post-event activity and strategic analysis

(A) Decision and search activity – targeting and 'pre-terrorism'

The selection of the particular target for an attack, and the identification of the means of that attack, is the first critical step in the terrorist event cycle. Targets are not random but are always deliberate. This can be more obvious when a significant political figure is attacked (e.g. the Sri Lanka Tamil Tigers movement have assassinated two heads of state), or when members or property of a symbolic institution is attacked (i.e. soldiers, police officers, or say, an embassy or foreign bank). It may be less obvious when the incidental individual attached has no special meaning, except that they happen to be where a bomb explodes.

In the following events, we can see this variety of target selection through a series of examples, beginning with events in Spain related to the Basque separatist movement, ETA. During the summer of 1996, a series of bombs exploded at holiday sites in northern Spain. On 20 July a bomb injured 35 holidaymakers at Reus Airport, an airport used by holiday flights to northern Spain. Other holiday locations were also bombed without injury to tourists or others. These included the ticket office of the Alhambra in Granada, in the south. A series of small bombs was also placed in holiday locations on the southern coast. Adequate warnings were given for the small devices that were planted to be made safe. On the one hand, these bombings, targeting Spain's important tourist industry, relate to ETA's 30-year campaign against the Spanish government, but they must also be understood in the context of the change towards a right-wing government in Spain, and attempts to force the pace of talks between ETA and the Spanish government.

At the same time as these overtly politically inspired attacks on tourist sites, in the northern Spanish town of Ordizia, ETA members shot and killed a construction firm chief, Isidro Usabiaga. He was shot in the face, stomach and leg, as he returned home from a city fiesta. This shooting had no particular links with the attacks on holiday locations, and local officials at the time said that Usabiaga had become a target for ETA after refusing to pay a so-called 'revolutionary tax', one of several means by which ETA raises money through extortion.

This attack illustrates another aspect of terrorist violence, where the agenda is not primarily the political objectives of the movement (although it may contribute to this in some general way by spreading fear), but the internal needs of the organization, and specifically the need to raise money. Thus, in these examples we can see the two major influences on target selection: the political context and organizational pressures.

Running a successful terrorist organization is an expensive endeavour. It was estimated that the PIRA, for example, needed an annual income of several million pounds per year to maintain its organization. Other smaller terrorist organizations have less financial needs, but the procurement of weapons, the support of various grades of members, etc., will always present financial as well as logistical problems. The PIRA developed a sophisticated array of activities for raising money, including at least one clear example of 'riding shotgun' (providing an armed escort for payment) on an international drugs shipment, cigarette smuggling, diesel laundering, and money-laundering schemes in the US, Northern Ireland and the Republic of Ireland. The latter involves the purchase of legitimate businesses with illegally obtained funds. Such businesses may then be run as commercial concerns, yielding 'legitimate' profit which finds its way back to the terrorist organization, or the businesses may be exploited using fraudulent or other means to maximize returns and avoid tax, the business then having been 'run into the ground', abandoned and/or sold on. 'Legitimately'-owned businesses have included private security firms, and taxi cabs in Belfast. They also included at least two known hackney cab services in Dublin, construction firms, shops, restaurants, courier services, guest houses, cars and machinery, and pubs, which at one time or another have included at least one in Boston in the United States, small pubs in Co. Dublin, Co. Donegal and Co. Cork with others scattered about the country. One of the best known and certainly widely reported sources of funds have come from armed robbery. Such activity in Northern Ireland, the Republic and England has long played a major role in obtaining hard cash for the PIRA, and a number of audacious bank robberies in the Republic of Ireland were conducted by members of the PIRA to raise money for the organization.

A special category of terrorist target selection concerns efforts on the part of the terrorist organization to directly maintain its own integrity and control. Terrorist organizations recognize the need to exercise and maintain discipline, and to preserve security. This may be important in an operational sense, it may relate to sustaining control over a particular locality or base of operations, or it may relate to the preservation of the organization from penetration by informants. All organizations in some sense face discipline problems, and the response to this is invariably the development of some form of punishment element within the organization. In Ireland, both the PIRA and Loyalist terrorist organizations have developed specialized internal security elements, as well as addressing other related problems again through the formation and development of specialized units. Less complex or small terrorist organizations may not have the same degree of specialization found in the Irish ones, but will exercise that function in some way.

The fact that a variety of kinds of targets can be chosen with differing objectives, sometimes at the *same* time, indicates the sense in which contemporary terrorism is a planned dynamic activity (and events in Iraq since the US-led invasion there support this to spectacular effect). It also emphasizes the role of leadership to take strategic decisions, and to have an overview of where the organization is, and how it might meet its goals. These goals are set at a variety of levels related to sometimes sophisticated political analyses on the one hand, and organizational pressures on the other. In large terrorist organizations, that leadership may well have access to considerable intellectual and planning resources (this was certainly the case in Ireland) either directly as members or more usually through sympathizers. However, whatever pressures there may be, an important task for any leadership in meeting long-term goals is the short-term acquisition of resources and their allocation between conflicting elements of the organization. These short-term goals exist within a practical context related to resources and manpower. In this respect at least, contemporary terrorism has a great deal in common with a large business organization if political and societal aspirations are substituted for financial objectives.

Concepts from the criminology literature once more may be useful to help us place this and the next phase of the terrorist incident cycle into context. This phase of the terrorist cycle corresponds in many ways to what Maurice Cusson[3] has termed the 'search' phase in his strategic analysis of crime. The next stage of the terrorist cycle, what is termed here preparation, relates to what Cusson terms the 'precriminal situation'. The 'search' phase identifies a suitable 'precriminal situation', which Cusson defines as the 'set of outside circumstances immediately preceding and surrounding the criminal event and making the offence more or less difficult, risky and profitable'. The search process is essentially therefore one of both evaluation and selection. In the case of terrorism, it may differ somewhat from crime in two main respects, to the extent that examples of terrorism strive towards an ostensibly political rather than financial goal, and because terrorist movements are complex, they typically demonstrate a greater degree of specialization of function than most criminal activity reveals.

The use of the term 'search' to characterize this phase also serves to draw our attention to a particular feature of the relationship between the terrorist movement and its environment. The security services represent the most significant environmental constraint on terrorist freedom of action. The reciprocal interaction of the terrorist with the security services implied by the 'search' and later 'precriminal' phase is an important factor driving the development of terrorist tactics. Opportunities for terrorist action (like most examples of predatory crime, including sexual offences for example) do not inadvertently occur, but are actively developed. The 'search' for suitable precriminal situations implies a deliberate exploration of targets' protective systems to find weak spots suitable to exploit.

To summarize the key critical points then, we can assert that:

1 Excepting all but the smallest of organizations, terrorist acts are planned and calculated acts of violence.
2 A leadership function of some sort takes decisions and influences the direction of activity.
3 To understand terrorist target selection, we must consider it within the broad context of both the needs and objectives of the organization that has committed the terrorist act, as well as in terms of the political and societal critique of the terrorist organization and the operating constraints imposed on the organization by the security services.
4 The act itself may well be either overtly political or criminal, and many target individuals or property having a direct political or symbolic role, uninvolved civilians, its own membership, or the membership of a rival organization, reflecting the complex dynamic of the situational context to the terrorist organization.
5 In strategic and criminological terms, this phase may be characterized as one of 'search' for a suitable precriminal (or in this context, perhaps more accurately 'pre-terrorism') situation.

(B) Preparation or 'pre-terrorist' activity

Having identified a target, or completed a successful search phase, the cycle moves onto the preparation or precriminal (or perhaps *pre-terrorist*) phase. Here the necessary preparations have to be put in place to exploit the potential event and make possible the execution of whatever the attack might be. The decision processes discussed above emphasize the strategic and policy functions of the central command of the organization. Preparing for an attack emphasizes the logistical and organizational issues involved. This phase might be seen as the tactical phase of a terrorist act, where having established an objective from a strategic perspective, the choices and activities to be used are identified and prepared to operationalize that objective. For any given situation, these phases may be well compounded and conflated, but the functions they represent can be readily enough identified.

Any terrorist event has a logistical, intelligence and financial aspect. In logistical terms, at a simple level someone has to *do* whatever the event requires to be executed, they have to *know* what to do, and they need some form of weaponry or equipment with which to do it. The simplest form of attack may be opportunistic, a random shooting at a police vehicle, for example, as it drives through an area. Even for this form of attack to take place, however, some form of strategic thinking is necessary to express the intention behind the attack. The intelligence function behind an attack of this form would naturally be limited – perhaps any police or army vehicle would do – but even here some kind of structure to give advance warning of the vehicle in the locality, and to guard against a second vehicle following that might come to the assistance of the first, would be prudent. The individual undertaking the attack needs a weapon, and needs to know how to fire it. This implies two clear functions, although they may be compounded in simple or small scale activities: a personnel function, in that someone has to make the attack and to have received sufficient training to complete it, and a logistic function, to obtain a serviceable weapon.

In more complex operations, for instance the 3/11 and 9/11 attacks, these functions become much more important and far more specialized: as a general rule, and as we might expect, attacks involving highly specific targets make many more intelligence demands than more general attacks. Although it may still be premature to attempt to analyse the complete background to the 9/11 attacks by Al Qaeda, there are many other precedents we can identify through cases in which our knowledge of events is more complete. The preparations for the spectacular assassination in November 1989 by the Red Army Faction of Alfred Herrhausen, for example, took two months, and involved complex and systematic surveillance activities. The bomb was detonated when the movement of Herrhausen's car interrupted a light beam generated via a photo-electric cell device in the side of the road. In this case, the identification of a potential site for a car bomb may be less complex, than say, identifying the specific airline jets to hijack as was the case for Al Qaeda's pre-9/11 preparations, but still requires preparation.

Personnel factors relate to two broad issues here then: the *identification* of an appropriate individual or team to undertake the attack, and making sure that they know *what to do*. At one level the personnel needs may be met by simply identifying someone who will not panic, and with a steady enough nerve to complete the operation. More complex operations may involve the recruitment, or tasking, of a range of specialists to complete the attack. The selection of individuals to undertake suicidal terrorist attacks represents another rather different kind of highly personalized and focused personnel selection problem.

At another level again, the personnel function might imply the placing of 'sleeper' terrorists in jobs in the target location so that they can be 'activated' when the need arises. Attacks by the PIRA in the United Kingdom very shortly after the PIRA announced the end of its ceasefire on 9 February 1996 appear to have been undertaken by individuals with no clear connections to the PIRA. These people were recruited, trained and put in place to be used at a future time, a process that implies a high degree of organization. One good example of this came to light on the 18 February 1996 when Edward O'Brien, a 21-year-old member of the Provisional IRA from the Irish Republic, was killed by the bomb he was carrying on a bus in London. The bomb appears to have been prematurely exploded, and does not appear to have been indicative of some sort of martyrdom attack. This was the fourth bombing of a campaign that started after the ending of the ceasefire. O'Brien was not known to be a member of the PIRA by the British security services, but perhaps more surprisingly he was not even known by his family to have been involved. The first the family knew of his involvement was when they were told of it by a PIRA 'welfare' officer, who visited the family home in Gorey, Co. Wexford, soon after the explosion. The neighbours near where he lived in London and his friends and acquaintances had no knowledge of his associations with the Republican movement. Furthermore, no one seemed to be aware of any suspicious circumstances surrounding the apartment where he lived, despite the police subsequently finding bomb-making equipment in the garden and under the floorboards of the house. O'Brien appeared to have moved to the United Kingdom from Ireland in 1994, and began then to organize munitions for a future bombing campaign. In addition, it is worth noting that this was during a period of ceasefire in the PIRA's bombing campaign in the UK.

The second personnel element involves *training*. Most terrorist organizations have some form of training capacity, and there is even evidence of formal structured terrorist training, not just at local level (e.g. the PIRA have had several training camps located around the Republic of Ireland, especially in places like Kerry, in the southwest of the country) but especially when states are involved as sponsors of terrorism as an element of a country's foreign or security police. The focus of such alleged sponsors of terrorism became sharpened after 9/11 with the US-led incursions into both Afghanistan and Iraq. The truth or otherwise of reports pertaining to the nature and extent of terrorist bases and training camps are of course difficult to verify, and since the fallout over the misleading basis to the Iraq invasion, such allegations must be viewed even more critically. That there is a measure of international support and shared training between terrorist organizations, however, is quite clear. It is well known, for example, that members of the PIRA have participated in training activities with Palestinian organizations, while the Philippines-based Abu Sayyaf ('Bearer of the Sword') appears to have received training from Al Qaeda. Recently, the PIRA was believed to have been supplying training and targeting expertise to the FARC organization in Colombia. These linkages imply a level of organization and competence that is rarely appreciated for what it implies in a practical sense. It also implies a measure of financial commitment from some source in order to sustain both the bases to and development of such activities.

This phase of the terrorist cycle, with its references to training, emphasizes the development of technical competence. Servicing a weapon may not be so complex a task, but arming and placing a bomb on the other hand may involve more skills. Designing, making and testing a bomb, a further step in the process can be a very complex task indeed. Furthermore, it is likely that the bomb has to be constructed in such a way that it can be armed and used by someone other than the bomb maker (as is the case perhaps most obviously for martyrdom terrorist operations). This calls on considerable technical skill, as well as equipment and explosive resources.

Gaining a competence in the construction of bombs does not, however, necessarily imply attendance at complex subversive training programmes. Anyone with access to the Internet can rapidly acquire bomb-making instructions, ranging from simple devices to complex bombs and grenades. Instructions for the construction of relatively simple pipe bombs, often used by Loyalist terrorists in Northern Ireland, and that which exploded during the 1996 Olympic Games in Atlanta, are readily available. The effectiveness of such a bomb, and its effectiveness as a terrorist weapon, is quite clear. It was made of simple and relatively available materials. The explosion of such a device in Atlanta killed two people and injured over one hundred. Access to this kind of information makes the construction of such devices a relatively easy task for any dissident group, political or otherwise, and the growth in the use of bombs in the United States reflects this ease of access. In 1989, the FBI reported 1,699 criminal bombings either attempted or carried out in the USA. By 1994, the number had risen to 3,163. Very many more attempts or failed bombings occurred. Many of these bombs were simple devices similar to the one that exploded in Atlanta.

The development of sophisticated technical capacity can sometimes extend in unexpected directions, to the terrorists actually engaging in what amounts to manufacturing activities to produce munitions. In September 1988, the Royal Ulster Constabulary raided a small engineering facility at a farm near to Ballynahinch, Co. Down. They found there the largest illegal weapons factory ever uncovered in Northern Ireland and possibly in Western Europe. It was run by the Loyalist terrorist organization, the Ulster Defence Association (UDA), and at the time of the raid the facility was close to the completion of 800 sub-machine guns, based on the design of the Israeli Uzi machine gun. Thirty machine guns were completed, and on testing found to be highly serviceable weapons. Surprisingly, little attention has ever been paid to this in accounts of terrorist activity in Northern Ireland, but it suggests a considerable level of technical skill within the UDA. The PIRA have a similar capacity, if less localized, to produce explosives and propulsion devices used to make mortars and other rocket-propelled armaments.

In summary, therefore, we can identify within the preparation phase:

1 A need for target identification and surveillance functions, including an evaluation of risk.
2 The identification and selection of appropriate personnel.
3 Training requirements, related to general preparation and specific target requirements.
4 Design, construction and manufacturing functions related to device construction.
5 Device testing and preparation.

Again, in strategic and criminological terms, we might characterize this phase as 'precriminal', or here *pre-terrorist*.

(C) Event execution

The terrorist event, whether it is a bombing, shooting, abduction or something else, is the only intended public phase of the whole terrorist cycle. But even the action itself can be thought of as consisting of a series of steps, only one of which is the actual bombing or shooting, or other activity. The event itself has certain logistical requirements that are essentially short term, as distinct from the broader capacity activities embraced in the preparation phase. Another very important element in this phase is the need to maintain security, in terms of avoiding detection before the event whilst materials are being assembled, successfully undertaking the action, merging into the post-event activities of effecting the escape of the terrorists after the event, and destroying evidence that might compromise the terrorists or their organization. It is these essentially situational logistical requirements and associated security needs that determine and shape the actual process of conducting the action.

To explore this further, we will take an example of a bombing. Given that the elements of a bomb (timing device or switching, detonator, explosives) are available, the first step is that these elements have to be brought to the locality chosen for the explosion. Small bombs designed to injure bystanders or cause disruption in a transportation system might be carried by hand. Large bombs require some other form of transportation, usually a vehicle. The bomb primarily made from homemade explosives that was placed by the 'Real' IRA (a breakaway splinter group from the Provisional IRA) in Omagh town centre, in August 1998, was estimated to weigh in excess of five hundred pounds. Clearly a bomb of this size presents transportation difficulties simply given size alone. It also presents security problems for the terrorists to move it on the public roads without detection. For a short-lasting action such as a shooting, a stolen vehicle with false registration plates can be used with reasonable safety to transport the terrorists. In the case of preparations for the Omagh bomb, two members of the Real IRA stole a

Vauxhall Cavalier from the town of Carrickmacross. The theft of a vehicle may be reported, but it is unlikely that for the brief usage of a shooting it would be detected. A bombing like that at Omagh, however, implies a relatively longer term setting up phase than, say, the frequent car bombings in Iraq during May to July 2004, and therefore a stolen vehicle has more chance of being noticed. A bomb of that size has to be prepared in a reasonably secure environment, and then transported to the scene (in this case, a former PIRA bomb maker, who lives near the Irish border, mixed the explosives in a farmhouse with the assistance of at least three other men, and about one week before the actual attack, readied a test version of the bomb which was detonated in a nearby mountainous area). In some circumstances, of course, the terrorists may be more likely to purchase a vehicle legally (or at least in a legitimate fashion).

In the case of a shooting, practices may vary between different terrorist organizations, but the need to maintain security is what ultimately drives the process. In the case of the PIRA, they have a well-developed procedure of keeping the weapon separate from the individual who will do the shooting until the actual attack. Indeed, it may well be disassembled, and the pieces hidden separately, often in the houses of sympathizers, with the pieces coming together for assembly only when the attack is to take place. After the attack, the weapon is then taken away, disassembled and hidden, freeing the actual terrorist from the incriminating evidence of the weapon. Indeed, in some instances, the terrorist may not know in fact who the intended victim is until just before the attack takes place. The terrorist may be told that he has a job to do, but will not necessarily know what that job is. Less well-structured organizations may not use such elaborate procedures, but the same general principles apply.

We can see from this, therefore, that the attack itself is the only element in the whole process described thus far that is designed to be public. But however well prepared in advance, those doing the attack necessarily have to take into account the situation of the moment. The individual placing the bomb, or shooting the weapon, has to adjust to the immediate situation as he or she finds it. The two Real IRA members who drove the Vauxhall car carrying the bomb to Omagh were accompanied by two men in another car who drove ahead on the lookout for any checkpoints that might be on the road. Both cars kept in touch by means of mobile telephone.

One revealing illustration of how individual assassins receive guidance on adjusting to the situation of the moment was revealed when the FBI announced that it had discovered a handwritten copy of a five-page Arabic document in a piece of luggage that belonged to the 9/11 hijack ringleader, Mohammad Atta. Atta's bag apparently did not get on the flight that departed from Logan Airport (it was retrieved at Portland, Maine from where Atta boarded the Boston–Los Angeles flight, which subsequently was crashed into the World Trade Center). The document was a guide to the hijacker's behaviour before and during the flight, making reference to ritual behaviours essentially aimed at reinforcing the terrorists' determination and maintaining focus during the final phases of the attack. The document makes reference to performing checks on the team members' luggage, clothing, documentation, etc., but in particular there are references to what the individual should do if any passenger should offer resistance:

> If God grants any one of you a slaughter, you should perform it as
> an offering on behalf of your father and mother, for they are owed
> by you. Do not disagree amongst yourselves, but listen and obey.

The Arabic word used to denote slaughter is 'zhabiha', from the noun 'zhabihatun', and is a colloquial term in Arabic used to denote the slaughter of an animal. The order to invoke zhabiha and not 'qatala' (any form of killing), Raufer[4] explains, suggests the importance of the ritual:

> [It] means slit the jugular vein of an animal or human being. It is a
> ritual slaughter, what Abraham was about to do to his son, sacrifice
> him on God's order. It is a physically close act, committed with a
> blade: the blood must actually flow. It's impossible to perform . . .
> from afar, with any other type of weapon.

On Atta's flight, American Airlines Flight 11, four of the hijackers cut the throat of one of the first-class passengers near whom they had been sitting during the flight. Incidentally, 'zhabiha' was also the word used in the video-taped ritual beheadings of US contractors Nicholas Berg and Paul Johnson in Iraq in 2004.

Necessarily, therefore, the action itself has a logic that is determined by immediate situational factors such as the movement of bystanders, the chance presence of other vehicles in chosen parking spots, the resistance of intended victims, etc. However, we should note that the decisional scope in this phase is limited in the extreme to either continuing with the attack, or aborting it.

For the terrorist event phase of the cycle, therefore, we can identify a number of significant issues:

1　The logistic demands of assembling both a device and the manpower to be used at the scene of the attack.
2　The maintenance of surveillance and broader security of the operation.
3　The dynamics of the actual event, which relate both to its immediate situational context and, where appropriate, the escape routes available.
4　Where appropriate, the securing of weapons after the attack.

(D) Post-event activity and strategic analysis

Immediately after an attack, the terrorists must effect their escape (excepting, obviously a very specific category of terrorist attack – martyrdom operations). From analyses of terrorist incidents, there are grounds for supposing that escape factors are both the primary determinant of whether or not a planned attack will actually take place, and the principal situational features that determine the precise location and features of an attack. Access to a main road to escape by a vehicle, access to a safe area, the availability of cover to escape by foot, the absence of security force patrols in the area, are all factors that determine the features of a particular attack. The logic of this becomes quite clear when the details of an attack are analysed.

The final element of the actual event, after the incident has taken place, the weapons removed and secured, and the attackers having escaped from the scene, is the destruction of evidence. This will involve burning any car stolen for transport, burning clothes worn during the attack, and eventually for the terrorist, bathing to eliminate residual chemical or bodily evidence. In general, terrorist organizations are very alert to the possibilities of forensic identification, and implement very stringent procedures to destroy or make difficult the identification through forensic examination of the terrorists involved.

Overall, it is rarely the case that the details of terrorist attacks are analysed in this way (in fact there has been only one recent example of such an analysis, that of Silke,[5] in examining the Shankill bombing of 23 October 1993 during which an IRA bomb killed ten people, including the bomber). In the following case example, that of an armed robbery by the Provisional IRA in the Republic of Ireland, we can see how many of these elements can come together to culminate in a strategic analysis with important outcomes based on pressures from within and outside the terrorist organization.

A case example: the murder of Garda Jerry McCabe

At 6.50 am, on Friday 7 June 1996, Detective Garda Jerry McCabe and Detective Garda Ben O'Sullivan, both Special Branch officers of An Garda Siochana (the Irish police force), were sitting in their unmarked police car, in plainclothes, as the post office van which they were escorting stopped outside the post office in Adare village in Co. Limerick. The van driver, William Jackson, was in the process of taking the post, which included pension and unemployment benefits, from the van into the post office, when he heard the sound of another vehicle crashing into the detectives' car. Three men wearing balaclavas and army fatigues jumped out of a Mitsubishi Pajero jeep and stood at either side of the police car. The detectives were still in a sitting position inside the car when the masked men opened fire, using Russian AK-47 Kalashnikov assault rifles. As gunfire raked the detectives' car, McCabe was shot eight times with rounds from the Kalashnikovs and died in his seat. The raiders immediately fled in the Pajero and ignored a £100,000 cash haul in the post office van.

While O'Sullivan underwent emergency surgery at Limerick Regional Hospital, Garda road-blocks were set up throughout Limerick County with Air Corps helicopters joining in the search for McCabe's killers. By that afternoon, the Gardai had discovered incendiary devices in two vehicles that pointed to Provisional IRA involvement. A Mitsubishi Lancer was found in an isolated lane beside a derelict cottage, about one mile from Granagh village, near Adare. It appears that the Lancer was driven up this lane, out of sight, and abandoned immediately. On the 6 o'clock news on Irish television that same evening, Gardai reported the discovery of the incendiary devices in two vehicles used by the four-man gang, the jeep vehicle (Pajero) used to ram the car, and an abandoned suspected getaway car (the Lancer). These developments, in conjunction with the use by the gunmen of the Kalashnikov automatic rifle and the paramilitary nature of the attack, was seen as pointing to only one possibility, that of PIRA involvement.

The PIRA swiftly distanced themselves from the shooting when the Gardai said they strongly suspected PIRA involvement. A statement was telephoned to the RTE offices with the caller using a recognized PIRA codeword, saying 'None of our volunteers or units were in any way involved in this morning's incident at Adare . . . there was absolutely no IRA involvement'. A written statement issued to RTE was signed 'P. O'Neill. Irish Republican Publicity Bureau, Dublin'. Reporters described the response as a 'damage limitation exercise' in view of the possible impact of the killing on the fragile Northern Ireland peace process. Initially, it was believed the killing was the result of a raid that went badly wrong. But later, when it was found that the big cash haul was ignored, Gardai began to speculate that the gang could have been on a 'more sinister straightforward murder mission' targeted at the two detectives. It emerged that both were friends of former Irish Minister for Justice and local politician Des O'Malley. O'Malley said, 'Because the money was not taken it makes me wonder whether the primary intention was a desire to murder the police'.

On Monday 10 June, *Irish Times* journalists Jim Cusack and Suzanne Breen reported Republican sources in Belfast confirming that the 'Munster unit led by senior IRA figures was behind the killing'.[6] They said that the men were members of an officially approved PIRA unit and did not belong to a breakaway faction. According to one of the journalists' sources, 'these are seasoned IRA activists who are respected in the Republican move-ment'. The source said that their 'evident access to IRA arms' showed they were not rebels outside the movement. He added that they seemed to have been indifferent to the effects the incident would have on the peace process: 'I don't think that Gerry Adams' difficulties are first and foremost in their minds . . . they would be out to do what they had to do'. This same source also pointed to the PIRAs 'Green Book' forbidding members from opening fire on Gardai. Cusack and Breen cited several Republican sources as saying 'harsh disciplinary action against the leaders of the unit was unlikely. The IRA members involved were of too high a standing for that. There was no question of the Army Council ordering [the] execution [of the PIRA members]'. The journalists proceeded to quote a Sinn Fein source as saying even if the IRA expressed regret and said it was an operation which went wrong, 'there would be complete political upheaval . . . our relationship with Dublin [the Irish Government] would be placed under severe strain'.

By Sunday 23 June, Gardai had finally established that the attack related to a 'bungled robbery' and indeed had been sanctioned by the then Operations Commander of the PIRA Southern Command in Dublin. That same day, the *Sunday Independent* journalist Veronica Guerin explained how much-needed support for Sinn Fein had gathered momentum during their recent 17-month ceasefire, but citing her own Garda sources noted that 'a lot of ground was lost when they murdered Jerry McCabe and it will be hard for them to get it back'.[7] This was effectively illustrated with an anonymous call from a member of the public to the Gardai, disclosing the secret site of a huge bomb-making factory in Co. Laois in the Republic, a major blow to the PIRA's arms stocks.

It is often the case within the PIRA that after a robbery has been committed, practice dictates that the haul can be collected by a person (not necessarily a member of the ASU who committed the robbery) and is sometimes stored locally, for use against local costs. The loot may also be passed along a chain of designated individuals, for storage so it can be submerged through money laundering at a later date. The weekly income for an ASU member from his superior(s) was low, and although reported to vary from member to member in different areas, it was certainly not enough to sustain family living. Weekly PIRA wages only supplemented social welfare payments, or income from part-time or full-time employment, varying from member to member, as operational roles are likewise varied. The prospect for earning more money was obviously therefore quite tempting. It appears that this particular ASU did not indeed seem too concerned about the implications which this kind of activity had on anyone, be it on the organization which these individual members claimed to represent or on members of their sympathetic audience in general (the disillusionment of one of whom led to the telephone call to the Gardai about the Laois site). A perennial challenge for security forces in the context of PIRA robberies is the difficulty in assessing whether any robbery involves units indulging in local fundraising (either to sustain local activities or to supplement their own pockets or to submit money to their finance department) or if the robbery is an example of a breakaway act of unsanctioned Republican activity, even while having the purpose of raising funds 'for the good of the Movement'. Indeed, some

PIRA leaders have spoken of their volunteers' tendency in 'going for it' (i.e. robbing without permission from higher source). However, as PIRA informer Martin McGartland describes: 'most of the IRA men who handled income from whatever source seemed to be meticulous in their accounting. There were also examples of punishment beatings handed to those few who misused IRA funds for their own ends. Those men would not only be beaten but would also earn the scorn and contempt of their IRA mates, friends and often their families'.[8] Another former PIRA member, Eamon Collins (murdered in January 1999), spoke of the breakdown of his 'romantic image' of the Republican campaign when, during a bombing operation in Warrenpoint, Co. Down, his colleague 'robbed the tills . . . took the shine off the operations and made the IRA look like common criminals'.

How the leadership body can view maverick acts of robbery was illustrated during the Sinn Fein damage-limitation exercises after the Adare attack. It is easy in retrospect for leadership figures to describe their own members' behaviour as 'unsanctioned' or 'breakaway' (whether such behaviour is actually sanctioned or not). This has particular usage during sensitive times, as was demonstrated on more than one occasion during the 1994–1996 ceasefire, an example of which became apparent when the PIRA denied it had authorized a robbery in Newry, Co. Down, when a PIRA ASU killed an elderly postal worker. The revolutionary theorist Regis Debray[9] noted that whenever terrorist organizations cease to have clearly defined political objectives, the movement may indeed continue to exist, but its activities tend to drift in focus towards other things they do well. For terrorist organizations such as the PIRA, these tend to be robberies, increases in the level of punishment attacks as a form of 're-directed violence' and other criminal acts. For the PIRA organization as a whole, it only emerged a week after the Adare shooting that the Southern Command OC, operating from his Dublin base, had indeed endorsed the operation. Even if the leadership had known about the OCs approval earlier there still would have been denials of PIRA involvement through its Publicity Bureau. The PIRA leadership had to deny knowledge of PIRA involvement in the Adare shooting until the Gardai uncovered the relevant forensic and other evidence.

The Southern Command OC of the PIRA had apparently permitted the robbery without the expressed consent of either peers or the superiors who expressed anger at his decision. For all intents and purposes then, the Adare attack was regarded as an unsanctioned, breakaway act, but committed by seasoned PIRA activists and not a breakaway group. The Southern Command OC in question, who was deemed prior to the Adare attack as 'letting things in Dublin get out of control', apparently remained 'Officer Commanding Southern Command' up until September 1996, but was later replaced by another man elected by the Northern Command and Army Council bodies.

The Adare attack serves as an example in which organizational functioning suffered a major breakdown and was proved to be highly embarrassing for the PIRA leadership, which has traditionally prided itself on control and discipline, as well as becoming a major source of political difficulty for Sinn Fein. While communication breakdown is commonly found in clandestine organizations, the significance of this particular breakdown is that it is one of the few clear examples that not only led to an internal PIRA reshuffle, but equally significantly to other changes. In the months following the Adare shooting, the PIRA leadership took the unprecedented step of changing the command and functional structures of the organization. The details remain unclear, but it led to the establishment of more regional command areas under the tight control of trusted brigadiers, with long experience in the PIRA. This move was to ensure that an attack such as that which unfolded in Adare could not be sanctioned again during the ceasefire. Control over particular groups of ASUs was apparently tightened, and members have been much more accountable to regional commanders than previously.

At another level, an important strategic and limiting factor to PIRA operations is revealed in the Green Book. The section entitled 'General Order No. 8' explicitly disallows military operations to be conducted against the 'Free State', i.e. the Irish Republic, stating:

> Volunteers are strictly forbidden to take any military action against 26 County forces under any circumstances whatsoever. The importance of this order in present circumstances especially in the border areas cannot be over-emphasised . . . At all times, Volunteers must make it clear that the policy of the Army [PIRA] is to drive the British forces of occupation out of Ireland.

In effect, General Order No. 8 appears to be a reminder to PIRA members, either based in the Republic or who travel to the Republic for operations, to keep a low profile. From the perspective of the PIRA leadership, the Southern Command area encompasses a population whose general passivity to the PIRA is to be exploited as fully as possible. For the PIRA, the repercussions of killing a member of the Gardai were tremendous, and had wide-ranging implications, not just in terms of how the localized passive support for the PIRA (frequently found in areas all over the Republic) turned against them, but in terms of how the PIRA's more active support suffered also. This active support encompassed those from a more general kind of sympathizer who, for example, could be persuaded to allow the PIRA to keep a stolen car or weapons on his farm, to those whose Republican sympathies play a role in the potential development of their own future terrorist behaviour with the appropriate organization. For those opposed to the killing of Gardai, the PIRA's practical assistance suffered significantly in the wake of the shooting.

While throughout the fledgling peace process there have been many emotive discussions about what is perceived to be an 'acceptable' level of terrorist violence, clearly killing Gardai does not qualify.

What we have through an analysis of the events during and after Adare, then, is a sense of strategic evaluation, brought about by an analysis of the outcome of the event itself, but feeding back into the beginning of the cycle. In sum, then, for the post-event phase of the cycle, we can identify a number of significant issues:

1   The situational factors affecting the escape of the individuals involved in the attack.
2   The destruction of evidence.
3   Post-event evaluation feeding into the post-event stage.

Psychological consequences and the context to terrorist events

It may appear disingenuous to attempt to separate or treat as distinct from the 'event' issues described above, the psychological processes that impinge upon the individual terrorist once a member of the organization and once expected to engage in (or continue engaging in) terrorist events. After all, and as has been argued since Chapter 3, group and organizational factors influence the individual at *whatever* stage of involvement or engagement in terrorism we examine. Indeed, we might go so far as to argue that, in psychological terms, perceptions relating to group and organizational factors in fact constitute the major controlling consequence for the context to the terrorist's acts as well as their continued nature, extent and direction. For the sake of clarity however, we will attempt to momentarily separate the 'event' issues from the other more overtly psychological processes that the individual terrorist is faced with upon (a) increased or prolonged involvement, often symbolized and catalysed by (b) engagement in terrorist activities.

If the group and organizational dimensions to terrorist activity are obvious, it follows then that these dimensions also reflect the broad nature of the factors and issues that can come to bear on the individual. Most terrorist organizations develop formal rules and regulations, and in the case of some groups (e.g. the Red Brigades and the Provisional IRA), general adherence to these rules greatly enhanced survival.

One major organizational staple relates to ensuring solidarity within the ranks, as well as ensuring strict obedience to authority. From the perspective of the leadership, a necessary primary concern is that the individual will perform his duty when required. Maintaining focus, commitment and discipline become paramount concerns then for the terrorist group, and as we have seen in the earlier examples, without these concerns firmly at the fore of the terrorist group, problems can emerge, and it is likely that such concerns become bolstered as a result of some prior experience leading to careful post-event analysis.

Ensuring the realization of these concerns involves training, but in the absence of the capabilities demonstrated by large-scale armies, the nature of social influence aimed at ensuring conformity, solidarity, unquestioned commitment to the group ideals, and the execution of specific orders must be perhaps even more direct, more explicit and more immediate for the individual terrorist, especially where there is any doubt or confusion about what the recruit is supposed to be doing or has done.

Obedience to an authority

The psychologist Stanley Milgram[10] demonstrated through a series of celebrated experiments that randomly chosen individuals are capable of exhibiting cruel behaviour in the right circumstances – those circumstances, Milgram explained, primarily involve simply being instructed to carry out certain functions by an authority figure. Milgram arranged for two subjects to participate in a simple experiment. One was assigned the role of 'teacher', while the other (in reality a confederate of Milgram) would be the 'learner'. The 'teacher' would engage the 'learner' on a simple learning task, on which the learner would perform well at the outset, but would gradually (on Milgram's instructions) perform increasingly poorly such that the 'teacher' would be required to engage in an activity that Milgram instructed would help the 'learner' perform better – this help involved the delivery of electric shocks, to be delivered with increasing severity depending on the ability of the learner to answer the items correctly. There were never any real electric shocks, but the learner would receive a cue as to when to feign injury and distress, which would be met by the visibly increasing discomfort by the teacher. If the learner did not answer the next question correctly, the teacher would be required to deliver another electric shock.

The teachers were, for the most part, visibly distressed and showed signs of reluctance throughout. However distressed though, the teacher would reluctantly continue, upon Milgram as the authority figure instructing: 'the experiment requires that you go on'. Alarmingly, some of the teachers went so far as to deliver electric shocks so severe that if real, would result in the death of the learner. One of the many interesting features of this work is that Milgram's subjects were not mindless agents, or sadists, and it is well accepted that most of them were in fact genuinely concerned about the welfare of the 'learners',[11] and genuinely found their participation in the task upsetting. Nevertheless, two-thirds of all 'teachers' continued to follow Milgram's instructions.

Milgram's experiments on obedience to authority are powerful in that they illustrate dramatically that for a person to engage in such extreme behaviour, in this case involving the (perceived) delivery of intense punishment, it does not necessarily follow that it reflects a pathological mental state or otherwise of the person – Milgram simply demonstrated the extraordinary power of the *situation*, when individual responsibility for inflicting harm became subjugated for the more important task of obedience to authority. This work in fact developed from attempts to explain the willing participation in genocide of the Nazis during the Second World War.

Kelman[12] identified two distinct ways in which obedience to authority functions within institutions. Some individuals come to feel, Kelman says, that they do not expect to be held personally responsible for the consequences of their actions because they accept themselves as 'agents and extensions of the authorities and thus by definition assured of their protection'. It is not uncommon, Kelman explains, for members of this group to over-identify with the authority system and exaggerate the moral claim that the authorities have on their loyalty. In the case of the Milgram experiments, many of the 'teachers', quick to adopt a subordinate role once doubt or discomfort began to emerge, made remarks to Milgram about his own responsibility for things 'going wrong' and that they themselves would not be held responsible for any subsequent trouble. Another type of individual likely to obey authority to extreme degrees can be the person who, while also believing that they have no choice but to obey, may feel that they are almost completely removed from the source of authority. In the context of Milgram's findings, this might appear unusual – in Milgram's case, he found that teachers would withdraw their participation much earlier in the experiment when the authority figure was absent. The prospect of 'doing well' in the furtherance of some collective goal, despite the immediate absence of an authority figure, can often elicit enthusiasm for those who want to be regarded as doing well in the hope that there may be a more distant, but still tangible, pay-off for their activity. In fact, sometimes, the sense of 'loneliness' in engaging in such behaviour by oneself can be seen as a praiseworthy feature, elevating the person beyond those subject to the conditions under which such behaviours would normally be expected to be elicited (i.e. following direct orders in the presence of an authority). Kelman described how Heinrich Himmler would praise the men in charge of the extermination procedures within the *Arbeitslager* for their 'courage and devotion to duty in carrying out repugnant acts'.[13]

There is a significant difference, however, between the conditions created through psychology experiments and life in a terrorist group. Naturally we might assume that it is easier for 'teachers' in a psychology experiment to withdraw from the laboratory than it would for a novice terrorist to withdraw from the group that he has worked so hard to gain entry to. Not only is the terrorist in many ways 'primed' for action against the enemy, but the recruit will already have a sense of what being involved will mean in a practical sense. The PIRA's Green Book makes this as explicit as possible under the heading 'What it means to be a Volunteer':

> All recruits, entering the Army declare that they shall obey all orders issued to them by their superior officers and by the Army Authority. This means what it is supposed to mean literally, that you obey all orders, whether you like them or not. Orders and instructions sometimes may be distasteful to the Volunteer, but this is what is involved in being a volunteer, and this is the meaning of being a volunteer – the ability to take orders and to carry them out to the best of your ability.
>
> Being a volunteer involves acting both militarily and practically. In THE MILITARY ASPECT, after an initial training, volunteers are expected to wage military war of liberation against a numerically superior force. This involves the use of arms and explosives. Firstly the use of arms. When volunteers are trained in the use of arms they must fully understand that guns are dangerous, and their main purpose is to take human life, in order words to kill people, and volunteers are trained to kill people. It is not an easy thing to take up a gun and go out to kill some person without strong convictions of justification. The Army, its motivating forces is based upon strong convictions, convictions of justification. It is these strong convictions which bonds the Army into one force and before any potential volunteer decides to join the Army he must have these strong convictions. Convictions which are strong enough to give him confidence to kill someone without hesitation and without regret. The same can be said about a bombing campaign. Again all people wishing to join the Army must fully realise that when life is taken, that could very well mean their own. If you go out to shoot soldiers or police you must fully realise that they too can shoot you. It is a dangerous thing to join the Army because of romantic notions of guerrilla warfare or a mental picture of guerrilla warfare. There certainly is no romance in war of any type, except perhaps less so in an underground army, and as for mental pictures or subjected ideas of guerrilla lifestyle, there is certainly nothing romantic or pleasant in it. Life in an underground army is extremely harsh and hard, cruel and disillusioning at times. So before any person decides to join the Army he should think seriously about the whole thing.[14]
>
> The Army as an organization claims and expects your total allegiance without reservation. It enters into every aspect of your life. It invades the privacy of your home, it fragments your family and friends, in other words claims your total allegiance.[15]

Adriana Faranda in the Red Brigades, explained:

When you get involved in a long-term project which absorbs you totally you have to accept certain rules. You accept for example that when there are political disagreements you follow the majority line. You support the others, it's a kind of pact of obedience. Even when you don't agree, you have to follow things through, bring them to completion.[16]

A blurring of escape routes from operations is a real feature of terrorist groups. A man with organizational duties within the Palestinian Islamic Jihad movement was interviewed by Hassan[17] and gives insight on the kinds of pressures faced by the individual within the movement with respect to the themes identified here:

> We ask this young man, and we ask ourselves, why he wishes so badly to become a human bomb? What are his real motives? Our questions are aimed at clarifying first and foremost for the boy himself his real reasons and the strength of his commitment. Even if he is a longtime member of our group, and has always wanted to become a martyr, he needs to be very clear that in such operations there is no drawing back.

Central to the readiness to obey authority figures is the extent to which the individual believes in the authority's ability to accept ultimate responsibility in sanctioning the activity to be carried out on the ground. For the PIRA Volunteer, the moral, legal and ethical authority to sanction military activity against the enemy rests with the PIRA Army Council, the leadership of the movement:

COMMITMENT

> Commitment to the Republican movement is the firm belief that its struggle both military and political is morally justified, that war is morally justified and that the Army is the direct representatives of the 1918 Dail Eireann parliament, and that as such they are the legal and lawful government of the Irish Republic, which has the moral right to pass laws for, and to claim jurisdiction over, the whole geographical fragment of Ireland, its maritime territory, air space, mineral resources, means of production, distribution and exchange and all its people regardless of creed or loyalty.
>
> This belief, this ethical fact, should and must give moral strength to all volunteers, and all members of every branch of the Republican Movement. The Irish Republican Army, its leadership, is the lawful government of the Irish Republic, all other parliaments or assemblies claiming the right to speak for and to pass laws on behalf of

129

the Irish people are illegal assemblies, puppet governments of a foreign power, and willing tools of an occupying force. Volunteers must firmly believe without doubt and without reservation that as members of the Irish Republican Army, all orders issued by the Army Authority, and all actions directed by the Army Authority are the legal orders and the lawful actions of the Government of the Irish Republic. This is one of the most important mainstays of the Republican Movement, the firm belief that all operations and actions directed by the Army are in effect the lawful and legal actions to the Government of all the Irish people.

MORAL SUPERIORITY

The Irish Republican Army as the legal represeentatives of the Irish people are morally justified in carrying out a campaign of resistance against foreign occupation forces and domestic collaborators. All volunteers are and must feel morally justified in carrying out the dictates of the legal government, they as the Army are the legal and lawful Army of the Irish Republic which has been forced underground by overwhelming forces. All volunteers must look upon the British Army as an occupying force.

Dehumanization and justification

We might describe such passages as part of the 'ideology' of the group (although ideology, in a psychological sense, and when thought of in terms of 'content' rather than process, might betray the relative lack of sophistication of the accounts themselves), but we also see in these mantras some surface features of what we might think of as the 'dehumanization' of the enemy. This is a potent feature of increased commitment to the special, focused community to which the terrorist now belongs. A byproduct of increased commitment to this community is the acquisition of special language that not only brings with it an ideological context to the terrorist's activities, but also delivers the basic elements required for the individual terrorist effectively to displace and diffuse responsibility for his behaviour. The Provisional IRA emphasize this tactical aspect explicitly, outlining the necessity and benefits of being able to articulate and justify the nature of the activities being conducted:

TACTICS

Get your defensive before your offensive . . . What [this means] is that before we go on the offensive politically or militarily we take the greatest defensive precautions possible to ensure success, e.g.

we do not advocate a United Ireland without being able to justify our right to such a state as opposed to partition; we do not employ revolutionary violence as our means without being able to illustrate that we have no recourse to any other means. Or in more everyday simple terms, we do not claim that we are going to escalate the war if we cannot do just that; we do not mount an operation without first having ensured that we have taken the necessary defensive precautions of accurate intelligence, security, that weapons are in proper working order with proper ammunition and that the Volunteers involved know how to handle interrogations in the event of their capture, etc., and of course that the operation itself enhances rather than alienates our supporters.

Evidence of this ability to 'talk the talk' is something that Hassan's interviewees in Hamas emphasized in candidates for martyrdom (once existing members of the group):

If [revenge] alone motivates the candidates, his martydom will not be acceptable to Allah. It is a military response, not an individual's bitterness, that drives an operation. Honor and dignity are very important in our culture. And when we are humiliated we respond with wrath.

Not only is the act of martyrdom then imbued with a sense of prestige (as we saw in the previous chapter), but the reality of the selection process is that there is also a sense of value associated with learning how to rationalize and justify the 'military response' in the first instance. Indeed at one point, the Italian Red Brigades limited membership only to those who had a good prior understanding of the Red Brigade ideology through its available documentation, while there is enough anecdotal evidence in Northern Ireland to suggest that the Green Book can be obtained easily enough, and this would almost certainly be examined by potential recruits prior to seeking involvement or increased involvement in the PIRA.

Another common aspect of this rationalization and normalization is a reference to the legitimacy of the specific tactics being pursued by the group, via a sort of legitimacy 'by comparison':[18]

NOTE ON CONVENTIONAL WARFARE

Conventional warfare takes place when a regime musters all its resources, personnel, material, technical, financial, in order to crush the enemy, civilian wise, material wise and militarily. Thus the great powers who deem us terrorists, sub-human, butchers, thugs, have employed cluster bombs, napalm bombs, atomic bombs against the civilian populations of their enemy causing in the last sixty years of this century alone hundreds of millions of civilian deaths and the attending consequences of sufferings, starvation, disease and dehumanization to the survivors.

The terrorist's acts, in a relative sense then, can come to seem almost inconsequential as the far lesser of two evils. This is a commonly found feature of terrorist 'morality'.

Routinization and deindividuation

Hannah Arendt[19] explained in great detail how although Adolf Eichmann's contempt for the Jews was evident, he never passionately hated the Jews, but like many of his colleagues, dealt with them in a 'passionless, businesslike way'.[20] In a consideration of how this might develop in the context of genocide, Kelman,[21] like Kurt Lewin suggested a focus not as much on what are the presumed factors that increase the strength of driving forces towards violence, but instead attempt to identify the factors that reduce the strength of restraining forces against violence.

In particular, Kelman explains that a process of 'routinization' fulfils two basic functions for the individual: (1) there is a reduction in the effort required for conscious, deliberate decision-making, thus, he describes, minimizing the likelihood of situations occurring where the individual has to engage in moral evaluation; and (2) the individual finds it easier to avoid the implications of their behaviour by 'focusing on the details of his job rather than on its meaning'. It is not difficult to see how this might develop in terrorist groups given the explicit language qualities laid down in the PIRA's Green Book and elsewhere.

Milgram himself argued that there were certain situational adjustment factors that served to distance his subjects from the effects of their behaviour on the victim. Physical proximity with the victim is a factor (it is always easier to justify killing from a distance), but Milgram noticed in particular how the teachers became very involved in the technical aspects of their task, 'tried to be competent at it, attributed the responsibility for the proceedings to the experimenter'[22] and hence, according to Heskin, their 'moral concern correspondingly diminished'. Milgram described the process as 'counteranthropomorphism', to illustrate just how his subjects began to 'deny the human element in what was an institutionalised procedure':[23] any normal reactions were suppressed to distress in others 'in the name of . . . scientific enquiry' (ibid.).

We know that the nature and extent of both conformity and obedience are susceptible to a variety of factors. Perhaps the most relevant here relates to the nature of the group. Terrorist movements are illegal, secretive and due to limited opportunities for targeting, combined with shared risks and threats, set the scene for exceptional degrees of internal pressure. Conformity is always strengthened when the group is more cohesive, bound together and unanimous, which makes orders difficult to resist especially when delivered by those with higher status and authority. Another common property of group membership, however, is that membership of a group in itself can lead to a lessening of restraints against impulsive or unusual forms of behaviour, behaviour that under normal conditions would be suppressed, if recognized at all. *Deindividuation* is a formal term given to the process whereby 'social restraints are weakened and impulsive and aggressive tendencies released as the person loses individual identity, usually as the result of being part of a large group or having his or her identity concealed in some way'.[24] Deindividuation helps understand why people who would normally not be aggressive, might join in a violent political protest, or join in with a group which loots a shop, for example. Dworetsky[25] explains how it is possible to become:

> so caught up in events and in the feeling of the group that we lose our individuality. Once our individuality has been reduced, we lose track of who we are and what our values are. This, in turn, causes us to become more impulsive, more sensitive to our present emotional state, and, to some degree, less able to regulate our own behaviour. Also, with such reduced individuality, we are less concerned about what other people think of us and what they might do to us. We are more concerned about responding as part of a group.

The qualities of deindividuation are evident at various points within the terrorism process, and as described in the Green Book examples above can play a role in strengthening the readiness of a PIRA Volunteer to follow orders and engage in an operation, but they can also come to bear on reassuring the Volunteer at any post-event phase and serve to minimize responsibility, doubt and lack of confidence in the moral justification of what has just happened. For some terrorists who have just engaged in their first operation, feelings of guilt or depression might occur, but can eventually dissipate through the processes described. And indeed, we can see how deindividuation works at a more basic, practical level. Silke[26] discovered that the use of disguises by Northern Irish terrorists was significantly associated with increased levels and variety of aggression at the scene of the crime. In addition, the injuries inflicted on victims tended to be more severe than those inflicted by perpetrators who did not wear masks.

Part of the dehumanization process entails another use of language that is frequently found in conventional military settings. Military discourse abounds with what Bandura[27] describes as *palliative expressions*. We are used to hearing soldiers speak of being taught to shoot at 'targets' and not 'people'. We should not understimate the importance of the power of words as a controlling or sustaining influence on behaviour: indeed such labels are not far removed from the types of expression used in response to the coalition bombing of suspected terrorist safehouses in Fallujah in mid-2004 that frequently resulted in the deaths of non-combatant civilians. Such targets were often the casualties of what was described as 'conscientiously deployed' weaponry.

The following excerpts illustrate the combined efforts at both conveying legitimacy whilst simultaneously encouraging dehumanization (not unlike the example described earlier, making comparisons between conventional warfare and the tactics being engaged in by the PIRA). In particular, we see from the PIRA example how locating legitimacy within the context of communal identity can be a powerful focusing influence:

THE BRIT AND THE I.R.A. VOLUNTEER[28]

The most obvious differences between the Brit and the I.R.A. volunteer, apart from the fact that the Brit is an uninvited armed foreigner who has no moral or historical justification for being here in the first place are those of support, motivation and freedom of personal initiative.

The Brits support, his billets, dumps, weapons, wages etc., are all . . . provided for by involuntary taxation. His people who pay the taxes have never indicated nor indeed have they been asked to indicate by any democratic means their assent to his being here at their expense. The I.R.A. volunteer recieves all his support voluntarily from his people.

The Brit, apart from the adventurist elements, has no motivation for being here. He simply obeys orders and arrives.

A member of the I.R.A. is such by his own choice, his convictions being the only factor which compels him to volunteer, his objectives the political freedom and social and economic justice for his people. Apart from the few minutes in the career of the average Brit that he comes under attack, the Brit has no freedom or personal initiative. He is told when to sleep, where to sleep, when to get up, where to spend his free time etc.

The I.R.A. volunteer except when carrying out a specific army task acts most of the time on his own initiative and must therefore shoulder that responsibility in such a way that he enhances our necessary stated task of ensuring that his conduct is not a contributory factor to the Brit attempt to isolate us from our people.

Rarely do we achieve a sense of how Al Qaeda denigrate the enemy in a similar manner. In March 2003, the group released the fifth and sixth in a series of important documents aimed at identifying and clarifying the context and focus to its activities, and in particular as a means of encouragement for Mujahideen fighters in Iraq. Saif Al-Adel, a former Egyptian special forces officer, became involved with Al Qaeda via the Epyptian Islamic Jihad (itself once managed by Ayman Al Zawahiri, Osama Bin Laden's second in command). The following is from an article entitled 'Message to our people in Iraq and Gulf [Region] specifically, and to our Islamic Ummah in general: the Islamic Resistance against the American Invasion of Kandahar and lessons learned':[29]

> We differ completely from our enemy in the psychological fight. While our enemy depended on creating lies about itself, magnifying its power [by saying that] it will not be defeated and the war will not exceed a week as it has sweeping power which can make miracles, and its program depended on terrorising the competitor because of the Crusaders' hopelessness in their deteriorating fighting level, we were working on bonding every one with his God and his relation with Him, and He is mighty strong and keen. Therefore our program depended on building the Muslim person who belives in the divine secrets, and who realises that the Book of Allah contains acts not understood except by Allah the Almighty.
>
> In fact we did not suffer much psychologically for the simple reason that we did not make it mandatory for the youth to join the training camps. We opened our nation's eyes on its issues and as a result, the youth came forward to fight for the dignity of Islam and Muslims, armed with the hope of becoming martyrs.
>
> This is the true motivation behind the heroic stand of the mujahideen, and their ability to handle extremely difficult tasks.

When combined with notions invoked by the Fundamental Attribution Error (described in Chapter 3), these issues form the basis of a powerful bias in explaining and rationalizing our own behaviour while also attempting to portray the motivation and behaviour of others in a negative light (and implicitly suggesting negative dispositional qualities inherent in 'the enemy'). As a result, there is denigration of the enemy, and simultaneously an avoidance of responsibility for any potentially necessary activities conducted against them. These processes collectively contribute towards an explanation of how barriers to engagement can be broken down, but from the individual perspective can also form the basis of important psychological tools, a special language, with which involvement and engagement can be rationalized, normalized and justified to oneself and others.

Social activity

One final pressure worth identifying here, because it relates to some of the properties of the processes described, relates to the social implications of the terrorist's engagement in operations and other activities. An unmistakable feature of being a terrorist entails both an obvious increase in activities related to terrorism, coupled with a consequent decrease in activities relevant to the terrorist's former (i.e. non-terrorism related) life. This dynamic differs in potency depending on the specific nature of the cell or group to which the member belongs, but the general feature is a real one for every member involved.

In particular, security concerns underpin almost every aspect of what it means to be a terrorist, and the reality of what this means for the terrorist quickly becomes tangible. The Green Book explains:

> The most important aspect of any organization, party, group or army is security. Security binds all people within that organisation together in confidence. Like a chain its strongest point is the weakest link, so all volunteers should regard themselves as links within an organised chain, bearing in mind that the continuity of struggle, the object of resistance, the confidence in victory depends on the individual himself. Any weakening in the individual means a weakening in his organisation as a whole, so volunteers should and must at all times be conscious of their own security . . .
>
> So the most important thing is security, that means you:- DON'T TALK IN PUBLIC OR IN PRIVATE PLACES; YOU DON'T TELL YOUR FAMILY, FRIENDS, GIRLFRIEND OR WORK- MATES THAT YOU ARE A MEMBER OF THE I.R.A.: DON'T EXPRESS VIEWS ABOUT MILITARY MATTERS. IN OTHER WORDS YOU SAY NOTHING to any person. Don't be seen in public marches, demonstrations or protests. Don't be seen in the company of known Repubicans, don't frequent known Republican houses. Your prime duty is to remain unknown to the enemy forces and the public at large.[30]

For Red Brigade members, leading a double life meant tackling the strain of social and psychological challenges. The 'intensification' of commitment would be obvious:

> when the [member] accustomed to spending his evenings with his wife or girlfriend at home or playing cards with his friends in the local bar became increasingly absent from his usual haunts, un- available because of unspecified 'meetings' and began making and receiving telephone calls from unknown 'friends', accusations of

suspicious activities or of infidelity frequently created pressure for an explanation. In the early years, the BR tended to be flexible over this and left it to the discretion of each member how much was told to a partner, whose shock and/or disapproval in some instances prevented further militancy.[31]

Clearly the move towards increased involvement in terrorism can result in a shift for the individual away from one kind of social relationship and into others. What the individual finds in the terrorist group, however, are others who have broadly similar experiences and whose relationships often solidify as a result of those shared past experiences, shared threats, shared illegal acts, all resulting in the formation of relationships whose sole purpose is to ensure continuing mutual validation and normalization of commitment to the group and the associated activity.

No terrorist engages in military operations on a continuous basis, but the terrorist will still engage in relevant (i.e. terrorism-related) 'non-offending' or non-event-related behaviour. We can probably only say in a limited way, however, that such activities are non-event related. In some clear ways they are not, and obviously do not constitute terrorist events, but for the individual who has engaged in terrorist activity, they can become powerful sustaining factors. In Northern Ireland, commemorative events constitute exceptionally important rituals, whether through song, music, parades or other activities. Sometimes the rituals can take the form of major events: in April 2002, over 400 families of dead PIRA members came together with the PIRA leadership and other senior Republicans to commemorate and honour their dead at a hotel dinner evening. Each dead PIRA member was represented by four family members who received an engraved plaque and special commemorative book on behalf of the PIRA leadership.

Conclusions

The 'being' phase can be considered a crystallization of what happens to the individual who is becoming increasingly involved in terrorism to the point of engaging in terrorist events. While we identified earlier the specific event factors important to understanding what issues impinge upon the active terrorist, the relevant process factors, we should remember, include: the rapid acquisition of skills, the fitting into a role, the acquisition of special language, an increased acceptance and embracing of that role (and the accompanying integration of personal fantasies), the increased sense of control and personal agency, and furthermore, the use of involvement as currency in acquisition of status. As with the 'becoming' phase, the reality of increased involvement in terrorism reflects a rational, conscious and effortful process.

The nature of the process that impinges upon the individual in remaining a terrorist is specific to that phase, and is not necessarily related to the reasons why people become involved in the first place, or, as we shall see, leave. The role of social and group processes is very powerful, with implicit and explicit conformity, compliance and obedience operating as powerful sustaining engagement process factors. The nature of terrorist groups is such that dissent is not tolerated easily within the group, with group conditions frequently becoming stifling as a result, but for the individual terrorist increasing psychological investment, or the process of becoming a more committed member, is shaped most remarkably through engagement in terrorist activities.

If we are to continue to attempt to develop the *risk assessment* or *risk management* metaphor hinted at in Chapter 4, the processes engaged by the individual terrorist at this phase can be identified as possible 'process' points of dangerousness also. For the individual terrorist then, these might include, in no particular order:

1 A sense of working towards the acquisition and articulation of a 'special' internal language of both (a) explanation and (b) rationalization, which is solidly ground in the social and political context in which the violence of the terrorist group emerges.
2 As a result of (1), a sense of growing empowerment, control and defensiveness.
3 As a result of increased engagement in events, a developing sense of engaging in risk-laden behaviours.
4 A probable sense of working through the development and devotion to personal fantasies.
5 Specifically in relation to the commission of terrorist activity, a lowering of inhibitions in relation to the expression of violent behaviour (with the group presence being a major controlling consequence of this).
6 As an overall consequence of increased involvement and particularly engagement in terrorist activity, an increase in very focused, purposive (i.e. terrorism-related) social activity, and as a result of this,
7 An overall decrease in non-focused, non-purposive (i.e. non-terrorism-related) social activity.

We saw in the previous chapter that issues that relate to why people become terrorists tend to be complex, difficult to pin down in specific ways (because individual factors vary in significance for everyone) and quite diffuse – with questions relating to why people become terrorists often unanswerable in any meaningful or complete way. Issues that relate to the emergence of terrorist events, however, are smaller, more identifiable and predictable, and relate primarily to the immediate context issues which the individual is facing, such as those relating to environment, opportunities, the political context, leadership relationships and so forth.

A further and crucial assertion to make from this is that issues to do with event factors can be thought of as under some measure of control by the security forces, while 'becoming' issues are not. The latter are based in some distant past, relating to the individual's background factors, idiosyncratic personal experiences and perceptions, and are much more resistant to any change.

We have also seen in this chapter that we can identify a number of factors that are crucial for maintaining engagement in terrorism for the individual. We might think of them in terms of 'risk management' in that they would indicate possible points of dangerousness for an individual who has developed through the initial phase of becoming involved. Recognizing the potential dangerousness of an individual does not necessarily offer a means of reducing that dangerousness, but focusing on these factors in specific contexts might offer practical benefits. If we consider some of these factors in terms of interrogation planning, for example, it might help gain a better understanding of that individual person. This is not new in the area of forensic psychology (in the context of sex offenders, for instance), where concepts of dangerousness are widely explored, but this is as yet unexplored in the context of involvement and engagement with terrorist activity.

In the following chapter, we will arrive at the final area of activity we will consider within the model that is developing. The next chapter involves those factors that lead to the individual moving away from, or disengaging from, terrorism.

6

DISENGAGING

Introduction

We have seen from the previous chapter that in recognizing terrorism as a group process, the consequences of what that recognition implies are obvious: psychological qualities of group membership in terrorism quickly become apparent for the extreme potential both to attract members as well as to bind them together via sustained commitment and engagement. Extreme conformity and strict obedience are organizational cornerstones that leaders put in place to enhance the effective maintenance of what is already a difficult, secret and, above all, illegal organization. It follows then that maintaining such conformity is paramount, and having a shared purpose or sense of unity and direction, which in itself is catalysed by having a clearly identifiable enemy, facilitates this. We have also seen that the distinction between where one lies with respect to the 'becoming' and 'being' a terrorist is in one sense as much a psychological issue as anything else, but thinking of participation in terrorist events as a possible delineation point is useful: any remaining hurdles of finally having one's identity reaffirmed within the terrorist group often comes through engagement in activity considered centrally valuable to the organization.

The final phase of the process model inevitably then concerns disengagement: how and why people *leave* terrorism and terrorist activity. At the outset, however, it must be stated this would appear to have been the basis for the shortest chapter of this book for one simple reason – we simply know too little about what happens for the individual terrorist to leave terrorism behind. It is obvious that the psychological research community has for far too long focused on issues to do with becoming involved, at the expense of other gaps in our knowledge. A disheartening reason for this is an ambivalent perception by researchers towards issues concerning, and arising from, disengagement. Many researchers assume that terrorists and their organizations are somehow no longer 'relevant', or deserving of serious, urgent study, once their involvement in terrorism has ceased, a fact that tells us more about the factors driving the direction of the research than anything else. In fact, James Dingley[1] suggested that academics who study terrorism would lose a major vested interest if terrorist campaigns were to come to an end. If he is correct, such a blinkered attitude on the part of researchers about what our subject matter 'ought' to represent (presumably active terrorists only) precludes then the valuable opportunities now available, for example, to researchers who prior to the recent peace initiatives in Ireland could barely contemplate the possibility of meeting and speaking with those involved in terrorism. Talking with terrorists is, as briefly described in Chapter 2, now an achievable reality[2] and our neglect of valuable research avenues will ultimately be reflected in future assessments of our knowledge of terrorist behaviour. This has been a persistent issue since terrorism research efforts began to gain momentum in the early 1980s, but if students and scholars of terrorism heeded theoretical issues and gaps in the literature to guide their research agendas, our knowledge and understanding of the processes involved in terrorism would be more complete. If only to attempt to broaden our subject perspective for the moment, and to complete the final phase of the model under development here, let us remember that despite even the best of intentions, more research on the same issue does not necessarily imply greater knowledge, and the need for us to consider disengagement issues, even speculatively, is important.

A starting point: understanding why terrorism ends

The focus of this chapter concerns individual issues in terrorist disengagement, but we must first consider the nature of the relevant broader processes. The terrorism literature has increasingly considered the broad factors that have contributed to the slow decline of traditional forms of terrorism since both the end of the Cold War and the changing nature and direction of many of the world's most intractable terrorist campaigns. The examples of ideological and revolutionary terrorism across Europe are familiar to most as contributing to the pre-9/11 public image of 'the terrorist', and include the Italian Red Brigades, the German Red Army Faction (RAF) and numerous other Marxist anti-imperialist groups born largely out of the spirit of revolt in the late 1960s. Europe's last 'Red terrorists' undoubtedly remain the November 17 group in Greece, but whilst ideological terror has failed to adapt to changing times and changing opinion, ethno-nationalist terrorist movements, allied with increasingly adept and influential political wings, have stood the test of time more firmly. In the case of the Provisional IRA, a popular base, tactical, strategic and organizational adaptability (often learned through harsh experience), financial backing and a successful political wing (Sinn Fein) have contributed to the remarkable persistence of this most intractable of groups: an unwavering belief in their own imminent victory and a gradual nuancing of once offensive Marxist ideology has helped to shape the Republican movement into a now effective and attractive political force in Ireland, and a gradual involvement in a wide array of activities often not usually associated with terrorism (both legal and illegal) have contributed to its survival. The recent rise of Sinn Fein across the whole of Ireland has been directly assisted by the movement's exploitation of government complacency and a persistent failure truly to appreciate the long-term strategic nature of Sinn Fein and the PIRA. Although the Irish Peace Process has been the subject of many, often naive, commentaries since it began in the early 1990s, some general principles can be identified to help understand the timing and pace of the PIRA's gradual de-escalation of terrorism and escalation of political activity since the early 1980s. These include, but are not limited to:

- A realization that terrorism alone was insufficient in achieving the movement's aspirations (leading to the increasingly tactical and largely discriminate use of terrorist attacks since the rise of Sinn Fein).
- A gradual willingness by the British Government to engage in secret discussions with Republicans on how to end the conflict, or at least allow for breathing space (i.e. ceasefires) through which other alternatives to violence could be encouraged.
- Successes both by counter-terrorism efforts and an increasingly belligerent Loyalist terror campaign against both the Republican movement and the wider nationalist community in Northern Ireland in the early 1990s, in itself contributing to public opinion desperate for stability in the region.

Despite a breakdown in the initial PIRA ceasefire (largely arising from accusations of bad faith: whether the original ceasefire was simply perceived as a breathing period for Republicans or a genuine move towards a greater peace settlement at the time, we will probably never know), in the years since the steps toward peace in Northern Ireland began, a number of concessions granted towards all paramilitary movements and their political wings has meant that their increasing involvement in the political process has ultimately contributed to the overall decline in the activity we most usually associate with terrorism – fatal shootings and bombings. There is no point in describing here the various ebbs and flows in the labyrinthine peace process with concession and counter-concession carefully choreographed in secrecy, but a more recent event has given great cause for questioning what happens to individual members of a terrorist movement when terrorism ends.

In the weeks following the 9/11 attacks, a press conference was called at Sinn Fein's former Belfast headquarters at Conway Mill. The Sinn Fein leaders, Gerry Adams and Martin McGuinness, announced that decommissioning of the PIRA's weapons (according to all perceived detractors of the Republican movement, the main obstacle to political stability in the region) was to become not a distant aim, but a current reality. To many non-Republicans this offered proof (if it was ever needed) that not only did international events overshadow the mighty PIRA's self-importance and unwavering demand for parity of political esteem in the continued absence of decommissioning, they also illustrated more obviously, as described in Chapter 2, that Sinn Fein and the PIRA do respond to pressure. All parties welcomed the breakthrough statement and there was no question that Sinn Fein was now finally on its way to gaining its place in the political process. To the public, the leadership portrayed the move as the PIRA having saved the peace process: the political deadlock broken thanks to the PIRA's 'courage'. The dissent within the movement was clear, however, and illustrated to the outside world just how little detail of this unprecedented move had been revealed to the rank-and-file supporters of the organization prior to this news conference. Upon leaving the meeting, it was reported that Adams was met with shouts and jeers from his own followers, cries of 'you sold us out Gerry' representing the new uncomfortable reality facing Republicans who had previously been facilitated in their commitment by an unwavering promise of 'not an ounce [of explosives], not a bullet'.

Although this is just a glimpse of a specific period of one terrorist campaign, the range of questions for research became clear. There are questions we need to answer in relation to what happens to people who leave terrorism, issues relating to what influences them to leave (either voluntarily or involuntarily), as well as the implications of such processes. Indeed, a broader issue here, and one that is especially relevant given the complexity of what 'becoming involved' seems to now suggest, concerns what we mean by 'disengaging' or 'leaving' at all. Leaving terrorism behind might suggest leaving behind the shared social norms, values, attitudes and aspirations so carefully forged while a member of a terrorist group. On the other hand it might indicate some adherence to these values and attitudes, but perhaps no longer engaging in actual terrorist activity. The more issues we consider, the more we will realize that to gain a fuller understanding of how and why people leave terrorism behind we need to bear in mind the varied and complex reasons as to why and how people join a terrorist group in the first place, and also how and why they remain in an organization. Some of the reasons that might help explain a sense of 'remaining' involved might further be considered as reasons that possibly inhibit or block exit routes (be they psychological – e.g. through disillusionment with some aspect the group – or physical – e.g. apprehension by the security services). To complicate matters further, we might think of each of these as either voluntary in origin (e.g. the decision that continued membership of the group is no longer as important as some overriding personal issue) or involuntary (e.g. an individual is forced to leave in the face of some external issue such as the reality of arms decommissioning, or some new legislative initiative, and the implications this has for organizational dissipation, possibly leading to an outright rejection of the group's ideals as a result). We already then have two broad possible categories within which we can consider the influences 'forcing' or 'attracting' a person to leave terrorism behind: voluntary and involuntary disengagement.

The seeds of psychological disengagement

We saw in the previous two chapters how it is in earning trust, respect and a place in the terrorist group that members encounter the psychological barriers that must be overcome or adapted to. If not, the seeds of what we might term 'psychological' disengagement will already begin to set, and indeed, a variety of influences appear directly or indirectly to facilitate (or even encourage) the prospect of leaving.

While we saw in Chapter 4 how the rewards involved in terrorist groups can include an enormous amount of excitement, status, purpose and admiration, coupled with what McCauley and Segal[3] refer to as 'mutual solidarity and feelings of comradeship', these supportive qualities of involvement are exceptionally important, especially given the kinds of new demands facing the terrorist recruit, as described in Chapter 5. Indeed, given illegal underground life more generally, these features can become quite potent. The reality of balancing out the negative features of increased, sustained and focused involvement with the positive supportive qualities is rarely so straightforward, however, and the negative intensity of the group is demonstrated by many accounts of members who have left the organization and have written memoirs or autobiographies.

For instance, Michael Baumann, a former member of the German 2nd June Movement,[4] reflects on the negative influence exercised by the power of the group:

> the group becomes increasingly closed. The greater the pressure from the outside, the more you stick together, the more mistakes you make, the more pressure is turned inward . . . this crazy concentration all day long, those are all the things that come together horribly at the end, when there's no more sensibility in the group: only rigid concentration, total pressure to achieve, and it keeps going, always gets worse.

Increased security becomes paradoxical with often greater pressure arising from attempts to safeguard against infiltration, or even internal disputes. In February of 1969, Japanese police discovered 14 bodies in the snowy mountains outside Tokyo. It transpired that all of them were members of the Japanese Red Army who were tortured and killed by their fellow members as a result of internal squabbling over ideological issues.

While some acquiesce to the pressures, others do not. Again, there are unfortunately too few reliable data on this issue, but we do know that individual terrorists do make requests to 'leave', having decided that the lifestyle is not for them. Anecdotal evidence suggests that sometimes this is not a problem given the implicit assumption that the member will 'not talk'. Indeed the Italian Red Brigades (on which Jamieson[5] gives perhaps the best glimpse into the factors affecting disengagement) appeared to have realized the importance of identifying probable 'drop-outs' from the outset: 'when a firing group went into action, one, or at the most two, "novices" were taken along to provide cover and to test their nerve and reliability under pressure'.[6] The Red Brigades adopted what was tantamount to a crude psychometric screening tool via assessment under extraordinary pressure.

For many facing self-doubt, however, leaving is not so easy. After all, regardless of what stage along the 'becoming' and 'being' continuum a person lies, the organization will seek a return on their investment and a promise to keep one's mouth shut may not be enough. The leadership of the Baader-Meinhof group never hesitated to clarify this: 'Whoever is in the group simply has to hold out, has to be tough',[7] later threatening that the only way out for any doubters would be 'feet first'. Similarly, Spire,[8] a former member of the French Communist Party, describes the fear of ostracization and marginalization if one 'challenges the ideology . . . or the fashionable beliefs'. Spire described in detail his own attempts to rationalize 'breaches of faith, oppression, and political crimes' because he felt 'terrified at the thought of being marginalized by beloved fellow comrades and colleagues'.[9] Adriana Faranda of the Italian Red Brigades also reflects on the pressures associated with membership, and the negative social and psychological consequences of sustained membership:[10]

> choosing to enter the Red Brigades – to become clandestine and therefore to break off relations with your family, with the world in which you'd lived until the day before – is a choice so total that it involves your entire life, your daily existence. It means choosing to occupy yourself from morning till night with problems of politics, or organisation, and fighting; and no longer with normal life – culture, cinema, babies, the education of your children, with all the things that fill other people's lives. These things get put to one side, ignored, because they simply do not exist any more. And when you remove yourself from society, even from the most ordinary things, ordinary ways of relaxing, you no longer share even the most basic emotions. You become abstracted, removed. In the long run you actually begin to feel different. Why? Because you are different. You become closed off, become sad, because a whole area of life is missing, because you are aware that life is more than politics and political work.

Another significant pressure that may later catalyse the move (psychological or physical) to leave is the uncomfortable individual realization that the initial aspirations and personal hopes expressed through seeking membership are quite removed from the day-to-day reality of what the duties and responsibilities of this new role involve. Brockner and Rubin[11] developed the notion of *psychological traps* that refer to situations where an individual, having decided upon some course of action that he or she expects will return a reward (in the broadest possible sense), for example joining a terrorist group or remaining in such a group, finds that the actual process of goal attainment requires a continuing and repeated 'investment' in some form over some degree of time. This 'repeated investment', in a psychological sense, will probably be required of that individual to sustain his or her involvement, but still the eventual goal may continue to be a very distant realization. Brockner and Rubin note that somewhere in this process is an inevitable stage when people find themselves in a 'decisional no-man's land', the realization that he or she has made quite a substantial investment but still not yet achieved his or her expected goal.

At this point, the individual experiences a decisional crisis and reaches a crossroads. The investment of time, energy and hope may seem too large (especially when combined with the intense pressures one must bear per se as a result of membership) given other circumstances to continue in the absence of a readily attainable goal. On the other hand, withdrawal means the abandonment of what has gone before, and the individual may feel a commitment if only to personally justify the investment already made.[12] The ensuing entrapment encompasses 'the spiralling of commitment, so frequently seen in members of terrorist groups'.[13]

Rubin[14] identifies three critical qualities of traps: (a) the ability to lure or distract the trap's victim into behaviour which may be quite socially psychologically costly to him, (b) the construction of the trap allows only decisions that permit greater movement into the trap, and (c) efforts to escape serve only to increase the trap's bite.[15] The longing for the once-normal life, with social contacts, the ability to walk the streets or simply to engage in a romantic relationship are all normal personal factors which, at any stage of the process, may become prioritized (perhaps arising from, and leading to, distinct emotional states that could be seen to characterize a greater openness to embracing such possibilities) and thereby facilitate at least the beginning of psychological disengagement (probably at the moment doubt arises). What path the member chooses to follow subsequently will be subjected to all of these and further influences.

Other psychological influences

Post[16] highlights the fact that the group pressures themselves have a variety of implications for decision-making within that group. Individual judgement in most decision-making groups tends to be 'suspended and subordinated to the group process'.[17] Groupthink occurs in situations where group cohesiveness is high, and the ability of the group to engage in critical decision-making processes is interfered with. Here, the attempts of group members to portray unanimity in the context of their decision-making appears to actually take precedent over their motivation to 'realistically appraise' alternative (and perhaps more effective) decisions.[18] The group becomes blind to the possibility that its decision might not be the most effective, and in reality this may prevent the group from attaining its goal. Post notes that there is an overwhelming sense of 'wishful thinking' in groups where this occurs, but emphasizes that the processes by which such faulty decision-making can occur are quite simple: when we join a group, and our views become evident from discussion, we may seek approval by sharing those views in an attempt to display a greater level of commitment to the group's ideal and thereby demonstrate our loyalty over time.[19]

There may often be a realization, however, that some of the closely held political ideals that would have contributed to the initial phase of becoming involved often have to give way and become compromised as a result of individual personalities, a stifling organizational 'climate' (often, in fact, a result of an individual personality) which can give rise to enormous dissent, whether expressed overtly or not. A good example of this comes from an interview conducted by the present author in Northern Ireland in early 1999. The interview segment, although brief, illustrates just how several factors can come into play: conformity, obedience, groupthink and the influence exerted by a minority might (eventually) lead to a change in direction for the group, and also contribute to one member's gradual disillusionment with the movement:

> The meeting was called, and we all knew there was going to be trouble. We were all told we had to be there and I'd say a lot of fellas were told they were going to be told off in front of everyone. [The leader] came in and called things to order. He went around to each of us and wanted reports. When he came to me I was last, but I had to speak up. I told him that our arms situation was in dire straits and unless we were going to do something about it quick, let alone about the lack of funds, that we were just shooting ourselves in the foot. I had the greatest faith in that man, but he had this way of not wanting to see the reality of things as they were. So I said, we need to elect a Quartermaster, and that person would have complete responsibility for the procuring of the stuff as well as managing it, you know? He wasn't pleased at that because like I said, his ideas about the organisation was that it was 'grand', 'no problem' like. When the meeting ended, one of the lads caught up with me on the steps, and I never liked the [man] anyway, but he

actually shook my hand! He said 'congratulations, that needed to be said'. No one else would have said it if I didn't open up my mouth.

The importance of this interviewee's comments becomes apparent in considering other relevant issues. The organization he belonged to was the Official IRA, a movement that became defunct in the early 1970s primarily because it was unable to develop an effective political presence. This interviewee, one of the founding members of the group, left the movement and eventually emigrated:

> I went to [country] for several years I was just so pissed off with the whole thing. We were originally established to espouse socialism. And I know we offended a lot of people [laughs] especially since we were simply spouting every party line that came from Moscow, but [the leader] brought the trouble on himself by not being in touch with the mood on the ground and I never really patched things up with him after that . . . It's miserable when you . . . believe in it, believe in the movement and the, ah, initial socialist ideals I suppose. I gave up my house, my car . . . you had people give up their farms, and for what in the end? Arguing about guns all the time because we'd no money.

This man's disillusionment appears to have developed over some time, and comparison with Alison Jamieson's[20] interviews with Faranda reveals unmistakable similarities. Faranda described her 'dissociation' from the Red Brigades as:

> a process which matured very gradually . . . it's not a traumatic leap, it's more a matter of a thousand little stages. It encompasses everything though; reasoning, valuations, questions which involve not just one action, not one way of conducting the armed struggle, not one revolutionary project – everything. It involves the revolution itself; Marxism, violence, the logic of enmity, of conflict, of one's relationship with authority, a way of working out problems, of confronting reality and of facing the future . . . I haven't taken one huge traumatic leap. It's not as if I was one person one day and a different one the next.

What is also significant here is that both of these accounts point to a gradual process of disengaging that appears similar to the process that characterizes involvement in terrorism in the first place.

For others, however, singular catalyst events appear, on the surface anyhow, to characterize a sudden move towards psychological disengagement. Sean O'Callaghan, the former PIRA terrorist who subsequently

148

became the most important informer against the PIRA for the Irish and British security services, describes one of his most important memories as a young PIRA member:[21]

> I come from the South. I come from a Republican family and was heavily influenced in 1969 by the pogroms in Belfast and loads of nationalist refugees fleeing south. I joined the Provisional IRA at 15 and I ended up in East Tyrone and started to become very aware that the Provisional campaign on the ground was extremely sectarian. That began to worry me. Once in 1975 I was sitting in a flat in Monaghan, along with about eight or ten people from the East Tyrone IRA who were on the run. A news item came on the television. A policewoman had been killed in a bomb explosion in Bangor. A person, who later became chief of staff at the IRA for many years, turned to me and said, 'I hope she's pregnant and we get two for the price of one'. I'd been brought up in a kind of romantic, nationalist background in the deep south and I wasn't prepared or able to cope with that kind of hate and bigotry.

O'Callaghan claims that this was the defining moment that caused him not only to question his own involvement in the movement, but subsequently to inflict damage on the movement (by turning informer). Of course, it is impossible to generalize from single examples, but as with the recalled and presumed significance of single events (either to characterize involvement or disengagement), their true significance is likely to emerge when acting upon some state of 'readiness' or openness towards disengagement. It is likely that O'Callaghan had been having some doubts about his commitment to the movement before the above event that seemed to propel him into greater certainty that he wanted to leave.

In summary, therefore, we can tentatively identify factors that appear to contribute to a move towards psychological disengagement:

1 Negative influences as a result of sustained, focused membership (e.g. the influence of unbearable group and organizational psychological pressures) and as a result,

2 A sense of changing priorities (e.g. the longing for a social/psychological state which (real or imaginary) the member feels is lacking, or existed before membership, often a result of self-questioning but mostly following prolonged social/psychological investment as a member from which little return appears evident).

3 A sense of growing disillusionment with the avenues being pursued (e.g. with the political aims (as illustrated in the Official IRA interviewee example); or with the operational tactics and the attitudes underpinning them (as illustrated by O'Callaghan's statement)).

Physical disengagement

In many ways, reasons for what might be called 'physical' disengagement are easier to identify. Relevant disengagement behaviours and their antecedents might be thought of as physical where there is a change in the role of an individual terrorist away from opportunities to engage in violent behaviour, but where this move may or may not necessarily result in a lessening of commitment to the group. Often there can be physical disengagement from terrorist activity per se, but no change or reduction in support. Indeed, in some cases physical disengagement from terrorism (in terms of being removed from the activity of committing terrorist violence) might involve any of the following, none of which should be considered exclusive:

- Apprehension by the security services, perhaps with subsequent imprisonment (or if not, forced movement by the leadership of the member into a role whereby he or she is less likely to risk arrest).
- Forced movement into another role as a result of disobeying orders: at the very least ostracization may occur, if not outright execution, but if there is some mitigating circumstance the member may instead be pushed into another functional role.
- An increase in 'other role' activity whereby the original role becomes displaced (e.g. an area of specialization that relates directly to the commission of terrorist offences such as exploiting one's technical acumen by assisting in the preparation of equipment), or increased involvement in political activity (often as a result of imprisonment which, ironically for some, represents a final consolidation of communal identity).
- Being ejected from the movement (e.g. for improper use of arms, money, etc. or some disrespectful behaviour that warrants dismissal but not execution).
- As with psychological disengagement, a change in priorities.

The crucial difference between physical and psychological disengagement in this sense, however, is that the terrorist may continue with his or her role in the movement but may later move into another role/function in order to facilitate new personal circumstances (e.g. getting married or having children, and moving into a support or ancillary role as a result): they may still continue to engage in 'terrorism'-related activities, but not 'terrorist events' per se. The other direction from which this role change might emerge is from the leadership, who may place a heavier emphasis on political activity in the months approaching an election. In simple practical terms, this might involve an active terrorist engaging in distributing posters or helping to organize political rallies.

A vital source from which we may be able to formulate hypotheses relating to disengagement processes is analysing the implications of organizational issues per se, as far as the terrorist leadership is concerned, both with respect to promoting engagement and inhibiting any form of, but especially psychological, disengagement.

Organizational issues

Terrorist organizations, as we have seen so far, must not only offer incentives to join, but must also prioritize 'action over talk'[22] to indirectly facilitate sustained, prolonged involvement. Citing Carlos Marighella, Crenshaw notes that 'action creates the vanguard': describing terrorists as 'often individuals who are impatient for action'.[23] Terrorist leaders in Northern Ireland have had to deal with the problem of dissuading disengagement during times of intense organizational difficulties. The long-time leaders of the Irish Republican movement, Gerry Adams and Martin McGuinness, were also intimately involved in the negotiations around the last substantial ceasefire in Northern Ireland in 1975. That ceasefire (or more accurately a series of small ceasefires) yielded little on the political front towards the Republican goal of a united Ireland, but did result in the emergence of serious organizational stressors and a weakening of community support (an issue upon which counter-terrorist policy at the time failed to capitalize). Gerry Adams seems to have recognized these stressors: 'When the struggle was limited to armed struggle, the prolongation of the truce meant that there was no struggle at all. There was nothing but confusion, frustration, and demoralization, arising directly from what I call "spectator politics"'.[24]

This comment clearly indicates the problems faced by Irish Republicanism in attempting to change the focus of the organization, but also recognizes the need to refocus 'the struggle' on a broad front in such circumstances, another challenge for the PIRA following the events surrounding the emergence of the Good Friday Agreement in 1998, and a problem which may have contributed to the flow of disaffected members to the radical splinter group, the Real IRA.

A lesson that stands out from this is the danger of allowing the organization to lose its direction and operational capacity when the focus on violence and attack against a clearly defined enemy is lost. In terms of organizational psychology, this makes good sense; any organization, terrorist or otherwise, can rapidly lose direction when the focus of its activities changes unless something is deliberately designed to sustain and control it. Regis Debray,[25] to whom we have referred earlier, noted that when terrorist organizations cease to have a political objective, they may continue to exist but drift towards other things that they do well, and in the case of terrorist organizations these tend to be robberies (as we saw in Chapter 5) and other criminal activities. The number of Republican punishment assaults rose dramatically during the ceasefire period, and this rise was sustained after the end of the ceasefire when the PIRA campaign was initially confined to the UK. Many of the assaults were savage in the extreme, resulting in serious wounding and physical damage to the people involved. Assaults were claimed to be directed against drug dealers or petty criminals, but some of those assaulted also seem to have had political connections as well. Punishment assaults, often of barbaric savagery, are used by all terrorist organizations in Northern Ireland to exercise control over recalcitrant members and to intimidate communities. It seems likely that the rise in such punishment assaults during the cease-fire (and afterwards) relate to control and maintenance factors as much as the preservation of good order in their respective communities. Punishment assaults are also a visible indication of the continuing presence of the terrorist groups as functioning organizations within their communities, and as such may well go some way to addressing the problems of lack of focus and activity.

A second way in which the PIRA attempted to sustain organizational solidarity during the ceasefire was by continuing its preparations and training for terrorist attacks. Evidence suggests that throughout this period, the PIRA and Loyalist organizations continued to acquire arms and prepare for attacks. Indeed, a great irony of the euphoria surrounding President Clinton's visit to Northern Ireland is that detailed preparations for the Canary Wharf bombing (which signalled the end of the ceasefire) were in fact in progress at the time. By retaining and developing the capacity for violence, the PIRA (and to a lesser extent the Loyalist paramilitaries) seems to have sustained the capacity for violence throughout the ceasefire period. However, it might be argued that sustaining the organization in this way necessarily jeopardized the ceasefire, and of course calls into question the claims of openness to a peace process. All of these dynamics might have important relevance for understanding the nature of prolonged ethno-nationalist terrorist campaigns more generally, and why, despite reductions in high-profile violence (e.g. bombings), ongoing low-intensity conflict plays a role in sustaining the unity of the movement.[26]

Implications of leaving

The focus of this chapter so far has been on identifying influences that might lead to disengagement. However, a further illustration of just how complex the issue is considers the implications of leaving. Terrorists who leave an organization (for whatever reason) might not necessarily have appreciated the extent to which certain aspects of their lives will be limited thereafter. The psychological pressures that follow the former terrorist wherever he or she goes sometimes become so intense as to convince him or her into surrendering. For instance, Kuldip Singh, a former member of the Khalistan Liberation Force, surrendered to the police in 2000 for crimes committed in 1991. Police reports stated that Singh's confession was spurred by his wish to start a new life following his trial. That same year, Hans Joachin Klein, a former colleague-in-arms of Carlos the Jackal, was tried before a court, 25 years after his role in the infamous Carlos-led attack on the Organization of Petroleum-Exporting Countries (OPEC) oil ministers' meeting in 1974 and a lifetime on the run from the authorities. And in the same year again, the founding member of the Japanese Red Army terror group, Fusako Shigenobu, was arrested in western Japan after more than 25 years underground. While protection from the enemy may not be enough to keep the members part of the group at the initial phase(s), there may be little to protect them from relentless law-enforcement and intelligence efforts to bring them to justice.

Security services often attempt to recruit ex-terrorists in an effort to persuade them to provide evidence against a terrorist movement. This may even become a factor in facilitating a way out of the group for an individual in the first place. Sean O'Callaghan regularly occupies a valuable educational role in raising awareness about the Provisional IRA. Eamon Collins, another PIRA informer, gave evidence (as did O'Callaghan) at the trial of an alleged PIRA leader. Government credibility is crucial if disengagement is to be promoted as a possible counter-terrorism strategy, but the tactics used by many governments have been less than tasteful in attempting to procure 'supergrasses' in Northern Ireland[27] or the more imaginative 'pentiti' in Italy.[28]

The Irish and British governments have attempted to facilitate organizational disengagement by Irish Republicans by reiterating their view that they do not see the PIRA's decommissioning as an act of 'surrender'. This in effect is a 'face-saving' strategy via which the PIRA leadership can attempt to de-escalate its campaign gradually (on all levels bar political). However, the reintegration of terrorists into society poses significant challenges. In Northern Ireland, despite the monumental progress made in the region, forgiveness does not come cheap, and while high-level terrorist violence may currently remain a thing of the past, the civil violence and naked sectarianism slowly destroying community-based peace efforts have not been encouraging signs of expected progress.

Even if the entire organization begins to dissipate, the route members may take can vary enormously. Some might drift towards other illegal activity (such as organized crime),[29] an option made easier if the individual was involved in similar activity whilst a member of the terrorist organization (e.g. in the context of fundraising). In such circumstances, the individual may still attempt to employ the nom de guerre of the movement in the face of threats from rival groupings. Others might drift into social isolation and the psychological problems this can create (depression, substance abuse, etc.), while others might find employment and a healthy life with new relationships.

Often the perceived availability of viable avenues might reflect such issues as: (a) the extent of the person's involvement in the group (e.g. very part-time, part-time or full-time), (b) the extent to which psychological support and identity comes solely from the terrorist group itself, and (c) whether or not the terrorist feels that his or her (perhaps lifetime) commitment to the group has actually been worth it. Following the decommissioning announce-ment, many Irish Republicans have continued their soul-searching, and some security analysts believe that it is possibly only because the other dissident groups in Ireland are perceived as either in complete disarray (i.e. the Real IRA) or too 'ideologically motivated' (i.e. the Continuity IRA) that there has not been a mass shifting of allegiance.

Understanding disengagement

At this stage, it is too ambitious to provide a comprehensive discussion of disengagement from terrorism from an individual perspective. If anything concrete has emerged from the preceding examples it is surely that our notion of 'leaving terrorism' is probably too simplistic and needs to be con-sidered in a more sophisticated way, with the same levels of complexity as the complex combination of factors that push and pull individuals into terrorism in the first place. This does not devalue the rational process model being developed, however, but we do need to recognize the disengagement phase as the least informed.

In the preceding discussion, we might well have considered disengagement from a variety of levels of analysis: in many cases, the 'ending' of terrorism is a process that for a terrorist organization begins and progresses over a signi-ficant period of time and is often started with the realization that terrorist violence on its own rarely, if ever, manages to achieve its aims. In the case of the Provisional IRA, the joint development of what senior Republican Danny Morrison once famously described as the 'ballet box and armalite strategy' – the pursuit of the movement's political aspirations but with an increasingly discriminate and tactical use of its 'armed struggle' – probably signalled the very beginning of the process that recently culminated in decommissioning.

It might be too obvious at this point to suggest that more research is needed, but given the lack of basic data (from which we might in the future move from the merely speculative more easily), at least the call for more research in this particular area should be forgiven. Most of the examples in this chapter derive from Northern Irish accounts, perhaps unsur-prisingly given that it is the most commonly studied terrorist movement (there is practically no data on these issues regarding movements like Al Qaeda). The preceding discussions have attempted to illustrate some of the issues relevant to thinking about disengagement, but there are many ques-tions to be answered and the following list of research issues might represent a modest beginning to such a process. Their common emphasis does not rest on identifying implications for law enforcement or policy concerns, but on illustrating psychological principles inherent in thinking about disengagement as an important research topic per se.

- Assessing and understanding the nature and extent of the roles played by individual terrorists within their organizations in terms of promoting either momentary or long-term de-escalation of tactical activity, strategic activity or indeed of an entire campaign.
- An exploration of the measures taken (if any) within terrorist organizations in the psychological preparation of organizational de-escalation (with an impending disintegration).
- An analysis of what terrorist documentation and training material has to say about individual disengagement.
- An exploration of what happens to members during temporary cessations of organizational terrorist activity (e.g. during ceasefires) and the steps taken (if any) to attempt to maintain organizational unity.
- An exploration of ex-member lives outside the terrorist structure – what are the psychological effects of increased isolation from the group? This might be considered at a variety of levels – personal, family, etc. – and explored as a function of varying pressures on the individual depending on the social, political or organizational climate.
- An exploration of the factors that lead to partial disengagement from role-specific behaviours: for example, voluntary movement away from involvement in actual operations (e.g. shootings, bombings) to voluntary involvement in other activities (e.g. political, organizational, financial etc.).
- An exploration of how and to what extent former terrorists express remorse, and what actions are taken (if any) to alleviate the associated stress.
- Comparative analyses of the experiences of involuntarily disengaged terrorists (e.g. imprisoned terrorists or those who have been moved into other roles, and those affected by organizational disintegration, etc.); similarly, comparative analyses between different forms of political extremism.
- An examination of the possibility that different roles and functions within terrorist organizations have varying attrition rates with respect to voluntary disengagement (e.g. fundraisers vs. gunmen vs. bombers vs. organizers vs. political actors, etc.): we might ask what are the psychological implications of performance within specific organizational functions and are some roles more likely than others to result in voluntary disengagement? This, incidentally, would serve a dual function in moving the nature and direction of other psychological research from

the profiling of 'terrorists' per se to the profiling of organizational roles and functions.

Conclusions

The most readily available data from which we might construct a model of disengagement comes from autobiographical sources (and old ones at that), and while more basic research using such sources ought to be encouraged (as is clear from the beginning of this book, it remains under-exploited, as does much primary source terrorist material, which is particularly disappointing in light of exciting new developments in both 'grounded theory' approaches and more traditional, if more valuable, content analysis), caution must be exercised in assessing the value of the data from such sources. Rather than attempting to seek some 'truth' in such sources, a more promising avenue would be to explore the nature of the accounts presented in such texts, perhaps in an effort to identify common processes. This would be one clear way of terrorist 'profiling' that would offer important benefits over vague attempts at constructing personality-based profiles for equally vague purposes.

Reliance on autobiographical sources will always suffer from a variety of problems, perhaps the most obvious being that there is little autobiographic material available. First-hand research, primarily via interview, is necessarily limited by a number of different practical issues, not least fears for personal safety. Although these issues were addressed in Chapter 2, it needs restating that such research is possible, and the experiences of a small number of researchers have demonstrated that terrorist organizations generally tend to co-operate and be facilitative of researchers' approaches (with the proviso that the researcher is assumed to play some potential role in achieving a greater audience, for instance), and in the context of disengagement we might be able to identify potential interviewee types as physically or psychologically disengaged, 'involuntarily disengaged' across either physical or psychological dimensions, as well as whether or not they are now to be viewed as 'repentant' or 'unrepentant' (this final dimension contains obvious implications for questioning styles and interrogative strategies on the part of the interviewer). Indeed, it is at this point that we ought to consider again James Dingley's sentiment about the future likelihood of research on the Northern Ireland conflict: ironically, it is in the dissolution of terrorist organizations that interviewing has become more possible than ever before, yet we continue to dismiss these opportunities as no longer pertinent to contemporary research.

To try to answer why people leave terrorism in straightforward terms obscures the impressive complexity of the question and the possible assumptions that underpin it. It is for this reason that the question 'Why do people leave terrorism?' is as conceptually and pragmatically difficult to answer as

'Why do people become terrorists?' Leaving terrorism may be the result of circumstances outside of one's control, or just like joining a terrorist group it may even resemble a decision made from an array of personal, social or occupational choices. If terrorism is a product of its own time and place, this thinking can also be extended to terrorist decision-making and to the processes influencing how terrorists see themselves.[30] Leaving terrorism from an individual perspective ought to be viewed with the same complexity as our now undeniably over-researched issues relating to the initial phase. If at some future point there are calls for a taxonomy of factors contributing to disengagement (some have been suggested here), researchers will need to accept the dynamic processes influencing individual behaviour regarding any stage, role or function of the terrorist group.

7

ANALYSIS, INTEGRATION, RESPONSE

Introduction

At the beginning of this book, it was pointed out that those wishing for a practical 'manual' to understand and/or 'deal with' the problem of terrorism would be disappointed. In addition, however, and something which might begin to be clear after the preceding six chapters is that those interested in seeing the potential of a 'psychology of terrorism' develop may be equally disappointed and perhaps surprised at our lack of progression. It might be easy to be flippant and to do disservice to the difficult efforts made to understand this complex area more generally, but we must face facts explicitly: although we can develop potential models of terrorist behaviour (as the last three chapters have demonstrated), and while we can begin to attempt to 'make terrorism known' in more accessible and straightfoward ways, the progress of psychological research is unsatisfactory. We are seriously lacking in the data needed not only to inform our theories, but to test even the most basic of hypotheses. As a result, and having (a) reviewed the psychological literature and (b) suggested new ways of understanding terrorism from psychological and criminological perspectives, it would be easy to rush to premature conclusions (and easier again to admit defeat and negatively suggest that we can do little or nothing in reality), and so we ought to proceed with particular caution at this juncture.

The history of both the use of terrorism and counter-terrorism offer us many valuable lessons. If we chose to ignore those lessons, we ought to be aware of the consequences of doing so. A valuable lesson, hinted at in earlier chapters, is that those who use terrorism as well as those affected by it are capable of holding a number of seemingly inconsistent and ambiguous views about both the nature of terrorism and the use of political violence more generally. From the opening sections of this book, we saw how the strategy of terrorism seems littered with paradoxes: in terms of publicly observed activities at least, terrorists aim to capture an audience's attention, and this is often through the propogation of atrocious and offensive actions.

In doing this, however, terrorist groups make it difficult for the state to even contemplate negotiation, let alone consider some sort of settlement.

Similar contradictions abound in analyses of counter-terrorism and at no time has this become more blatantly obvious than during the War on Terrorism. We may well be aware of how certain responses to terrorist movements actually increase support for the use of terrorism against the state, yet governments find it inhuman and absurd to resist engaging terrorists in ways other than those we asssume are deserved by cowards. Naturally it is easier, always, to attempt to prevent future instances of some action by immediately 'punishing' it than it is to try and find some other way of perhaps (a) redirecting the behaviour, or (b) attempting objectively to verify what underpins it (i.e. the expected consequences of engaging in that behaviour) at any point in the process. This idea might seem unusual because by implication then, and given the long history of terrorism and equally long debates about responses to it, we already know how, in several ways, we probably should *not* respond to terrorism (at whatever level of the problem we are tackling). The issue then suddenly becomes not so much 'how do we fight terrorists?', as opposed to 'why aren't we doing it in ways we all seem to agree on as being appropriate and grounded in evidence as being effective?'

Sooner or later, we must debate another controversial and uncomfortable assertion: terrorism may be complex, but we can no longer hide behind the façade that it is somehow incomprehensible or mysterious. That being said, however, and not meaning to contradict this point, another equally valid reality is that we are still nowhere near an agreed *understanding* of terrorism. That academic analysts guiltily presuppose a certain level of thinking at the political level about terrorism is part of this, but that we cannot agree on the nature of terrorism reflects confusion and a lack of prioritization of our goals. As above, it is ironic that our responses to terrorism at a political level are often such that we only engage in and sustain the problems we think we are trying to prevent or achieve some sort of limiting control over.

We can, however, identify three possible starting points that would seem to emerge from current debates about terrorism to help clarify answers to problems of this kind, and all are relevant to some of the issues that have driven psychological research in particular:

1   That the person who engages in terrorism is different or special in a psychological sense (this argument has always become heightened when we limit our perception of 'terrorism' to planting bombs or engaging in other acts of violence); and related to this,

2   The label 'terrorism' is misleading and utterly skews our perception and by default, our understanding of the problem. This has nothing to do with arguments about the perceived legitimacy of armed resistance by an insurgent political group or any related 'moral' argument, but it relates to the conceptual issue highlighted throughout this book: if we

broaden our thinking on the concept, then 'terrorism' encompasses much more activity and more people (a point forcefully clear from the terrorist incident cycle described in Chapter 5, whereby we only publicly see the end result of a complex chain of events).

3   And finally, the admission that 'we don't really know enough' – but still assume that a core 'causal' factor in terrorism lies in the connection between the broader conditions and individual perceptions of those conditions – an area that might be understood with reference to the qualities of ideological control.

An overreliance (although constantly changing in nature) on the first assertion has led to attempts to identify common features of the terrorist in terms of presumed inner or mental qualities of those who engage in the process. Such inner qualities, as we have seen from Chapter 3, were (and still are by many) assumed to play a significant role in predisposing a supposed 'type' towards terrorist violence as well as actually causing terrorism. In the twenty-first century, notions of personality and simplistic profiles should be exposed as the refuge of weak analysis, with bizarre uses of psychometric assessment as a way of supposedly making informed, testable judgements. We are simply wasting valuable opportunities by continuing what appears to be an obsession with such efforts.

On a footing that is assumed to be a little firmer, the notion of a 'terrorist profile' may be administratively attractive, even seductive, because we believe it enables us to simplify an enormously complicated process into misleading and simplistic answers. But, we must realize, it is unhelpful, carrying with it equally misleading (if implicit) assumptions about what might be needed to tackle the problem (interestingly we have seen similar mistaken assumptions come to light in late 2004 about the presumed role that terrorist finances had on limiting terrorist activity and the realization that addressing the problem in a financial sense is practically worthless from the point of view of 'preventing' terrorism). It is clear from any appreciation of the heterogeneity of both the concept of terrorism and those who partake in it (at whatever level), let alone any careful examination of the research, that many of the personal traits or characteristics we attempt to identify as belonging to the terrorist are neither specific to the terrorist nor serve to distinguish one 'type' of terrorist from another (even within the same group, let alone between different groups). Nor are the routes into and through (and indeed, away from) terrorism distinct in a psychological sense from other kinds of social movements nor are such features (as described in Chapters 4, 5 and 6) necessarily homogeneous in nature or extent *between* terrorist movements: we still neglect the fact that terrorist incidents represent a limited (albeit public and dramatic) element of much broader activity in some of the larger extremist movements. It is still the case in the psychological literature of today that many of the psychological attributes presumed unique to terrorist profiles are implicitly suggested and interpreted accordingly as social or psycho-logical deficiencies. We have already engaged in this discussion in detail in Chapter 3, but let us conclude that while such accounts will always present to policy-makers as neat, plausible ways of reducing what is in reality a complex interactive set of idiosyncratic circumstances and events that shape individual attitudes (and subsequently, behaviours), in doing so our understanding is confused (although we may not appreciate this at the time) and severely limited. There are, simply, no easily identifiable a priori qualities of the terrorist that enable us to predict the likelihood of risk of involvement and engagement in any particular person or social group that is either valid or reliable over a meaningful period of time.

A major part of the problem here has been a dogmatic preoccupation with the term 'terrorism'. On the one hand we have seen how the label 'terrorism' skews the nature and scope of analyses of both those who engage in terrorism as well as a fuller understanding of the broader processes that give rise to and emerge from political violence. Where psychological analyses have com-pletely failed to assert their relevance, however, is in clearly identifying the behaviours associated with all stages of the terrorism process – i.e. in terms of the behaviours related to becoming involved, 'being' or remaining involved and engaging in terrorist events, and disengaging. Whatever label we put on those who participate in this type of behaviour, the behaviours themselves, and the ways in which they develop, do not change. They remain consistent. The process of becoming a terrorist involves a cumulative, incrementally sustained process of behaviours that culminate in increased, sustained and focused commitment to the group. The important point again, though, is that regardless of any short-term policy changes, or as we have seen post 9/11, regardless of political attempts to fundamentally alter our thinking about who or what is a terrorist, the central behaviours do not change. What has changed are perceptions from policy-makers about where the focus and scope of preventative or control efforts ought to be directed. The additional fact then that counter-terrorism is rarely evidence- or outcome-based ensures that the range of terrorism-related behaviours that receive attention is in constant flux, with little or no sense of what factors drive that change (naturally, we assume that what drives it is something about the terrorist group itself, often phrased in terms of how terrorism seems to have 'changed').

Furthermore, and outside of the legal context, the real issue we must eventually address is not, perhaps surprisingly, 'what is terrorism?', but how do disaffected groups (or 'lazy' groups, or groups lacking broad appeal, or any highly motivated single-issue organization) change and influence the political process. The critical factor then becomes the instrumental quality of violence for that organization at that time, and in that particular place, and its use falls neatly into the optimizing frameworks identified collectively through Chapters 4, 5, and 6. Violence, even extreme violence, is available to anyone and everyone in the world to use; as has so often been asserted, it is clearly one of the great democratizers of our world. The use of violence is then just one aspect of the 'toolbox', and its adequacy or otherwise for any particular extremist organization is the critical issue. The Provisional IRA recognized this in the early 1980s when its dual role with Sinn Fein (as the 'public' face) developed. The next step then is to try to understand what 'instrumental' actually means for different terrorist organizations – intent, of course, becomes a quality of this, but all sorts of other issues also become relevant. One of the challenges of terrorism to the state is that it effectively undermines and breaks its monopoly control over instrumental violence (we remember President Bush's comments about anyone who 'supports' terrorism being equated to a 'terrorist' as an attempt to deligitimize any challenge to the state).

All of these points, in a very clear way, reflect a pressing problem that is endemic to issues of counter-terrorism. All too often, a prioritization of effort in terms of practical counter-terrorism measures bears little real relevance to the reality of terrorism and where it comes from, how it develops and so forth. The point ought not to be interpreted as an overly cynical criticism of law enforcement policies or the intelligence services (which are not being discussed in detail here), but it is true that we rarely appreciate how both law enforcement and intelligence agencies can strategically respond to the broad 'terrorist threat' in ways that enable them to develop what they perceive to be their own agenda. Within the criminal context, problems about assembling evidence are not unique to terrorism, of course, but the political sensitivities that emerge following terrorist incidents (9/11 being the obvious case in point) allows for the emergence of arguments about changing rules, language and the very meaning of terrorism that would, at another level, never be made about the problems of combating car theft, for instance. We easily reach a difficult conundrum – the political process is almost completely ineffective in so many ways in dealing with terrorism, so it looks to locate the solution to the problem elsewhere, for example, in the intelligence services or in law enforcement. A vicious circle then emerges where the police accept a sense of ownership of the problem as a means of reaching increased resources and importance, but eventually find that they too cannot 'solve' the problem of terrorism. Because law enforcement does not admit to not being able to solve terrorism, the search for the solution is then pushed back onto the structural and systems-level weaknesses we have – in other words, the problem eventually becomes a political one, and often we see how frustration can sometime lead the government to admit that the War on Terrorism, for example, is essentially unwinnable. Once again, the choice of words, reflecting the way in which the problem is thought about, is self-defeating. If we are to effectively break this vicious circle, we must be prepared to challenge traditional and essentially comfortable views that the 'security' solution to terrorism is the most appropriate one.

We must prioritize our efforts then – what is it that we want to do? If the overall goal in discussions of counter-terrorism is one of prevention, then the starting point is an acceptance that, deriving from the foregoing analytic principles described in Chapters 4, 5, and 6 for instance, prevention can only be understood in terms of what position and time in the terrorism process we are facing. For the same reason that the headcounting of captured or killed terrorists tells us relatively little about the progress of a broad counter-terrorist campaign (which represents a good example of how developments in Iraq in 2004 go completely misunderstood in the wider world), shooting terrorist suspects (or terrorists), infringing human rights, or corrupting the democratic process (and language itself) will never work because it only feeds political violence by sustaining the legitimization of the 'imperative' for terrorism by the extremist group.

Terrorism as process

An effort to view terrorism as a process, as this book has done, might on the one hand clearly help us develop our understanding of psychological approaches to terrorism (if only for us to assess which kind of psychological approaches to terrorism are more beneficial and conceptually helpful) and perhaps efforts more generally. Some approaches have been developed here, and it is perhaps useful to attempt to identify the emergent implications from such an approach.

To try and summarize the collective analysis (and chapter-specific conclusions) of Chapters 4, 5 and 6, we might run the risk of oversimplifying the 'message': for example, one conclusion might be expressed in the assertion that in terms of trying to understand the development, maintenance, and decline of involvement and engagement in terrorism, terrorism ought to be primarily considered as a group and organizational process. This assertion on its own, however, can be misleading and we run the risk of again oversimplifying the debate (by, for example, attempting to isolate and treat as distinct, psychological factors from strategic and/or ideological factors). Perhaps we might more usefully think about this conclusion couched in terms that reflect the process that has been described. For example, from the analysis developed through Chapters 4, 5 and 6:

- We have a *clear* and *unambiguous* way of identifying focus points of dangerousness and risk assessment for both initial involvement in terrorism (Chapter 4), continued involvement in terrorism (i.e. focused, sustained, terrorism-relevant activity) and engagement in terrorist incidents (Chapter 5), and in disengaging from terrorism (Chapter 6).
- We can appreciate and understand the signficance of changed attitudes, thoughts and behaviours as factors in the escalation of involvement and engagement with terrorism, as ground in social, group and organizational

influences that reinforce focused, sustained, terrorism-relevent activity, and discourage (and shape against) broader, non-terrorism-relevant social activity.

- We can also now clearly establish the nature of the relationship between terrorism-relevant activity and other forms of both illegal and legal social and political activity.

A process-based approach to terrorism is valuable for many other reasons, although the fuller social and political implications of such an approach we have not yet opened up to considering more fully, perhaps because although seemingly straightforward and maybe even obvious in parts (with hindsight anyway), this direct analysis is elusive in many circles. By adopting such an approach for analysis, we immediately see in psychological terms how disparities in profiles, individual backgrounds and routes into terrorism can become focused against and resistant to the consequences of counter-terrorism operations (which, from the terrorists' perspective, serves a vital psychological function in terms of sustaining internal solidarity and cohesion against a backdrop of constant danger, threat and stress from external sources). It is extremely important to realize that a process model of terrorist behaviour need not invalidate such disparities in backgrounds, etc., but that its true value allows us to see how different people, with different back-grounds and characteristics, engage with the process in different ways, and consequently move through the process in different ways. This represents a critical issue for further exploration.

In slightly more practical terms, however, it can help us draw distinctions between phases of the process and to develop policy focuses, as argued above. The significance of this analytical framework should not be under-estimated in terms of its potential to contribute to policy. One all too obvious example derives from some issues related to the the terrorist 'incident cycle' which we explored earlier. In Chapter 5, we identified a pathway and logic to terrorist events that, upon closer inspection, revealed some circular (but no less helpful) qualities. For instance, although we can identify features to terrorist incidents that run parallel to how other forms of criminal activity (e.g. burglary) may occur and develop, the post-event analysis in some obvious ways does not necessarily belong at the 'end' of an event: it is not only a part of 'getting away with' an incident, but also relates centrally to the decision to commit the activity in the first place. We can see how it is a factor in the decisional process which has to occur before the offence (and any subsequent incident) is committed. We can see this very clearly in the case of suicidal terrorist attacks where post-event analysis in terms of escape does not emerge.

A further point may appear obvious here and it is one that needs to feed directly into policy appraisals of the potential contribution of psychological research: issues to do with 'psychological qualities' of individual terrorists might be relevant in terms of personnel selection and broader organizational issues, but clearly on the other hand have little or no role to play in the type of analysis of incidents suggested by incident-cycle frameworks. This is an important conceptual point we ought to consider more closely (ironically it may be such that this is a useful practical way of highlighting the limitations of personality-focused explanations of terorrism, which when considered in light of the analysis of terrorist incidents, loses all meaning and purpose).

One feature lacking in the cycle framework, but perhaps now clearer in the broader analysis is the distinction between the 'incident' and 'inclination' (or 'predisposition') associated with the terrorist. Whatever reasons have led an individual person to acquire, create or see the emergence of criminal or terrorist inclinations (influenced by, we can assume, various social, psychological, religious, physiological, individual, group and organizational influences), a focus on criminal and terrorist targets assumes that the necessary preconditions to lead an individual to prepare and engage with these events has actually occurred. It is concerned, therefore, with the process whereby the actual terrorist event is expressed and fulfilled (or not), rather than with the origins of the activity, and the process whereby an individual person becomes involved in terrorist activity. Distinguishing between an 'inclination' and an 'incident' marks an important conceptual advance, enabling us to consider how we might develop a much more focused approach to policy and practice through changing events and situations, rather than people (which presumably is the implicit, if not obviously unreachable, goal of personality-driven accounts).

A further assumption ought to be included: analysis of terrorist incidents, because each and every incident (as we saw in Chapter 5) is particular and grounded in its own special situational context, should be 'crime-specific'. Clearly, the category of 'terrorism' is too broad to be meaningful – this should be clear from the analysis thus far. It may well be that some active members of terrorist movements are opportunistic in their choice of targets, and may engage in a range of illegal incidents, rather than engage solely in a single, focused activity. However, the process whereby a particular terrorist incident emerges is necessarily incident-specific, in that it relates to the context and circumstances of a particular situation. This has important implications in the development of operational planning – in simple terms, one size (or counter-terrorism strategy or plan) does not fit all. An important related issue that might follow from this might relate to the question of whether or not there are groupings of terrorist events that go together, or, we might ask, whether or not they are all idiosyncratic and completely unique? One obvious implication of this is that it is important that we develop case studies of terrorist incidents and attempt to identify the features of such incidents in light of a cycle-type framework.

Although there are signs that we are beginning to critically examine our perspectives on terrorism more than ever before, problems of perspective remain a reflection of the complex bases of the wide array of terrorism-related activity. Another obvious and signficant ongoing challenge is one of integration of analysis – for example, how the broader social problems (assumed to be, and unhelpfully described as, 'root causes of terrorism') relate to smaller, individual issues. On the one hand, we have an array of socio-political issues that would seem in some way to be relevant to the creation of a readiness for conflict within and between societies and groups. On the other hand, we have smaller individual qualities that drive action, but the relevance of which we frequently misinterpret, often through needless interdisciplinary tension and misrepresentation of different perspectives (both from within and outside academia): as anyone with even a passing interest in the psychology of terrorist behaviour might suppose – individual qualities within the process of terrorism are important. A driving force in much of the psychological research to date has been predictable: given the extent of the conditions assumed to generate conflict, why is it still that so few people engage in terrorism? Interestingly, we rarely ask the opposing empirical question – why is that so many do *not* engage in terrorism? Posing the questions in different ways generates different issues and challenges for the kind of analysis we undertake. And needless to say, perhaps, but the answer to questions such as that will continue to vary enormously depending on what level and range of activity we are willing to classify as 'terrorism'. In some ways, the thinking here is not new (criminologists will agree), but it is new in terms of how we think about terrorism. Not all individuals will follow the cumulative process inherent in becoming a terrorist: indeed, we often spend much time attempting to decide whether or not 'unusual' cases (e.g. people who appear to become terrorists within a very short period of time, and appear to reach the 'engagement' phase with little exposure to the behaviours and related changes associated with becoming involved) nullify or invalidate particular theories. Again, this is an unhelpful exercise and reveals limited thinking.

What do we do? What we want to do

The picture we might frame from this discussion is a depressing one. How can we then move forward? Part of the solution is not difficult to identify. In my opinion, the solutions both to the management of the problem of terrorism and its understanding (if these can be temporarily separated for a moment) is based on a need for us to prioritize our objectives. What is it that we want to do? If the elimination of terrorists is a primary objective for a government, then the implications become obvious, as we are seeing in many territories around the world today. If 'understanding' terrorism is our objective, then we need to be clear on where terrorism comes from, how it emerges, develops and ends. To achieve this objective, and perhaps to then attempt to discover how such understanding might better inform policy, we must be open to accepting the realities of our own actions in attempting to suppress terrorism. Often, as argued at the beginning of this chapter, the actions encouraged by counter-terrorism policies merely encourage further terrorism – subsequent activities by the terrorists then reinforce a self-fulfilling prophecy for the counter-terrorism personnel that the problem can only be dealt with in one way. Hence the basis for a cycle of violence emerges.

A crucial imperative here involves recognizing the social, political and psychological conditions in which we are more likely to condone actions against terrorists that in the long run do more harm than good. In the immediate climate post-11 September, to convey this statement would probably have led to (and probably still does in certain quarters) a view about the analyst that 'understanding terrorism' equates to somehow 'forgiving' the terrorist and sympathizing with his plight. Of course it should never imply such identification with the aggressor, but it reflects a reality of political violence – terrorists frequently claim victimization as a justification for further violence (often conducted on behalf of a 'represented' community). Terrorism remains a social problem and a social process, and therefore we must realize that while the communities the terrorist claim to 'represent' often disavow that representation in times of terrorist atrocity, a broader level of sympathy may exist towards the goals of the terrorist. We must not reinforce this broad sympathy by actions that are rooted in responses we subsequently come to regret. This important dynamic is something we must acknowledge and understand, because it contains the key to undermining and ultimately disrupting terrorist activity.

It is unfortunate that even within the discipline of psychology, we continue to speak about terrorism in polarized ways. The problem continues to be viewed as either mysteriously complex or devastatingly clear. Often, what influences which view is taken is access to information, or a particular view of the world which is rooted in our backgrounds, education or training. A single word or phrase in a presentation or document can betray an allegiance, political viewpoint or academic perspective, and given the overwhelming volume of material being churned out of a veritable terrorism 'industry', it is easy for us to castigate contributions accordingly or assume irrelevance due to ignorance. Again, at the heart of this issue is a problem of assessing value. One way forward to help us ascertain the quality of academic research and to develop the agendas needed for short to medium-term future intelligence analyses is for both academia and policy-makers to demonstrate their practical applicability and *mutual* relevance. There is a dual onus of responsibility on academics to show how their analyses are relevant in the real world, and for, in particular, intelligence analysts to recognize the value in the information they collect, classify and file on a routine basis. Indeed, as above, recognizing the value of reliable, validated information is probably at the heart of useful collaboration. Often what restricts the sharing of information are issues of mutual mistrust and suspicion and sometimes poor past experiences, and naturally, of course, issues of national security. Most of the time, however, it relates to more basic issues of power and control, but again, the mutually beneficial subject is one of value – how can both communities benefit from some sort of increased involvement with one another? Academia will probably have to produce the vanguard here by demonstrating the relevance of theories and analyses of terrorism, whilst those tasked with responding to the problem of terrorism must consistently voice their needs and concerns accordingly and appropriately. In short, neither side can truly benefit the other, nor in turn the wider community, unless they know what each other wants, needs and is willing to be clear about what each can, in practice, deliver.

Conclusions

The 11 September attacks and the War on Terrorism illustrate how the drama and emotion surrounding terrorism can hinder the emergence of a systematic, coherent strategy both to prevent future attacks and address root causes and triggering factors of terrorism. Paul Wilkinson has often said that terrorism is too important a problem to leave to politicians, and his words were never more relevant than they are today. It is time for academic researchers to start taking some ownership of the problem of terrorism in ways perhaps never dared before, and moreover it is time for us to begin to critically assess what contributions our analyses can offer. This book has hopefully made a case for sound, sustained investment in objective, independent, empirical data-driven research on terrorist behaviour. Unless psychological research on terrorism begins to develop systematically, we are, it is obvious now, unlikely to achieve either the evidence nor perspectives necessary to inform policy properly and reliably. The research and other problems described at length in some of the chapters of this book are certainly not insurmountable, that must be made clear one final time, neither has the rather short-sighted vision by psychological research to date been a waste of time. That is, it is not a waste of time and effort if we can learn from what mistakes we have made, and we also take the time to consider the implications of the enormous gaps in our knowledge. We are, quite simply, pre-paradigmatic.

   If academic research is constantly several battles behind the terrorism war, psychological research is even further behind, and chance predictions of particular terrorist scenarios do not bestow psychic qualities upon academic researchers: the harsh reality is that we are, we will eventually admit, failing to appreciate the value of what conceptual tools we already have at our disposal. We ought, then, to perhaps take closer stock of where we are, and where it is we eventually want to reach.

NOTES

PREFACE

1 X. Raufer, 'Al Qaeda: A Different Diagnosis', *Studies in Conflict and Terrorism*, 26, 6 (2003), pp. 391–398.

1 WHAT IS TERRORISM?

1 L. Richardson, 'Terrorists as Transnational Actors', in M. Taylor and J. Horgan (eds), *The Future of Terrorism* (London: Frank Cass, 2000), pp. 209–219.
2 N. Friedland and A. Merari, 'The Psychological Impact of Terrorism: A Double-Edged Sword', *Political Psychology*, 6, 4 (1985), pp. 591–604.
3 B.M. Jenkins, 'The Future Course of International Terrorism', in P. Wilkinson and A.M. Stewart (eds), *Contemporary Research on Terrorism* (Aberdeen: Aberdeen University Press, 1987), p. 583.
4 M. Dillon, *The Enemy Within: The IRA's War Against the British* (London: Doubleday, 1994), p. 165.
5 A.P. Schmid, 'Defining Terrorism: The Response Problem as a Definition Problem', in A.P. Schmid and R.D. Crelinsten (eds), *Western Responses to Terrorism* (London: Frank Cass, 1993), p.11.
6 Friedland and Merari, 'The Psychological Impact of Terrorism: A Double-Edged Sword', p. 592.
7 R. Thackrah, 'Terrorism: A Definitional Problem', in P. Wilkinson and A.M. Stewart (eds), *Contemporary Research on Terrorism* (Aberdeen: Aberdeen University Press, 1987), p. 24.
8 Schmid, 'Defining Terrorism: The Response Problem as a Definition Problem'; also see A.P. Schmid and A.J. Jongman (eds), *Political Terrorism (Second Edition)* (Amsterdam: North Holland Publishing Company, 1988).
9 Thackrah, 'Terrorism: A Definitional Problem', p. 27.
10 C. McCauley, 'Terrorism, Research and Public Policy: An Overview', *Terrorism and Political Violence*, 3, 1 (1991), p. 127.
11 N. Friedland, 'Becoming a Terrorist: Social and Individual Antecedents', in L. Howard (ed.), *Terrorism: Roots, Impacts, Responses* (New York: Praeger, 1992), p. 81.
12 B. Hoffman and D. Claridge, 'The Rand-St. Andrews Chronology of International Terrorism and Noteworthy Domestic Incidents 1996', *Terrorism and Political Violence*, 10, 2 (1998), pp. 135–180.
13 Ibid., p. 139; also see Thackrah, 'Terrorism: A Definitional Problem', pp. 26–27.

14 M. Taylor and E. Quayle, *Terrorist Lives* (London: Brassey's, 1994).

15 Ibid.

16 W. Lacqueur, 'Reflections on Terrorism', *Foreign Affairs*, 65, 1 (1986), pp. 86–100.

17 K. Heskin, 'Political Violence in Northern Ireland', *Journal of Psychology*, 119, 5 (1985), pp. 481–494.

18 B. Hoffman, *Inside Terrorism* (London: Victor Gollancz, 1998), p. 31.

19 Schmid and Jongman, *Political Terrorism (Second Edition)*, p. 17.

20 Heskin, 'Political Violence in Northern Ireland', p. 481.

21 Taylor and Quayle, *Terrorist Lives*, p. 10.

22 D. Veness, 'Single Issue Terrorism', paper presented at *51st International Criminological Conference*, Warsaw, 3 September 1995.

23 See R. Monaghan, 'Animal Rights and Violent Protest', *Terrorism and Political Violence*, 9, 4 (1997), pp. 106–116; also see R. Monaghan, 'Single Issue Terrorism: A New Phenomenon?', paper presented at *European Association of Psychology and Law/American Psychology and Law Joint Annual Conference*, Dublin, 6–9 July 1999.

24 A.P. Schmid and J. de Graaf, *Violence as Communication: Insurgent Terrorism and the Western News Media* (London: Sage, 1982), p. 176.

25 Thackrah, 'Terrorism: A Definitional Problem', p. 25.

26 Hoffman, *Inside Terrorism*, p. 34.

27 R. Linn, 'Terrorism, Morality and Soldiers' Motivation to Fight – An Example from the Israeli Experience in Lebanon', *Terrorism*, 11, 2 (1988), pp. 139–149.

28 'What is Terrorism?', *The Economist*, 2 March, 1996. Retrieved from the World Wide Web: economist.iconnect.net/issue/02–03–96/sf1.html

29 Thackrah, 'Terrorism: A Definitional Problem', p. 25.

30 J.K. Anderson, 'Terrorism'. Retrieved from the World Wide Web: www.gocin.com/probe/terror.htm.

31 T. Harnden, *Bandit Country* (London: Hodder and Stoughton, 1999); also see F. Keane, 'IRA Sniper Kills Nine in One Area', *Sunday Tribune* (16 January 1994), p. A8.

32 Keane, 'IRA Sniper Kills Nine in One Area', p. A8.

33 M. Taylor and J. Horgan, 'Future Developments of Terrorism in Europe', in M. Taylor and J. Horgan (eds), *The Future of Terrorism* (London: Frank Cass, 2000), pp. 83–93.

34 Hoffman, *Inside Terrorism*, p. 131.

35 H.H.A. Cooper, 'The Terrorist and the Victim', *Victimology*, 1, 2 (1976), pp. 229–239; also see Hoffman, *Inside Terrorism*.

36 Reuters World Service, 'Algerian Press Describes Bus Slaughter' (Reuters Group plc., 12 December 1996).

37 Ibid.

38 See J. Swain, 'Ramadan Killers Leave 250 Dead in City of Blood', *Sunday Times* (26 January 1997) p. 17; also see X. Raufer, 'Terreur en Algerie: Le GIA comme OVNI: Organization Violente Non Indentifiee', *Notes d'Information de Laboratoire MINOS* (Paris: Centre des Hautes Etudes de L'Armament, 1996).

39 Schmid, 'Defining Terrorism: The Response Problem as a Definition Problem'.

40 Ibid., p. 7.

41 M. Dartnell, 'A Legal Inter-Network for Terrorism: Issues of Globalization, Fragmentation and Legitimacy', in M. Taylor and J. Horgan (eds), *The Future of Terrorism* (London: Frank Cass, 2000), pp. 197–208.

42 Schmid, 'Defining Terrorism: The Response Problem as a Definition Problem', p. 13.

43 Thackrah, 'Terrorism: A Definitional Problem'.

44 United States Department of State, *Patterns of Global Terrorism: 1996* (Washington, DC: Government Printing Office, 1997).

45 A.P. Schmid, 'Terrorism and the Use of Weapons of Mass Destruction: From Where the Risk?', in M. Taylor and J. Horgan (eds), *The Future of Terrorism* (London: Frank Cass, 2000), pp. 106–132.

46 Taylor and Horgan, 'Future Developments of Terrorism in Europe'.

47 Ibid., p. 88.

2 UNDERSTANDING TERRORISM

1 For example, see A.P. Schmid and A.J. Jongman, *Political Terrorism (Second Edition)* (Amsterdam: North Holland Publishing Company, 1988); also see A.P. Silke (ed.), *Research on Terrorism: Trends, Achievements and Failures* (London: Frank Cass, 2004).

2 Schmid and Jongman, *Political Terrorism (Second Edition)*, p. 189; also see A. Merari, 'Academic Research and Government Policy on Terrorism', *Terrorism and Political Violence*, 3, 1 (1991), pp. 88–102.

3 D.C. Rapoport, 'Introduction', in D.C. Rapoport (ed.), *Inside Terrorist Organisations* (London: Frank Cass, 1988), pp. 1–10.

4 E. Cairns and R. Wilson, 'Stress, Coping, and Political Violence in Northern Ireland', in J.P. Wilson and B. Raphael (eds), *International Handbook of Traumatic Stress Syndromes* (New York: Plenum Press, 1992), pp. 365–376.

5 R. Thackrah, 'Terrorism: A Definitional Problem', in P. Wilkinson and A.M. Stewart (eds), *Contemporary Research on Terrorism* (Aberdeen: Aberdeen University Press, 1987), p. 31.

6 A.H. Miller, 'Book Review', *Terrorism and Political Violence*, 1, 3 (1989), pp. 391–396.

7 Ibid.

8 See especially the commentaries in Silke, *Research on Terrorism: Trends, Achievements and Failures*.

9 Wilkinson and Stewart, *Contemporary Research on Terrorism*, p. xvii.

10 A. Gordon, 'Terrorism Dissertations and the Evolution of a Speciality: An Analysis of Meta-Information', *Terrorism and Political Violence*, 11, 2 (1999), pp. 141–150; also see A. Gordon, 'Terrorism and Computerised Databases: An Examination of Multidisciplinary Coverage', *Terrorism and Political Violence*, 7, 4 (1995), pp. 171–177; A. Gordon, 'Research Note: The Spread of Terrorism Publications – A Database Analysis', *Terrorism and Political Violence*, 10, 4 (1998), pp. 192–196; E.F. Reid, *An Analysis of Terrorism Literature: A Bibliographic and Content Analysis Study*, Unpublished Doctoral Dissertation (University of South Carolina, 1983).

11 R.D. Crelinsten, 'Terrorism as Political Communication: The Relationship Between the Controller and the Controlled', in Wilkinson and Stewart, *Contemporary Research on Terrorism*, pp. 3–23.

12 For example, see M. Taylor, *The Terrorist* (London: Brassey's, 1988), and M. Taylor, *The Fanatics* (London: Brassey's, 1991); also see M. Taylor and E. Quayle, *Terrorist Lives* (London: Brassey's, 1994).

13 In particular see the excellent debates in B. Hoffman, 'Why Terrorists Don't Claim Credit', *Terrorism and Political Violence*, 9, 1 (1997), pp. 1–6; D. Pluchinsky, 'The Terrorism Puzzle: Missing Pieces and No Boxcover', *Terrorism and Political Violence*, 9, 1 (1997), pp. 7–10; D.C. Rapoport, 'To Claim or Not to Claim: That is the Question – Always!', *Terrorism and Political Violence*, 9, 1 (1997), pp. 11–17.

NOTES

14 J. Horgan and M. Taylor, 'The Provisional Irish Republican Army: Command and Functional Structure', *Terrorism and Political Violence*, 9, 3 (1997), pp. 1–32.

15 R.W. White, 'Issues in the Study of Political Violence: Understanding the Motives of Participants in Small Group Political Violence', paper presented at the *Future Developments in Terrorism* Conference, University College, Cork, 3–5 March 1999.

16 Ibid., pp. 10–11.

17 J.M. Post, 'Group and Organizational Dynamics of Political Terrorism: Implications for Counterterrorist Policy', in Wilkinson and Stewart, *Contemporary Research on Terrorism*, pp. 307–317.

18 R. Kearney, 'Myth and Terror', *The Crane Bag*, 2, 1–2 (1978), pp. 273–285.

19 A. Merari, 'A Classification of Terrorist Groups', *Terrorism*, 1, 3–4 (1978), pp. 331–346.

20 United States Department of State, *Patterns of Global Terrorism: 1996* (Washington, D.C.: Government Printing Office, 1997), p. 1; also see M. Dartnell, 'A Legal Inter-Network for Terrorism: Globalisation, Fragmentation and Legitimacy', in M. Taylor and J. Horgan (eds), *The Future of Terrorism* (London: Frank Cass, 2000), pp. 197–208.

21 H.H.A. Cooper, 'Voices from Troy: What Are We Hearing?', in *Outthinking the Terrorist – An International Challenge: Proceedings of the 10th Annual Symposium on the Role of Behavioral Science in Physical Security* (Washington, D.C.: Defence Nuclear Agency, 1985), p. 95.

22 X. Raufer, 'Al Qaeda: A Different Diagnosis', *Studies in Conflict and Terrorism*, 26, 6 (2003), pp. 391–398.

23 W. Reich (ed.), *Origins of Terrorism: Psychologies, Ideologies, Theologies, States of Mind* (New York: Cambridge University Press, 1990).

24 G. Wardlaw, *Political Terrorism: Theory, Tactics and Counter-Measures (Second Edition)* (Cambridge: Cambridge University Press, 1989), p. 171.

25 Post, 'Group and Organisational Dynamics of Political Terrorism', p. 307.

26 See B. Cordes, 'Euroterrorists Talk About Themselves: A Look at the Literature', in Wilkinson and Stewart, *Contemporary Research on Terrorism*, pp. 318–336; also see M. Crenshaw, 'The Psychology of Political Terrorism', in M.G. Hermann (ed.), *Political Psychology: Contemporary Problems and Issues* (London: Jossey-Bass, 1986), pp. 379–413.

27 M. Baumann, *Terror or Love?: Bommi Baumann's Own Story of His Life as a West German Urban Guerrilla* (New York: Grove Press, 1979).

28 S. MacStiofáin, *Memoirs of a Revolutionary* (London: Gordon Cremonisi, 1975).

29 M. Maguire, *To Take Arms: A Year in the Provisional IRA* (London: Quartet, 1974).

30 L. Khaled, *My People Shall Live: The Autobiography of a Revolutionary* (London: Hodder and Stoughton, 1973).

31 M. McGartland, *Fifty Dead Men Walking* (London: Blake, 1997).

32 E. Collins (with M. McGovern), *Killing Rage* (London: Granta, 1997).

33 R. Gilmour, *Dead Ground: Infiltrating the IRA* (London: Little, Brown and Company, 1998).

34 S. O'Callaghan, *The Informer* (London: Bantam, 1998).

35 J. Mallin, 'Terrorism as a Military Weapon', in J.D. Elliott and L.K. Gibson (eds), *Contemporary Terrorism: Selected Readings* (Maryland: International Association of Chiefs of Police, 1978), pp. 117–128.

36 D. Pluchinsky, 'Terrorist Documentation', *Terrorism*, 14 (1991), pp. 195–207, 241–252.

37 Rapoport, *Inside Terrorist Organisations*, p. 1.

38 M. Crenshaw, 'Questions To Be Answered, Research To Be Done, Knowledge To be Applied', in Reich, *Origins of Terrorism: Psychologies, Ideologies, Theologies, States of Mind*, pp. 247–260.

39 G. Adams, *Before the Dawn: An Autobiography* (London: Heinemann/Brandon, 1996), p. 2.

40 F. O'Toole, 'The Premature Life of Gerry Adams', *Irish Times – Weekend Section* (28 September 1996), p. 9.

41 S. O'Callaghan, 'Shots in the Propaganda War', *Sunday Times – Book Supplement* (22 September 1996), p. 3.

42 T. Strentz, 'A Terrorist Psychosocial Profile: Past and Present', *FBI Law Enforcement Bulletin*, April (1987), pp. 13–19.

43 M. Crenshaw, 'Current Research on Terrorism: The Academic Perspective', *Studies in Conflict and Terrorism*, 15, 1 (1992), pp. 1–11.

44 White, 'Issues in the Study of Political Violence', p. 7; also see Crenshaw, 'Questions To Be Answered, Research To Be Done, Knowledge To Be Applied', p. 248.

45 See Crenshaw, 'Questions To Be Answered, Research To Be Done, Knowledge To Be Applied', p. 248; J. Horgan, 'Issues in Terrorism Research', *The Police Journal*, 50, 3 (1997), pp. 193–202; also see J. Horgan, 'The Case for Firsthand Research', in Silke, *Research on Terrorism: Trends, Achievements and Failures*, pp. 30–56.

46 White, 'Issues in the Study of Political Violence'.

47 A. Jamieson, *The Heart Attacked: Terrorism and Conflict in the Italian State* (London: Marian Boyars, 1989); and A. Jamieson, 'Entry, Discipline and Exit in the Italian Red Brigades', *Terrorism and Political Violence*, 2, 1 (1990), pp. 1–20; A. Jamieson, 'Identity and Morality in the Red Brigades', *Terrorism and Political Violence*, 2, 4 (1990), pp. 508–520.

48 Taylor, *The Terrorist*; Taylor, *The Fanatics*; Taylor and Quayle, *Terrorist Lives*.

49 White, 'Issues in the Study of Political Violence', p. 8.

50 A.P. Schmid, 'Defining Terrorism: The Response Problem as a Definition Problem', in A.P. Schmid and R.D. Crelinsten (eds), *Western Responses to Terrorism* (London: Frank Cass, 1993), pp. 7–13.

51 K. Kellen, 'Ideology and Rebellion: Terrorism in West Germany', in Reich, *Origins of Terrorism: Psychologies, Ideologies, Theologies, States of Mind*, pp. 43–58.

52 W. Lacqueur, 'The Futility of Terrorism', in Elliott and Gibson, *Contemporary Terrorism: Selected Readings*, pp. 285–292.

53 Copy in author's possession.

54 Copy in author's possession.

55 J. Bowyer-Bell, *The Secret Army: The IRA 1916–1979* (Dublin: Academy Press, 1979).

56 Horgan, 'Issues in Terrorism Research'.

57 K. Heskin, *Northern Ireland: A Psychological Analysis* (Dublin: Gill and Macmillan, 1980), p. 79.

58 Taylor and Quayle, *Terrorist Lives*, p. 24.

59 J. Bowyer-Bell, *The Dynamics of the Armed Struggle* (London: Frank Cass, 1998), p. xv.

60 See for example, T.P. Coogan, *The IRA* (London: HarperCollins, 1995), pp. ix–x; also see T.P. Coogan, *The Troubles: Ireland's Ordeal 1966–1995 and the Search for Peace* (London: Hutchinson, 1995), p. xi.

61 Taylor and Quayle, *Terrorist Lives*, p. 24.

62 Bowyer-Bell, *The Dynamics of the Armed Struggle*, p. xv.

63 See especially Horgan, 'Issues in Terrorism Research'.

64 Ibid., also see Horgan, 'The Case for Firsthand Research'.

65 Horgan and Taylor, 'The Provisional Irish Republican Army: Command and Functional Structure'.

66 Coogan, *The IRA*, p. 479.

67 Cited in Horgan, 'Issues in Terrorism Research', p. 199.

68 R.M. Lee, *Dangerous Fieldwork* (New York: Sage, 1995), pp. 22–23.

69 Horgan, 'Issues in Terrorism Research'.

70 Horgan and Taylor, 'The Provisional Irish Republican Army: Command and Functional Structure'.

71 See the discussion on 'snowball sampling' procedures in G.J. Knowles, 'Dealing Crack Cocaine: A View from the Streets of Honolulu', *FBI Law Enforcement Bulletin*, 65, July (1996), p. 7.

72 Taylor and Quayle, *Terrorist Lives*.

73 Horgan, 'Issues in Terrorism Research', and Horgan, 'The Case for Firsthand Research'.

74 J. Sluka, *Hearts and Minds, Water and Fish: Support for the IRA and INLA in a Northern Irish Ghetto* (Greenwich, CT: JAI Press, 1989), p. 22. Jeffrey Sluka's work is one of the truly outstanding empirical research efforts on the Northern Ireland conflict.

75 Horgan, 'Issues in Terrorism Research', p. 197.

76 Crenshaw, 'Questions To Be Answered, Research To Be Done, Knowledge To Be Applied', p. 248.

77 Ibid.

78 F. Ferracuti, 'Ideology and Repentance: Terrorism in Italy', in Reich, *Origins of Terrorism: Psychologies, Ideologies, Theologies, States of Mind*, pp. 59–64.

79 Also see Cordes, 'Euroterrorists Talk About Themselves'.

80 Crenshaw, 'Questions To Be Answered, Research To Be Done, Knowledge To Be Applied', p. 248.

81 See the discussion in Horgan, 'Issues in Terrorism Research'; also see C. McCauley, 'Terrorism, Research and Public Policy: An Overview', *Terrorism and Political Violence*, 3, 1 (1991), pp. 126–144.

82 Crenshaw, 'Questions To Be Answered, Research To Be Done, Knowledge To Be Applied', p. 247; also see especially McCauley, 'Terrorism, Research and Public Policy'; Merari, 'Academic Research and Government Policy on Terrorism'; P. Wilkinson, 'Foreword – Terrorism: An International Research Agenda?', in Wilkinson and Stewart, *Contemporary Research on Terrorism*, pp. xi–xx.

3 INDIVIDUAL APPROACHES

1 British Broadcasting Corporation, *Third World War: Al Qaeda* (broadcast on 24 February 2004).

2 R. Carroll, 'Beatings Take On New Form – Victim Loosed Like An Animal', *Irish News* (10 December 1996).

3 S. Anderson, 'Making a Killing', *Harper's Magazine*, 288 (1 February 1994).

4 H.H.A. Cooper, 'The Terrorist and the Victim', *Victimology*, 1, 2 (1976), pp. 229–239.

5 R.R. Corrado, 'A Critique of the Mental Disorder Perspective of Political Terrorism', *International Journal of Law and Psychiatry*, 4, 3–4 (1981), pp. 293–309; also see H.H.A. Cooper, 'What is a Terrorist?: A Psychological Perspective', *Legal Medical Quarterly*, 1 (1977), pp. 16–32; H.H.A. Cooper, 'Psychopath as Terrorist', *Legal Medical Quarterly*, 2 (1978), pp. 253–262; H.H.A. Cooper, 'Whither Now? Terrorism on the Brink', in J.D. Elliott and L.K. Gibson (eds), *Contemporary Terrorism: Selected Readings* (Maryland: International Associa-

tion of Chiefs of Police, 1978), pp. 269–284; F.J. Hacker, *Crusaders, Criminals, Crazies: Terror and Terrorism in our Time* (New York: W.W. Norton, 1976); C. Hassel, 'Terror: The Crime of the Privileged – An Examination and Prognosis', *Terrorism*, 1 (1977), pp. 1–16; K. Kellen, *Terrorists: What Are They Like? How Some Terrorists Describe Their World and Actions: Rand Publication N-1300–SL* (Santa Monica, CA: Rand, 1979); K. Kellen, *On Terrorists and Terrorism: A Rand Note N-1942–RC* (Santa Monica, CA: Rand, 1982); K.I. Pearce, 'Police Negotiations', *Canadian Psychiatric Association Journal*, 22 (1977), pp. 171–174.

6 Cooper, 'The Terrorist and the Victim', p. 232.

7 J. Bowyer-Bell, *The Secret Army: The IRA 1916–1979* (Dublin: Academy Press, 1979); J. Bowyer-Bell, *The IRA: 1968–2000* (London: Frank Cass, 2000); F. Burton, *The Politics of Legitimacy: Struggles in a Belfast Community* (London: Routledge and Kegan Paul, 1978); T.P. Coogan, *The IRA* (London: HarperCollins, 1995); A. Jamieson, *The Heart Attacked: Terrorism and Conflict in the Italian State* (London: Marian Boyars, 1989); A. Jamieson, 'Entry, Discipline and Exit in the Italian Red Brigades', *Terrorism and Political Violence*, 2, 1 (1990), pp. 1–20; A. Jamieson, 'Identity and Morality in the Red Brigades', *Terrorism and Political Violence*, 2, 4 (1990), pp. 508–520.

8 M. Taylor and E. Quayle, *Terrorist Lives* (London: Brassey's, 1994), p. 107.

9 M. Taylor, *The Terrorist* (London: Brassey's, 1988), p.88.

10 Ibid.

11 Cooper, 'The Terrorist and the Victim', p. 237.

12 Kellen, *On Terrorists and Terrorism*, p. 23.

13 For other interesting data on this, see Burton, *The Politics of Legitimacy*.

14 K. Heskin, 'The Psychology of Terrorism in Northern Ireland', in Y. Alexander and A. O'Day (eds), *Terrorism in Ireland* (Kent: Croom Helm, 1984), pp. 85–105.

15 Kellen, *On Terrorists and Terrorism*, p. 18.

16 A.P. Silke, 'Cheshire-Cat Logic: The Recurring Theme of Terrorist Abnormality in Psychological Research', *Psychology, Crime and Law*, 4 (1998), pp. 51–69.

17 W. Baeyer-Katte, D. Claessens, H. Feger and F. Neidhart (eds), *Analysen Zum Terrorismus 3: Gruppeprozesse* (Darmstadt: Westedeutcher Verlag, 1982); also see H. Jager, G. Schmidtchen and L. Sullwold, *Analysen Zum Terrorismus 2: Lebenslauf-Analysen* (Opladen: Westdeutcher Verlag, 1982).

18 For reviews of the material (in English), see Taylor's *The Terrorist* and M. Crenshaw, 'The Psychology of Political Terrorism', in M.G. Hermann (ed.), *Political Psychology: Contemporary Problems and Issues* (London: Jossey-Bass, 1986), pp. 379–413.

19 Taylor, *The Terrorist*, p. 145.

20 M. Crenshaw, 'The Psychology of Political Terrorism', p. 387.

21 Ibid., p. 389.

22 For example, see R. Pearlstein, *The Mind of the Political Terrorist* (Wilmington: Scholarly Resources, 1991); and especially J.M. Post, 'Notes on a Psychodynamic Theory of Terrorist Behaviour', *Terrorism*, 7 (1984), pp. 241–256; J.M. Post, 'Group and Organisational Dynamics of Political Terrorism: Implications for Counterterrorist Policy', in P. Wilkinson and A.M. Stewart (eds), *Contemporary Research on Terrorism* (Aberdeen: Aberdeen University Press, 1987), pp. 307–317; J.M. Post, 'Rewarding Fire With Fire: The Effects of Retaliation on Terrorist Group Dynamics', *Terrorism*, 10 (1987), pp. 23–35; and also J.M. Post, 'Terrorist Psycho-Logic: Terrorist Behavior as a Product of Psychological Forces', in W. Reich (ed.), *Origins of Terrorism: Psychologies, Ideologies, Theologies, States of Mind* (New York: Cambridge University Press, 1990), pp. 25–40.

23 Crenshaw, 'The Psychology of Political Terrorism'.

24 Also see F. J. Lanceley, 'The Anti-Social Personality as Hostage Taker', *Journal of Political Science and Administration*, 9 (1981), p.28.

25 Post, 'Group and Organisational Dynamics of Political Terrorism', p. 308.

26 Crenshaw, 'The Psychology of Political Terrorism', p. 382.

27 K. Heskin, *Northern Ireland: A Psychological Analysis* (Dublin: Gill and Macmillan, 1980); also see Heskin, 'The Psychology of Terrorism in Northern Ireland'.

28 For example, see E. Cairns, 'Understanding Conflict and Promoting Peace in Ireland: Psychology's Contribution', *Irish Journal of Psychology*, 15, 2–3 (1994), pp. 480–493.

29 N. Friedland, 'Becoming a Terrorist: Social and Individual Antecedents', in L. Howard (ed.), *Terrorism: Roots, Impacts, Responses* (New York: Praeger, 1992), pp. 81–93.

30 W. Reich, 'Understanding Terrorist Behavior: The Limits and Opportunities of Psychological Enquiry', in W. Reich (ed.), *Origins of Terrorism*, pp. 261–279.

31 Friedland, 'Becoming a Terrorist', pp. 82–83.

32 For example, see D. Birrell, 'Relative Deprivation as a Factor in Conflict in Northern Ireland', *Sociopolitical Review*, 20 (1972), pp. 317–343; Corrado, 'A Critique of the Mental Disorder Perspective of Political Terrorism'; Hassel, 'Terror: The Crime of the Privileged – An Examination and Prognosis'; Heskin, *Northern Ireland: A Psychological Analysis*; Heskin, 'The Psychology of Terrorism in Northern Ireland'; H.H. Tittmar, 'Urban Terrorism: A Psychological Perspective', *Terrorism and Political Violence*, 4, 3 (1992), pp. 64–71; P. Watzlawick, 'The Pathologies of Perfectionism', *Et Cetera*, 34, 1 (1977), pp. 12–18.

33 Tittmar, 'Urban Terrorism: A Psychological Perspective'.

34 L. Berkowitz, 'Some Aspects of Observed Aggression', *Journal of Personality and Social Psychology*, 12 (1965), pp. 359–369.

35 Friedland, 'Becoming a Terrorist', p. 83.

36 F. Ferracuti, 'A Sociopsychiatric Interpretation of Terrorism', *The Annals of the American Academy (AAPSS)*, 463 (1982), pp. 129–140.

37 For instance, see the discussion in A. Merari and N. Friedland, 'Social Psychological Aspects of Political Terrorism', in S. Oskamp (ed.), *Applied Social Psychology Annual 6: International Conflict and National Public Policy Issues* (London: Sage, 1985), pp. 185–205.

38 Ferracuti, 'A Sociopsychiatric Interpretation of Terrorism', p. 139.

39 Friedland, 'Becoming a Terrorist', p. 85.

40 Merari and Friedland, 'Social Psychological Aspects of Political Terrorism', p. 187.

41 T.R. Gurr, *Why Men Rebel* (Princeton: Princeton University Press, 1970); also see Birrell, 'Relative Deprivation as a Factor in Conflict in Northern Ireland'; Friedland, 'Becoming a Terrorist'; and Heskin, *Northern Ireland: A Psychological Analysis*.

42 Friedland, 'Becoming a Terrorist', p. 85.

43 H.A. Kampf, 'Terrorism, The Left-Wing, and The Intellectuals', *Terrorism*, 13, 1 (1990), pp. 23–51.

44 Hassel, 'Terror: The Crime of the Privileged – An Examination and Prognosis'; also see Watzlawick, 'The Pathologies of Perfectionism'.

45 Reich, 'Understanding Terrorist Behavior'.

46 For example, see Hassel, 'Terror: The Crime of the Privileged – An Examination and Prognosis'; C. Lasch, *The Culture of Narcissism* (New York: W.W. Norton,

1979); Pearlstein, *The Mind of the Political Terrorist*; Post, 'Notes on a Psycho-dynamic Theory of Terrorist Behavior'; Post, 'Group and Organisational Dynamics of Political Terrorism'; Post, 'Rewarding Fire With Fire'.

47 Pearlstein, *The Mind of the Political Terrorist*, p. 7.

48 Ibid., p. 28.

49 See for example, W. Rasch, 'Psychological Dimensions of Political Terrorism in the Federal Republic of Germany', *International Journal of Law and Psychiatry*, 2 (1979), pp. 79–86.

50 For example, see Corrado, 'A Critique of the Mental Disorder Perspective of Political Terrorism'.

51 Pearlstein, *The Mind of the Political Terrorist*, p. 171.

52 Ibid., p. 7.

53 Ibid., p. 46.

54 M. Taylor, *The Terrorist*, p. 140.

55 For example, see G. Bartalotta, 'Psicologia Analitica e Terrorismo Politico', *Rivista di Psicologia Analitica*, 12, 24 (1981), pp. 21–30; L. Brunet, 'Le Phenomene Terroriste et ses Effets sur les Object Internes', *Revue Quebecoise de Psychologie*, 10, 1 (1989), pp. 2–15; F. Ferracuti and F. Bruno, 'Psychiatric Aspects of Terrorism in Italy', in I.L. Barak-Glantz and C.R. Huff (eds), *The Mad, The Bad and The Different: Essays in Honor of Simon Dinitz* (Lexington, MA: Heath, 1981), pp. 199–213; P.W. Johnson and T.B. Feldmann, 'Personality Types and Terrorism: Self-Psychology Perspectives', *Forensic Reports*, 5 (1992), pp. 293–303; I. Kent and W. Nicholls, 'The Psychodynamics of Terrorism', *Mental Health and Society*, 4, 1–2 (1977), pp. 1–8; P.A. Olsson, 'The Terrorist and The Terrorized: Some Psychoanalytic Consideration', *Journal of Psycho-history*, 16, 1 (1988), pp. 47–60; Pearlstein, The Mind of the Political Terrorist; R. Turco, 'Psychiatric Contributions to the Understanding of International Terrorism', *International Journal of Offender Therapy and Comparative Criminology*, 31, 2 (1987), pp. 153–161; M.N. Vinar, 'La Terreur, Le Politique, La Place d'un Psychanalyste', *Patio*, 11 (1988), pp. 43–51.

56 Kellen, *On Terrorists and Terrorism*.

57 Ibid., p. 18.

58 Ibid.

59 A. Kaplan, 'The Psychodynamics of Terrorism', in Y. Alexander and J.M. Gleason (eds), *Behavioural and Quantitative Perspectives on Terrorism* (Elmsford, NY: Pergamon, 1981), pp. 35–51; also see W. Lacqueur, *Terrorism* (London: Weidefeld and Nicolson, 1977).

60 E. Erikson, *Identity, Youth and Crisis* (London: Faber and Faber, 1968).

61 Also see E. Cairns, 'Social Identity and Intergroup Conflict: A Developmental Perspective', in J. Harbinson (ed.), *Growing Up in Northern Ireland* (Belfast: Stranmillis College, 1989), pp. 115–130; E. Cairns and G. Mercer, 'Social Identity in Northern Ireland', *Human Relations*, 37, 12 (1984), pp. 1095–1102.

62 Crenshaw, 'The Psychology of Political Terrorism'.

63 Taylor, *The Terrorist*.

64 Crenshaw, 'The Psychology of Political Terrorism', pp. 391–392.

65 J. Knutson, 'Social and Psychodynamic Pressures Toward a Negative Identity: The Case of an American Revolutionary Terrorist', in Alexander and Gleason, *Behavioural and Quantitative Perspectives on Terrorism*, pp. 105–150.

66 Silke, 'Cheshire-Cat Logic: The Recurring Theme of Terrorist Abnormality in Psychological Research', p. 53.

67 For example, see C. McCauley, 'Terrorism, Research and Public Policy: An Overview', *Terrorism and Political Violence*, 3, 1 (1991), pp. 126–144;

C. McCauley and M.E. Segal, 'Social Psychology of Terrorist Groups', in C. Hendrick (ed.), *Review of Personality and Social Psychology 9* (Beverly Hills: Sage, 1987), pp. 231–256.

68 G. Morf, *Terror in Quebec – Case Studies of the FLQ* (Toronto: Clark, Irwin, 1970).

69 Rasch, 'Psychological Dimensions of Political Terrorism in the Federal Republic of Germany'.

70 McCauley, 'Terrorism, Research and Public Policy', p. 132.

71 Corrado, 'A Critique of the Mental Disorder Perspective of Political Terrorism'.

72 Jamieson, *The Heart Attacked*, p. 48.

73 H.A. Lyons and H.J. Harbinson, 'A Comparison of Political and Non-Political Murderers in Northern Ireland 1974–1984', *Medicine, Science and the Law*, 26 (1986), pp. 193–198.

74 Cited in C. Ryder, *Inside the Maze: The Untold Story of the Northern Ireland Prison Service* (London: Methuen, 2000) p. xiii.

75 Ibid., p. xiii.

76 Cited in Heskin, *Northern Ireland: A Psychological Analysis*, p. 78.

77 Taylor, *The Terrorist*, p. 92.

78 Heskin, 'The Psychology of Terrorism in Northern Ireland'.

79 Crenshaw, 'The Psychology of Political Terrorism'.

80 See Silke, 'Cheshire-Cat Logic: The Recurring Theme of Terrorist Abnormality in Psychological Research'; Taylor, *The Terrorist*.

81 Taylor, *The Terrorist*.

82 See Silke, 'Cheshire-Cat Logic: The Recurring Theme of Terrorist Abnormality in Psychological Research'.

83 For example, A. Beck, 'Prisoners of Hate', *Behavior Research and Therapy*, 40, 3 (2002), pp. 209–216; Johnson and Feldmann, 'Personality Types and Terrorism: Self-Psychology Perspectives'; Pearlstein, *The Mind of the Political Terrorist*.

84 Ferracuti, 'A Sociopsychiatric Interpretation of Terrorism', p. 129.

85 Kellen, *On Terrorism and Terrorists*, p. 15.

86 Ferracuti, 'A Sociopsychiatric Interpretation of Terrorism', pp. 3–6.

87 Ibid., p. 130.

88 Ibid.

89 Kellen, *On Terrorism and Terrorists*, p. 23.

90 Ibid., p. 19.

91 Silke, 'Cheshire-Cat Logic: The Recurring Theme of Terrorist Abnormality in Psychological Research', p. 64.

92 Ibid., pp. 66–67.

93 Taylor, *The Terrorist*.

94 Silke, 'Cheshire-Cat Logic: The Recurring Theme of Terrorist Abnormality in Psychological Research', p. 56.

95 R. Blackburn, 'Psychopathy and Personality Disorder in Relation to Violence', in K. Howells and C.R. Hollin (eds), *Clinical Approaches to the Mentally Disordered Offender* (Chichester, UK: Wiley, 1989), pp. 61–88.

96 Ibid., p.63.

97 Merari and Friedland, 'Social Psychological Aspects of Political Terrorism', p. 187.

98 J.S. Handler, 'Socioeconomic Profile of an American Terrorist: 1960s and 1970s', *Terrorism*, 13 (1990), pp. 195–213.

99 Ibid., p. 198; also see especially p. 195 and p. 199.

100 Cited in Taylor, *The Terrorist*, p. 124.

101 T. Strentz, 'A Terrorist Psychosocial Profile: Past and Present', *FBI Law Enforcement Bulletin*, April (1987), pp. 13–19.

102 Also see H.H.A. Cooper, 'Voices from Troy: What Are We Hearing?', in *Outthinking the Terrorist – An International Challenge: Proceedings of the 10th Annual Symposium on the Role of Behavioral Science in Physical Security* (Washington, D.C.: Defence Nuclear Agency, 1985), p. 95.

103 Taylor, *The Terrorist*, p. 124.

104 Blackburn, 'Psychopathy and Personality Disorder in Relation to Violence', p. 63.

105 Friedland, 'Becoming a Terrorist', p. 83.

106 Crenshaw, 'The Psychology of Political Terrorism', p. 387.

107 C.J.M. Drake, *Terrorists' Target Selection* (London: Macmillan, 1998).

108 Interviewed by the author in the Republic of Ireland in early 1997.

109 Taylor, *The Terrorist*.

110 Taylor and Quayle, *Terrorist Lives*.

111 Taylor, *The Terrorist*, p. 145.

112 Merari and Friedland, 'Social Psychological Aspects of Political Terrorism', p. 187; also see Merari, 'A Classification of Terrorist Groups', *Terrorism*, 1, 3–4 (1978), pp. 331–346.

113 Merari and Friedland, 'Social Psychological Aspects of Political Terrorism', p. 187.

4 BECOMING A TERRORIST

1 D. Farrington, 'Explaining the Beginning, Progress and Ending of Antisocial Behaviour from Birth to Adulthood', in J. McCord (ed.), *Facts, Frameworks and Forecasts: Advances in Criminological Theory, Volume 3* (New Brunswick: Transactional Publishers, 1992).

2 T. Björgo (ed.), *Terror from the Extreme Right* (London: Frank Cass, 1995).

3 With notable exceptions, e.g. M. Taylor, *The Terrorist* (London: Brassey's, 1988). See especially the extremely important Chapter 8.

4 R.V.G. Clarke and D.B. Cornish, 'Modeling Offenders' Decisions: A Framework for Research and Policy', in M. Tonry and N. Morris (eds), *Crime and Justice: An Annual Review of Research, Volume 6* (Chicago: University of Chicago Press, 1985).

5 Also see Farrington, 'Explaining the Beginning, Progress and Ending of Antisocial Behaviour from Birth to Adulthood'.

6 T. Hirschi, 'On the Compatibility of Rational Choice and Social Control Theories of Crime', in D.B. Cornish and R.V.G. Clarke (eds), *The Reasoning Criminal: Rational Choice Perspectives on Offending* (New York: Springer-Verlag, 1986).

7 T. Björgo (ed.), *Root Causes of Terrorism: Findings from an International Expert Meeting in Oslo 9–11 June 2003* (Oslo: Norwegian Institute of International Affairs (NUPI)).

8 Ibid., pp. 234–237

9 Ibid., p. 234.

10 B. Cordes, 'Euroterrorists Talk About Themselves: A Look at the Literature', in P. Wilkinson and A.M. Stewart (eds), *Contemporary Research on Terrorism* (Aberdeen: Aberdeen University Press, 1987), pp. 318–336.

11 M. Taylor and E. Quayle, *Terrorist Lives* (London: Brassey's, 1994).

12 B.M. Miller, *The Language Component of Terrorism Strategy: A Text-Based Linguistic Case Study of Contemporary German Terrorism*, Unpublished Doctoral

Thesis (Washington, D.C.: Georgetown University, 1987); also Cordes, 'Euro-terrorists Talk About Themselves'.

13 Taylor and Quayle, *Terrorist Lives*.

14 Cordes, 'Euroterrorists Talk About Themselves: A Look at the Literature'.

15 M. Burgess, N. Ferguson and I. Hollywood, 'From Individual Discontent to Collective Armed Struggle: Personal Accounts of the Impetus for Membership or Non-membership in Paramilitary Groups', Unpublished Draft (Liverpool: Department of Psychology, Liverpool Hope University College, 2003).

16 Ibid.

17 See for example, the discussions in J.M. Post, 'Notes on a Psychodynamic Theory of Terrorist Behaviour', *Terrorism*, 7 (1984), pp. 241–256; J.M. Post, 'Group and Organisational Dynamics of Political Terrorism: Implications for Counterterror-ist Policy', in Wilkinson and Stewart, *Contemporary Research on Terrorism*, pp. 307–317; J.M. Post, 'Rewarding Fire With Fire: The Effects of Retaliation on Terrorist Group Dynamics', *Terrorism*, 10 (1987), pp. 23–35; and also J.M. Post, 'Terrorist Psycho-Logic: Terrorist Behavior as a Product of Psycho-logical Forces', in W. Reich (ed.), *Origins of Terrorism: Psychologies, Ideologies, Theologies, States of Mind* (New York: Cambridge University Press, 1990), pp. 25–40.

18 N. Hassan, 'Letter from Gaza: An Arsenal of Believers – Talking to the Human Bombs', *The New Yorker* (19 November 2001).

19 J.M. Post and L.M. Denny, 'The Terrorists in their Own Words: Interviews With 35 Incarcerated Middle Eastern Terrorists'. This was the original unpublished draft, which was later published (but without some of the detail mentioned here) as J.M. Post, E. Sprinzak and L.M. Denny, 'The Terrorists in their Own Words: Interviews with 35 Incarcerated Middle Eastern Terrorists', *Terrorism and Political Violence*, 15, 1 (2003), pp. 171–184.

20 Burgess, Ferguson and Hollywood, 'From Individual Discontent to Collective Armed Struggle'.

21 A.P. Silke, 'Becoming a Terrorist', in A.P. Silke (ed.), *Terrorists, Victims and Society: Psychological Perspectives on Terrorism and Its Consequences* (London: Wiley, 2003), pp. 29–53.

22 S. Atran, 'Social Science Review: Genesis of Suicide Terrorism', *Science*, 299 (7 March 2003), pp. 1534–1539.

23 C. Crawford, *Inside the UDA: Volunteers and Violence* (Dublin: Pluto, 2003).

24 K. Kellen, 'On Terrorism and Terrorists', (1982)

25 Taylor, *The Terrorist*; Taylor and Quayle, *Terrorist Lives*.

26 J. Horgan and M. Taylor, 'The Provisional Irish Republican Army: Command and Functional Structure', *Terrorism and Political Violence*, 9, 3 (1997), pp. 1–32.

27 Copy in author's possession.

28 For example, E. Collins (with M. McGovern), *Killing Rage* (London: Granta, 1997); M. McGartland, *Fifty Dead Men Walking* (London: Blake, 1997); S. O'Callaghan, *The Informer* (London: Bantam, 1998).

29 C. McCauley and M.E. Segal, 'Terrorist Individuals and Terrorist Groups: The Normal Psychology of Extreme Behavior', in J. Groebel and J.H. Goldstein (eds), *Terrorism* (Seville: Publicaciones de la Universidad de Sevilla, 1989), p. 45.

30 R.P. Clark, 'Patterns in the Lives of ETA Members', *Terrorism*, 6, 3 (1983), pp. 423–454; also see R.P. Clark, *The Basque Insurgents: ETA 1952–1980* (Madison: University of Wisconsin Press, 1983).

31 A. Jamieson, *The Heart Attacked* (London: Marian Boyars, 1989), pp. 266–267.

32 R.W. White and T. Falkenberg White, 'Revolution in the City: On the Resources of Urban Guerrillas', *Terrorism and Political Violence*, 3, 4 (1991), pp. 100–132.

33 O. Billig, 'Case History of a German Terrorist', *Terrorism*, 7 (1984), pp. 1–10.
34 A. Jamieson, 'Entry, Discipline and Exit in the Italian Red Brigades', *Terrorism and Political Violence*, 2, 1 (1990), pp. 1–20.
35 See R.P. Clark, 'Patterns in the Lives of ETA Members', and *The Basque Insurgents: ETA 1952–1980*.
36 McCauley and Segal, 'Terrorist Individuals and Terrorist Groups', p. 55.
37 Hassan, 'Letter from Gaza: An Arsenal of Believers'.
38 J.K. Zawodny, 'Internal Organizational Problems and the Sources of Tensions of Terrorists Movements as Cataylsts of Violence', *Terrorism*, 1, 3–4 (1978), pp. 277–285.
39 B. Barber, *Heart and Stones: Palestinian Youth from the Intifada* (New York: Palgrave, 2003).
40 Hassan, 'Letter from Gaza: An Arsenal of Believers'.
41 White and Falkenberg White, 'Revolution in the City', p. 115.
42 Taylor and Quayle, *Terrorist Lives*, pp. 34–35.
43 For example see the interviews conducted by Hassan, in 'Letter from Gaza: An Arsenal of Believers'.

5 BEING A TERRORIST

1 J. Horgan, 'Social and Psychological Characteristics of Terrorism and Terrorists', in T. Björgo (ed.), *Root Causes of Terrorism* (London: Routledge, *in press*).
2 Ibid.
3 M. Cusson, 'A Strategic Analysis of Crime: Criminal Tactics as Responses to Pre-criminal Situations', in R.V. Clarke and M. Felson (eds), *Routine Activity and Rational Choice* (New Brunswick, NJ: Transaction, 1993), pp. 295–304.
4 X. Raufer, 'Al Qaeda: A Different Diagnosis', *Studies in Conflict and Terrorism*, 26, 6 (2003), pp. 391–398.
5 A.P. Silke, 'Beyond Horror: Terrorist Atrocity and the Search for Understanding – the Case of the Shankill Bombing', *Studies in Conflict and Terrorism*, 26 (2003), pp. 37–60.
6 J. Horgan and M. Taylor, 'Playing the Green Card: Financing the Provisional IRA – Part 1', *Terrorism and Political Violence*, 11, 1 (1999), pp. 1–38.
7 Ibid.
8 Ibid.
9 R. Debray, *Revolution in the Revolution* (New York: MR Press, 1967).
10 S. Milgram, 'Behavioral Study of Obedience', *Journal of Abnormal and Social Psychology*, 67 (1963), pp. 371–378; also see S. Milgram, 'Some Conditions of Obedience and Disobedience to Authority', in I.D. Steiner and M. Fishbein (eds), *Current Studies in Social Psychology* (New York: Holt, 1965).
11 J.P. Dworetsky, *Psychology (Third Edition)* (St. Paul, MN: West, 1991).
12 H.C. Kelman, 'Violence Without Moral Restraint: Reflection on the Dehumanization of Victims and Victimisers', *Journal of Social Issues*, 29, 4 (1973), pp. 25–61.
13 Ibid., p. 45.
14 The IRA's *Green Book* (copy in author's possession), pp. 8–9.
15 Ibid., p. 9.
16 A. Jamieson, 'Entry, Discipline and Exit in the Italian Red Brigades', *Terrorism and Political Violence*, 2, 1 (1990), pp. 1–20.
17 N. Hassan, 'Letter from Gaza: An Arsenal of Believers – Talking to the Human Bombs', *The New Yorker* (19 November 2001).
18 See the IRA's *Green Book*, p. 33.

19 H. Arendt, *Eichmann in Jerusalem: A Report on The Banality of Evil* (New York: Viking, 1963).
20 Kelman, 'Violence Without Moral Restraint', p. 36.
21 Ibid., p. 38.
22 K. Heskin, 'The Psychology of Terrorism in Northern Ireland', in Y. Alexander and A. O'Day (eds), *Terrorism in Ireland* (Kent: Croom Helm, 1984), pp. 85–105.
23 Ibid., p. 101.
24 Dworetsky, *Psychology*, p. 571.
25 Ibid.
26 A.P. Silke, 'Deindividuation, Anonymity, and Violence: Findings from Northern Ireland', *Journal of Social Psychology*, 143, 4 (2003), pp. 493–499.
27 A. Bandura, 'Mechanisms of moral disengagement', in W. Reich (ed.), *Origins of Terrorism: Psychologies, Ideologies, Theologies, States of Mind* (New York: Cambridge University Press, 1990), pp. 161–191.
28 The IRA's *Green Book*, pp. 38–39.
29 Translated by Venzke and Ibrahim, 2003.
30 The IRA's *Green Book*, p. 4.
31 Jamieson, 'Entry, Discipline and Exit in the Italian Red Brigades', p. 3.

6 DISENGAGING

1 J.C. Dingley, 'Peace Processes in Northern Ireland: Squaring Circles?', *Terrorism and Political Violence*, 11, 3 (1999), pp. 32–52.
2 In particular, see the various contributions in A.P. Silke (ed.), *Research on Terrorism: Trends, Achievements, Failures* (London: Frank Cass, 2004).
3 C. McCauley and M.E. Segal, 'Terrorist Individuals and Terrorist Groups: The Normal Psychology of Extreme Behavior', in J. Groebel and J.H. Goldstein (eds), *Terrorism* (Seville: Publicaciones de la Universidad de Sevilla, 1989).
4 Cited in Y. Alexander and K.A. Myers (eds), *Terrorism in Europe* (London: Croom Helm, 1982), p. 174; see also M. Baumann, *Terror or Love?: Bommi Baumann's Own Story of his Life as a West German Urban Guerrilla* (New York: Grove, 1979).
5 A. Jamieson, *The Heart Attacked: Terrorism and Conflict in the Italian State* (London: Marian Boyars, 1989).
6 Ibid., p. 5.
7 J.M. Post, 'Group and Organisational Dynamics of Political Terrorism: Implications for Counterterrorist Policy', in P. Wilkinson and A.M. Stewart, *Contemporary Research on Terrorism* (Aberdeen: Aberdeen University Press), pp. 307–317.
8 A. Spire, 'Le Terrorisme Intellectuel', *Patio*, 11 (1988), pp. 150–158.
9 Ibid., p. 150.
10 In Jamieson, *The Heart Attacked* (see especially pp. 267—268).
11 J. Brockner and J.Z. Rubin, *Entrapment in Escalating Conflicts* (New York: Springer-Verlag, 1985).
12 M. Taylor, *The Terrorist* (London: Brassey's, 1988).
13 Ibid., p. 168.
14 Cited in Taylor, *The Terrorist*, p. 168.
15 K. Lewin, 'Group Decision and Social Change', in T.M. Newcomb and E.L. Hartley (eds), *Readings in Social Psychology* (New York: Holt, 1947).
16 Post, 'Group and Organisational Dynamics of Political Terrorism'.
17 Ibid., p. 312.
18 Ibid.

19 M. Crenshaw, 'The Psychology of Political Terrorism', in M.G. Hermann (ed.), *Political Psychology: Contemporary Problems and Issues* (London: Jossey-Bass, 1986), pp. 379–413.
20 Jamison, *The Heart Attacked*.
21 Sean O'Callaghan, cited in S. Clare, 'Ceasefire Was Never Genuine – IRA Killer', *Press Association Newswire* (9 December 1996).
22 M. Crenshaw, 'An Organisational Political Approach to the Analysis of Political Terrorism', *Orbis*, 29, 3 (1985), pp. 465–489.
23 Ibid., p. 474.
24 Cited in L. Clarke, *Broadening the Battlefield: The H-Blocks and the Rise of Sinn Fein* (Dublin: Gill and Macmillan, 1987), p. 29.
25 R. Debray, *Revolution in the Revolution* (New York: MR Press, 1967).
26 See also K.L. Oots, 'Bargaining With Terrorists: Organisational Considerations', *Terrorism*, 13 (1989), pp. 145–158.
27 D.P.J. Walsh, 'The Impact of the Antisubversive Laws on Police Powers and Practices in Ireland: The Silent Erosion of Individual Freedom', *Temple Law Review*, 62, 4 (1989), pp. 1099–1129.
28 R.H. Evans, 'Terrorism and Subversion of the State: Italian Legal Responses', *Terrorism and Political Violence*, 1, 3 (1989), pp. 324–352; Jamieson, *The Heart Attacked*.
29 For example, see S. Bruce, *The Red Hand: Protestant Paramilitaries in Northern Ireland* (Oxford: Oxford University Press, 1992); also see J. Horgan and M. Taylor, 'Playing the Green Card: Financing the Provisional IRA – Part 1', *Terrorism and Political Violence*, 11, 1 (1999), pp. 1–38; J. Horgan and M. Taylor, 'Playing the Greed Card: Financing the Provisional IRA – Part 2', *Terrorism and Political Violence*, 15, 2 (2003), pp. 1–60.
30 See especially the exciting analysis developed by K. Tololyan, 'Narrative Culture and Terrorist Motivation', in J. Shotter and K.J. Gergen (eds), *Texts of Identity – Inquiries in Social Construction Series* (London: Sage, 1989), pp. 99–118.

BIBLIOGRAPHY

Adams, G., *Before the Dawn: An Autobiography* (London: Heinemann/Brandon, 1996).

Alexander, Y. and Myers, K.A. (eds), *Terrorism in Europe* (London: Croom Helm, 1982).

Anderson, J.K., 'Terrorism'. Retrieved from the World Wide Web: www.gocin.com/probe/terror.htm.

Anderson, S., 'Making a Killing', *Harper's Magazine*, 288 (1 February 1994).

Arendt, H., *Eichmann in Jerusalem: A Report on The Banality of Evil* (New York: Viking, 1963).

Atran, S., 'Social Science Review: Genesis of Suicide Terrorism', *Science*, 299 (7 March 2003), pp. 1534–1539.

Baeyer-Katte, W., Claessens, D., Feger, H. and Neidhart, F., (eds), *Analysen Zum Terrorismus 3: Gruppeprozesse* (Darmstadt: Westedeutcher Verlag, 1982).

Bandura, A., 'Mechanisms of Moral Disengagement', in W. Reich (ed.), *Origins of Terrorism: Psychologies, Ideologies, Theologies, States of Mind* (New York: Cambridge University Press, 1990), pp. 161–191.

Barber, B., *Heart and Stones: Palestinian Youth from the Intifada* (New York: Palgrave, 2003).

Bartalotta, G., 'Psicologia Analitica e Terrorismo Politico', *Rivista di Psicologia Analitica*, 12, 24 (1981), pp. 21–30.

Baumann, M., *Terror or Love?: Bommi Baumann's Own Story of His Life as a West German Urban Guerrilla* (New York: Grove Press, 1979).

Beck, A., 'Prisoners of Hate', *Behavior Research and Therapy*, 40, 3 (2002), pp. 209–216.

Berkowitz, L., 'Some Aspects of Observed Aggression', *Journal of Personality and Social Psychology*, 12 (1965), pp. 359–369.

Billig, O., 'Case History of a German Terrorist', *Terrorism*, 7 (1984), pp. 1–10.

Birrell, D., 'Relative Deprivation as a Factor in Conflict in Northern Ireland', *Socio-political Review*, 20 (1972), pp. 317–343.

Björgo, T. (ed.), *Terror from the Extreme Right* (London: Frank Cass, 1995).

Björgo, T. (ed.), *Root Causes of Terrorism: Findings from an International Expert Meeting in Oslo 9–11 June 2003* (Oslo: Norwegian Institute of International Affairs).

Blackburn, R., 'Psychopathy and Personality Disorder in Relation to Violence', in K. Howells and C.R. Hollin (eds), *Clinical Approaches to the Mentally Disordered Offender* (Chichester, UK: Wiley, 1989), pp. 61–88.

Bowyer-Bell, J., *The Secret Army: The IRA 1916–1979* (Dublin: Academy Press, 1979).

Bowyer-Bell, J., *The Dynamics of the Armed Struggle* (London: Frank Cass, 1998).

Bowyer-Bell, J., *The IRA: 1968–2000* (London: Frank Cass, 2000).

British Broadcasting Corporation, *Third World War: Al Qaeda* (broadcast on 24 February 2004).

Brockner, J. and Rubin, J.Z., *Entrapment in Escalating Conflicts* (New York: Springer-Verlag, 1985).

Bruce, S., *The Red Hand: Protestant Paramilitaries in Northern Ireland* (Oxford: Oxford University Press, 1992).

Brunet, L., 'Le Phenomene terroriste et ses effets sur les object internes', *Revue Quebecoise de Psychologie*, 10, 1 (1989), pp. 2–15.

Burgess, M., Ferguson, N. and Hollywood, I., 'From Individual Discontent to Collective Armed Struggle: Personal Accounts of the Impetus for Membership or Non-membership in Paramilitary Groups', Unpublished Draft (Liverpool: Department of Psychology, Liverpool Hope University College, 2003).

Burton, F., *The Politics of Legitimacy: Struggles in a Belfast Community* (London: Routledge and Kegan Paul, 1978).

Cairns, E., 'Social Identity and Intergroup Conflict: A Developmental Perspective', in J. Harbinson (ed.), *Growing Up in Northern Ireland* (Belfast: Stranmillis College, 1989), pp. 115–130.

Cairns, E., 'Understanding Conflict and Promoting Peace in Ireland: Psychology's Contribution', *Irish Journal of Psychology*, 15, 2–3 (1994), pp. 480–493.

Cairns, E. and Mercer, G., 'Social Identity in Northern Ireland', *Human Relations*, 37, 12 (1984), pp. 1095–1102.

Cairns, E. and Wilson, R., 'Stress, Coping, and Political Violence in Northern Ireland', in J.P. Wilson and B. Raphael (eds), *International Handbook of Traumatic Stress Syndromes* (New York: Plenum Press, 1992), pp. 365–376.

Carroll, R., 'Beatings Take On New Form – Victim Loosed Like An Animal', *Irish News* (10 December 1996).

Clare, S., 'Ceasefire Was Never Genuine – IRA Killer', *Press Association Newswire* (9 December 1996).

Clark, R.P., 'Patterns in the Lives of ETA Members', *Terrorism*, 6, 3 (1983), pp. 423–454.

Clark, R.P., *The Basque Insurgents: ETA 1952–1980* (Madison: University of Wisconsin Press, 1983).

Clarke, L., *Broadening the Battlefield: The H-Blocks and the Rise of Sinn Fein* (Dublin: Gill and Macmillan, 1987).

Clarke, R.V.G., and Cornish, D.B., 'Modeling Offenders' Decisions: A Framework for Research and Policy', in M. Tonry and N. Morris (eds), *Crime and Justice: An Annual Review of Research, Volume 6* (Chicago: University of Chicago Press, 1985).

Collins, E. (with M. McGovern), *Killing Rage* (London: Granta, 1997).

Coogan, T.P., *The IRA* (London: HarperCollins, 1995).

Coogan, T.P., *The Troubles: Ireland's Ordeal 1966–1995 and the Search for Peace* (London: Hutchinson, 1995).

Cooper, H.H.A., 'The Terrorist and the Victim', *Victimology*, 1, 2 (1976), pp. 229–239.

Cooper, H.H.A., 'What is a Terrorist?: A Psychological Perspective', *Legal Medical Quarterly*, 1 (1977), pp. 16–32.

Cooper, H.H.A., 'Psychopath as Terrorist', *Legal Medical Quarterly*, 2 (1978), pp. 253–262.

Cooper, H.H.A., 'Whither Now? Terrorism on the Brink', in J.D. Elliott and L.K. Gibson (eds), *Contemporary Terrorism: Selected Readings* (Maryland: International Association of Chiefs of Police, 1978), pp. 269–284.

Cooper, H.H.A. 'Voices from Troy: What Are We Hearing?', in *Outthinking the Terrorist – An International Challenge: Proceedings of the 10th Annual Symposium on the Role of Behavioral Science in Physical Security* (Washington, D.C.: Defence Nuclear Agency, 1985).

Cordes, B., 'Euroterrorists Talk About Themselves: A Look at the Literature', in P. Wilkinson and A.M. Stewart (eds), *Contemporary Research on Terrorism* (Aberdeen: Aberdeen University Press, 1987), pp. 318–336.

Corrado, R.R., 'A Critique of the Mental Disorder Perspective of Political Terrorism', *International Journal of Law and Psychiatry*, 4, 3–4 (1981), pp. 293–309.

Crawford, C., *Inside the UDA: Volunteers and Violence* (Dublin: Pluto, 2003).

Crelinsten, R.D., 'Terrorism as Political Communication: The Relationship Between the Controller and the Controlled', in P. Wilkinson and A.M. Stewart, (eds), *Contemporary Research on Terrorism* (Aberdeen: Aberdeen University Press, 1987), pp. 3–23.

Crenshaw, M., 'An Organisational Political Approach to the Analysis of Political Terrorism', *Orbis*, 29, 3 (1985), pp. 465–489.

Crenshaw, M., 'The Psychology of Political Terrorism', in M.G. Hermann (ed.), *Political Psychology: Contemporary Problems and Issues* (London: Jossey-Bass, 1986), pp. 379–413.

Crenshaw, M., 'Questions To Be Answered, Research To Be Done, Knowledge To be Applied', in W. Reich (ed.), *Origins of Terrorism: Psychologies, Ideologies, Theologies, States of Mind* (New York: Cambridge University Press, 1990), pp. 247–260.

Crenshaw, M., 'Current Research on Terrorism: The Academic Perspective', *Studies in Conflict and Terrorism*, 15, 1 (1992), pp. 1–11.

Cusson, M., 'A Strategic Analysis of Crime: Criminal Tactics as Responses to Pre-criminal Situations', in R.V. Clarke and M. Felson (eds), *Routine Activity and Rational Choice* (New Brunswick, NJ: Transaction, 1993), pp. 295–304.

Dartnell, M., 'A Legal Inter-Network for Terrorism: Globalisation, Fragmentation and Legitimacy', in M. Taylor and J. Horgan (eds), *The Future of Terrorism* (London: Frank Cass, 2000), pp. 197–208.

Debray, R., *Revolution in the Revolution* (New York: MR Press, 1967).

Dillon, M., *The Enemy Within: The IRA's War Against the British* (London: Doubleday, 1994).

Dingley, J.C., 'Peace Processes in Northern Ireland: Squaring Circles?', *Terrorism and Political Violence*, 11, 3 (1999), pp. 32–52.

Drake, C.J.M., *Terrorists' Target Selection* (London: Macmillan, 1998).

Dworetsky, J.P., *Psychology (Third Edition)* (St. Paul, MN: West Publishing, 1991).

Economist, 'What is Terrorism?' (2 March, 1996). Retrieved from the World Wide Web: economist.iconnect.net/issue/02–03–96/sf1.html (14 December 1999).

Erikson, E., *Identity, Youth and Crisis* (London: Faber and Faber, 1968).

Evans, R.H., 'Terrorism and Subversion of the State: Italian Legal Responses', *Terrorism and Political Violence*, 1, 3 (1989), pp. 324–352.

Farrington, D., 'Explaining the Beginning, Progress and Ending of Antisocial Behaviour from Birth to Adulthood', in J. McCord (ed.), *Facts, Frameworks and Forecasts: Advances in Criminological Theory, Volume 3* (New Brunswick: Transactional Publishers, 1992).

Ferracuti, F., 'A Sociopsychiatric Interpretation of Terrorism', *The Annals of the American Academy (AAPSS)*, 463 (1982), pp. 129–140.

Ferracuti, F., 'Ideology and Repentance: Terrorism in Italy', in W. Reich (ed.), *Origins of Terrorism: Psychologies, Ideologies, Theologies, States of Mind* (New York: Cambridge University Press, 1990), pp. 59–64.

Ferracuti, F. and Bruno, F., 'Psychiatric Aspects of Terrorism in Italy', in I.L. Barak-Glantz and C.R. Huff (eds), *The Mad, The Bad and The Different: Essays in Honor of Simon Dinitz* (Lexington, MA: Heath, 1981), pp. 199–213.

Friedland, N., 'Becoming a Terrorist: Social and Individual Antecedents', in L. Howard (ed.), *Terrorism: Roots, Impacts, Responses* (New York: Praeger, 1992), pp. 81–93.

Friedland, N. and Merari, A. 'The Psychological Impact of Terrorism: A Double-Edged Sword', *Political Psychology*, 6, 4 (1985), pp. 591–604.

Gilmour, R., *Dead Ground: Infiltrating the IRA* (London: Little, Brown and Company, 1998).

Gordon, A., 'Terrorism and Computerised Databases: An Examination of Multi-disciplinary Coverage', *Terrorism and Political Violence*, 7, 4 (1995), pp. 171–177.

Gordon, A., 'Research Note: The Spread of Terrorism Publications – A Database Analysis', *Terrorism and Political Violence*, 10, 4 (1998), pp. 192–196.

Gordon, A., 'Terrorism Dissertations and the Evolution of a Speciality: An Analysis of Meta-Information', *Terrorism and Political Violence*, 11, 2 (1999), pp. 141–150.

Gurr, T.R., *Why Men Rebel* (Princeton: Princeton University Press, 1970).

Hacker, F.J., *Crusaders, Criminals, Crazies: Terror and Terrorism in our Time* (New York: W.W. Norton, 1976).

Handler, J.S., 'Socioeconomic Profile of an American Terrorist: 1960s and 1970s', *Terrorism*, 13 (1990), pp. 195–213.

Harnden, T., *Bandit Country* (London: Hodder and Stoughton, 1999).

Hassan, N., 'Letter from Gaza: An Arsenal of Believers – Talking to the Human Bombs', *The New Yorker* (19 November 2001).

Hassel, C., 'Terror: The Crime of the Privileged – An Examination and Prognosis', *Terrorism*, 1 (1977), pp. 1–16.

Heskin, K., *Northern Ireland: A Psychological Analysis* (Dublin: Gill and Macmillan, 1980).

Heskin, K., 'The Psychology of Terrorism in Northern Ireland', in Y. Alexander and A. O'Day (eds), *Terrorism in Ireland* (Kent: Croom Helm, 1984), pp. 85–105.

Heskin, K., 'Political Violence in Northern Ireland', *Journal of Psychology*, 119, 5 (1985), pp. 481–494.

Hirschi, T., 'On the Compatibility of Rational Choice and Social Control Theories of Crime', in D.B. Cornish and R.V.G. Clarke (eds), *The Reasoning Criminal: Rational Choice Perspectives on Offending* (New York: Springer-Verlag, 1986).

Hoffman, B., 'Why Terrorists Don't Claim Credit', *Terrorism and Political Violence*, 9, 1 (1997), pp. 1–6.

Hoffman, B., *Inside Terrorism* (London: Victor Gollancz, 1998).

Hoffman, B. and Claridge, D., 'The Rand-St. Andrews Chronology of International Terrorism and Noteworthy Domestic Incidents 1996', *Terrorism and Political Violence*, 10, 2 (1998), pp. 135–180.

Horgan, J., 'Issues in Terrorism Research', *The Police Journal*, 50, 3 (1997), pp. 193–202.

Horgan, J., 'The Case for Firsthand Research', in A.P. Silke (ed.), *Research on Terrorism: Trends, Achievements and Failures* (London: Frank Cass, 2004), pp. 30–56.

Horgan, J., 'Social and Psychological Characteristics of Terrorism and Terrorists', in T. Björgo (ed.), *Root Causes of Terrorism* (London: Routledge, *in press*).

Horgan, J. and Taylor, M., 'The Provisional Irish Republican Army: Command and Functional Structure', *Terrorism and Political Violence*, 9, 3 (1997), pp. 1–32.

Horgan, J. and Taylor, M., 'Playing the Green Card: Financing the Provisional IRA – Part 1', *Terrorism and Political Violence*, 11, 1 (1999), pp. 1–38.

Horgan, J. and Taylor, M., 'Playing the Greed Card: Financing the Provisional IRA – Part 2', *Terrorism and Political Violence*, 15, 2 (2003), pp. 1–60.

Jager, H., Schmidtchen, G. and Sullwold, L., *Analysen Zum Terrorismus 2: Lebenslauf-Analysen* (Opladen: Westdeutcher Verlag, 1982).

Jamieson, A., *The Heart Attacked: Terrorism and Conflict in the Italian State* (London: Marian Boyars, 1989).

Jamieson, A., 'Entry, Discipline and Exit in the Italian Red Brigades', *Terrorism and Political Violence*, 2, 1 (1990), pp. 1–20.

Jamieson, A., 'Identity and Morality in the Red Brigades', *Terrorism and Political Violence*, 2, 4 (1990), pp. 508–520.

Jenkins, B.M., 'The Future Course of International Terrorism', in P. Wilkinson and A.M. Stewart (eds), *Contemporary Research on Terrorism* (Aberdeen, Aberdeen University Press: 1987), p. 583.

Johnson, P.W. and Feldmann, T.B., 'Personality Types and Terrorism: Self-Psychology Perspectives', *Forensic Reports*, 5 (1992), pp. 293–303.

Kampf, H.A., 'Terrorism, The Left-Wing, and The Intellectuals', *Terrorism*, 13, 1 (1990), pp. 23–51.

Kaplan, A., 'The Psychodynamics of Terrorism', in Y. Alexander and J.M. Gleason (eds), *Behavioural and Quantitative Perspectives on Terrorism* (Elmsford, NY: Pergamon, 1981), pp. 35–51.

Keane, F., 'IRA Sniper Kills Nine in One Area', *Sunday Tribune* (16 January 1994), p. A8.

Kearney, R., 'Myth and Terror', *The Crane Bag*, 2, 1–2 (1978), pp. 273–285.

Kellen, K., *Terrorists: What Are They Like? How Some Terrorists Describe Their World and Actions: Rand Publication N-1300–SL* (Santa Monica, CA: Rand, 1979).

Kellen, K., *On Terrorists and Terrorism: A Rand Note N-1942-RC* (Santa Monica, CA: Rand, 1982).

Kellen, K., 'Ideology and Rebellion: Terrorism in West Germany', in W. Reich (ed.), *Origins of Terrorism: Psychologies, Ideologies, Theologies, States of Mind* (New York: Cambridge University Press, 1990), pp. 43–58.

Kelman, H.C., 'Violence Without Moral Restraint: Reflection on the Dehumanisation of Victims and Victimisers', *Journal of Social Issues*, 29, 4 (1973), pp. 25–61.

Kent, I. and Nicholls, W., 'The Psychodynamics of Terrorism', *Mental Health and Society*, 4, 1–2 (1977), pp. 1–8.

Khaled, L., *My People Shall Live: The Autobiography of a Revolutionary* (London: Hodder and Stoughton, 1973).

Knowles, G.J., 'Dealing Crack Cocaine: A View from the Streets of Honolulu', *FBI Law Enforcement Bulletin*, 65, July (1996), p. 7.

Knutson, J., 'Social and Psychodynamic Pressures Toward a Negative Identity: The Case of an American Revolutionary Terrorist', in Y. Alexander and J.M. Gleason (eds), *Behavioural and Quantitative Perspectives on Terrorism* (Elmsforth, NY: Pergamon, 1981), pp. 105–150.

Lacqueur, W., *Terrorism* (London: Weidefeld and Nicolson, 1977).

Lacqueur, W., 'The Futility of Terrorism', in J.D. Elliott and L.K. Gibson (eds), *Contemporary Terrorism: Selected Readings* (Maryland: International Association of Chiefs of Police, 1978), pp. 285–292.

Lacqueur, W., 'Reflections on Terrorism', *Foreign Affairs*, 65, 1 (1986), pp. 86–100.

Lanceley, F.J., 'The Anti-Social Personality as Hostage Taker', *Journal of Political Science and Administration*, 9 (1981), p. 28.

Lasch, C., *The Culture of Narcissism* (New York: W.W. Norton, 1979).

Lee, R.M., *Dangerous Fieldwork* (New York: Sage, 1995).

Lewin, K., 'Group Decision and Social Change', in T.M. Newcomb and E.L. Hartley (eds), *Readings in Social Psychology* (New York: Holt, 1947).

Linn, R., 'Terrorism, Morality and Soldiers' Motivation to Fight – An Example from the Israeli Experience in Lebanon', *Terrorism*, 11, 2 (1988), pp. 139–149.

Lyons, H.A. and Harbinson, H.J., 'A Comparison of Political and Non-Political Murderers in Northern Ireland 1974–1984', *Medicine, Science and the Law*, 26 (1986), pp. 193–198.

MacStiofáin, S., *Memoirs of a Revolutionary* (London: Gordon Cremonisi, 1975).

Maguire, M., *To Take Arms: A Year in the Provisional IRA* (London: Quartet, 1974).

Mallin, J., 'Terrorism as a Military Weapon', in J.D. Elliott and L.K. Gibson (eds), *Contemporary Terrorism: Selected Readings* (Maryland: International Association of Chiefs of Police, 1978), pp. 117–128.

McCauley, C., 'Terrorism, Research and Public Policy: An Overview', *Terrorism and Political Violence*, 3, 1 (1991), pp. 126–144.

McCauley, C. and Segal, M.E., 'Social Psychology of Terrorist Groups', in C. Hendrick (ed.), *Review of Personality and Social Psychology 9* (Beverly Hills: Sage, 1987), pp. 231–256.

McCauley, C. and Segal, M.E., 'Terrorist Individuals and Terrorist Groups: The Normal Psychology of Extreme Behavior', in J. Groebel and J.H. Goldstein (eds), *Terrorism* (Seville: Publicaciones de la Universidad de Sevilla, 1989), p. 45.

McGartland, M., *Fifty Dead Men Walking* (London: Blake, 1997).

Merari, A., 'A Classification of Terrorist Groups', *Terrorism*, 1, 3–4 (1978), pp. 331–346.

Merari, A., 'Academic Research and Government Policy on Terrorism', *Terrorism and Political Violence*, 3, 1 (1991), pp. 88–102.

Merari, A. and Friedland, N., 'Social Psychological Aspects of Political Terrorism', in S. Oskamp (ed.), *Applied Social Psychology Annual 6: International Conflict and National Public Policy Issues* (London: Sage, 1985), pp. 185–205.

Milgram, S., 'Behavioral Study of Obedience', *Journal of Abnormal and Social Psychology*, 67 (1963), pp. 371–378.

Milgram, S., 'Some Conditions of Obedience and Disobedience to Authority', in I.D. Steiner and M. Fishbein (eds), *Current Studies in Social Psychology* (New York: Holt, 1965).

Miller, A.H., 'Book Review', *Terrorism and Political Violence*, 1, 3 (1989), pp. 391–396.

Miller, B.M., *The Language Component of Terrorism Strategy: A Text-Based Linguistic Case Study of Contemporary German Terrorism*, Unpublished Doctoral Thesis (Washington, D.C.: Georgetown University, 1987).

Monaghan, R., 'Animal Rights and Violent Protest', *Terrorism and Political Violence*, 9, 4 (1997), pp. 106–116.

Monaghan, R., 'Single Issue Terrorism: A New Phenomenon?', paper presented at the *European Association of Psychology and Law/American Psychology and Law Joint Annual Conference*, Dublin, 6–9 July 1999.

Morf, G., *Terror in Quebec – Case Studies of the FLQ* (Toronto: Clark, Irwin, 1970).

O'Callaghan, S., 'Shots in the Propaganda War', *Sunday Times – Book Supplement* (22 September 1996), p. 3.

O'Callaghan, S., *The Informer* (London: Bantam, 1998).

O'Toole, F., 'The Premature Life of Gerry Adams', *Irish Times – Weekend Section* (28 September 1996), p. 9.

Olsson, P.A., 'The Terrorist and The Terrorized: Some Psychoanalytic Consideration', *Journal of Psychohistory*, 16, 1 (1988), pp. 47–60.

Oots, K.L., 'Bargaining With Terrorists: Organisational Considerations', *Terrorism*, 13 (1989), pp. 145–158.

Pearce, K.I., 'Police Negotiations', *Canadian Psychiatric Association Journal*, 22 (1977), pp. 171–174.

Pearlstein, R., *The Mind of the Political Terrorist* (Wilmington: Scholarly Resources, 1991).

Pluchinsky, D., 'Terrorist Documentation', *Terrorism*, 14 (1991), pp. 195–207, 241–252.

Pluchinsky, D., 'The Terrorism Puzzle: Missing Pieces and No Boxcover', *Terrorism and Political Violence*, 9, 1 (1997), pp. 7–10.

Post, J.M., 'Notes on a Psychodynamic Theory of Terrorist Behaviour', *Terrorism*, 7 (1984), pp. 241–256.

Post, J.M., 'Rewarding Fire With Fire: The Effects of Retaliation on Terrorist Group Dynamics', *Terrorism*, 10 (1987), pp. 23–35.

Post, J.M., 'Group and Organizational Dynamics of Political Terrorism: Implications for Counterterrorist Policy', in P. Wilkinson and A.M. Stewart (eds), *Contemporary Research on Terrorism* (Aberdeen: Aberdeen University Press, 1987), pp. 307–317.

Post, J.M., 'Terrorist Psycho-Logic: Terrorist Behavior as a Product of Psychological Forces', in W. Reich (ed.), *Origins of Terrorism: Psychologies, Ideologies, Theologies, States of Mind* (New York: Cambridge University Press, 1990), pp. 25–40.

Post, J.M., Sprinzak, E. and Denny, L.M., 'The Terrorists in their Own Words: Interviews with 35 Incarcerated Middle Eastern Terrorists', *Terrorism and Political Violence*, 15, 1 (2003), pp. 171–184.

Rapoport, D.C., 'Introduction', in D.C. Rapoport (ed.), *Inside Terrorist Organisations* (London: Frank Cass, 1988), pp. 1–10.

Rapoport, D.C., 'To Claim or Not to Claim: That is the Question – Always!', *Terrorism and Political Violence*, 9, 1 (1997), pp. 11–17.

Rasch, W., 'Psychological Dimensions of Political Terrorism in the Federal Republic of Germany', *International Journal of Law and Psychiatry*, 2 (1979), pp. 79–86.

Raufer, X., 'Terreur en Algerie: Le GIA comme OVNI: Organisation Violente Non Indentifiee', *Notes d'Information de Laboratoire MINOS* (Paris: Centre des Hautes Etudes de L'Armament, 1996).

Raufer, X., 'Al Qaeda: A Different Diagnosis', *Studies in Conflict and Terrorism*, 26, 6 (2003), pp. 391–398.

Reich, W., (ed.), *Origins of Terrorism: Psychologies, Ideologies, Theologies, States of Mind* (New York: Cambridge University Press, 1990).

Reich, W., 'Understanding Terrorist Behavior: The Limits and Opportunities of Psychological Enquiry', in W. Reich (ed.), *Origins of Terrorism: Psychologies, Ideologies, Theologies, States of Mind* (New York: Cambridge University Press, 1990), pp. 261–279.

Reid, E.F., *An Analysis of Terrorism Literature: A Bibliographic and Content Analysis Study*, Unpublished Doctoral Dissertation (University of South Carolina, 1983).

Reuters World Service, 'Algerian Press Describes Bus Slaughter' (Reuters Group plc., 12 December, 1996).

Richardson, L., 'Terrorists as Transnational Actors', in M. Taylor and J. Horgan (eds), *The Future of Terrorism* (London: Frank Cass, 2000), pp. 209–219.

Ryder, C., *Inside the Maze: The Untold Story of the Northern Ireland Prison Service* (London: Methuen, 2000).

Schmid, A.P. 'Defining Terrorism: The Response Problem as a Definition Problem', in A.P. Schmid and R.D. Crelinsten (eds), *Western Responses to Terrorism* (London: Frank Cass, 1993), p. 7–13.

Schmid, A.P., 'Terrorism and the Use of Weapons of Mass Destruction: From Where the Risk?', in M. Taylor and J. Horgan (eds), *The Future of Terrorism* (London: Frank Cass, 2000), pp. 106–132.

Schmid, A.P. and de Graaf, J., *Violence as Communication: Insurgent Terrorism and the Western News Media* (London: Sage, 1982).

Schmid, A.P. and Jongman, A.J. (eds), *Political Terrorism (Second Edition)* (Amsterdam: North Holland Publishing Company, 1988).

Silke, A.P., 'Cheshire-Cat Logic: The Recurring Theme of Terrorist Abnormality in Psychological Research', *Psychology, Crime and Law*, 4 (1998), pp. 51–69.

Silke, A.P., 'Becoming a Terrorist', in A.P. Silke (ed.), *Terrorists, Victims and Society: Psychological Perspectives on Terrorism and Its Consequences* (London: Wiley, 2003), pp. 29–53.

Silke, A.P., 'Beyond Horror: Terrorist Atrocity and the Search for Understanding – the Case of the Shankill Bombing', *Studies in Conflict and Terrorism*, 26 (2003), pp. 37–60.

Silke, A.P., 'Deindividuation, Anonymity, and Violence: Findings from Northern Ireland', *Journal of Social Psychology*, 143, 4 (2003), pp. 493–499.

Silke, A.P. (ed.), *Research on Terrorism: Trends, Achievements, Failures* (London: Frank Cass, 2004).

Sluka, J., *Hearts and Minds, Water and Fish: Support for the IRA and INLA in a Northern Irish Ghetto* (Greenwich, CT: JAI Press, 1989).

Spire, A., 'Le Terrorisme Intellectuel', *Patio*, 11 (1988), pp. 150–158.

Strentz, T., 'A Terrorist Psychosocial Profile: Past and Present', *FBI Law Enforcement Bulletin*, April (1987), pp. 13–19.

Swain, J., 'Ramadan Killers Leave 250 Dead in City of Blood', *Sunday Times* (26 January 1997) p. 17.

Taylor, M., *The Terrorist* (London: Brassey's, 1988).

Taylor, M., *The Fanatics* (London: Brassey's, 1991).

Taylor, M. and Horgan, J., 'Future Developments of Terrorism in Europe', in M. Taylor and J. Horgan (eds), *The Future of Terrorism* (London: Frank Cass, 2000), pp. 83–93.

Taylor, M. and Horgan, J. (eds), *The Future of Terrorism* (London: Frank Cass, 2000).

Taylor, M. and Quayle, E., *Terrorist Lives* (London: Brassey's, 1994).

Thackrah, R., 'Terrorism: A Definitional Problem', in P. Wilkinson and A.M. Stewart (eds), *Contemporary Research on Terrorism* (Aberdeen: Aberdeen University Press, 1987).

Tittmar, H., 'Urban Terrorism: A Psychological Perspective', *Terrorism and Political Violence*, 4, 3 (1992), pp. 64–71.

Tololyan, K., 'Narrative Culture and Terrorist Motivation', in J. Shotter and K.J. Gergen (eds), *Texts of Identity – Inquiries in Social Construction Series* (London: Sage, 1989), pp. 99–118.

Turco, R., 'Psychiatric Contributions to the Understanding of International Terrorism', *International Journal of Offender Therapy and Comparative Criminology*, 31, 2 (1987), pp. 153–161.

United States Department of State, *Patterns of Global Terrorism: 1996* (Washington, DC: Government Printing Office, 1997).

Veness, D., 'Single Issue Terrorism', paper presented at *51st International Criminological Conference*, Warsaw, 3 September 1995.

Vinar, M.N., 'La Terreur, Le Politique, La Place d'un Psychanalyste', *Patio*, 11 (1988), pp. 43–51.

Walsh, D.P.J., 'The Impact of the Antisubversive Laws on Police Powers and Practices in Ireland: The Silent Erosion of Individual Freedom', *Temple Law Review*, 62, 4 (1989), pp. 1099–1129.

Wardlaw, G., *Political Terrorism: Theory, Tactics and Counter-Measures (Second Edition)* (Cambridge: Cambridge University Press, 1989).

Watzlawick, P., 'The Pathologies of Perfectionism', *Et Cetera*, 34, 1 (1977), pp. 12–18.

White, R.W., 'Issues in the Study of Political Violence: Understanding the Motives of Participants in Small Group Political Violence', paper presented at the *Future Developments in Terrorism* Conference, University College, Cork, 3–5 March 1999.

White, R.W. and Falkenberg White, T., 'Revolution in the City: On the Resources of Urban Guerrillas', *Terrorism and Political Violence*, 3, 4 (1991), pp. 100–132.

Wilkinson, P., 'Foreword – Terrorism: An International Research Agenda?', in P. Wilkinson and A.M. Stewart (eds), *Contemporary Research on Terrorism* (Aberdeen: Aberdeen University Press, 1987), pp. xi–xx.

Zawodny, J.K., 'Internal Organizational Problems and the Sources of Tensions of Terrorists Movements as Cataylsts of Violence', *Terrorism*, 1, 3–4 (1978), pp. 277–285.

INDEX

acclimatization to terrorism 4, 14
Adams, Gerry 28, 36, 49, 142–3, 151
Afghanistan 115
aims of terrorism 1, 2, 3
Al Qaeda 2, 5, 24, 72; dehumanization
134–5; Madrid train bombing 110;
September 11th attacks 114
Al Qassam 100
Al Zawahiri, Ayman 135
Al-Adel, Saif 135
Algeria 17
Algerian Armed Islamic Group (GIA)
12, 17
An Phobacht 41
'anarchic-ideologue' groups 91
Anderson, J.K. 13, 50
Animal Liberation Front (ALF) 8
Arendt, Hannah 132
associates/helpers of terrorists 108
Atlanta, Olympic Games 1996 116
Atran, S. 94
Atta, Mohammad 35, 118–19
attacks *see* terrorist event cycle
attitudes to terrorism 5–6, 7
authoritarian personalities 55
'auto-propaganda' 89

Baader-Meinhof group 60, 63, 145
Bali, Indonesia 47
Bandura, A. 133
Barber, B. 101
Basque ETA 11, 31, 43, 45, 97, 99;
Alhambra, Granada 110; Ordizia
110; Reus Airport 110; targeting
110–11
Baumann, Michael 35, 36, 144
becoming a terrorist 80–106, 161;
acquisition of skills 99–100, 105;
catalyst events 87–90; competing
alternatives 103; 'currency' of roles
100–1; as gradual process 97–101,
105; and group organization/
recruitment 95–7, 103; identification
with group/community 90–5, 99; life
experiences 102, 103; predisposition
to 101–3, 105, 165; *process model*
80–1, 104, 165; in the Provisional
IRA 86–7; 'pushed' by external forces
89–90; social context 102, 105, 167;
and terrorist events
109–10, *see also* being a terrorist;
personality of terrorists; terrorist
groups/movements
being a terrorist 82, 126–39, 161;
dehumanization of the enemy 130,
132, 133–5; deindividuation 133;
distancing from the victim 132;
justification 130–2; obedience to
authority 126–30, 140; 'routinization'
132; and social activity 135–7
Berg, Nicholas 119
Berger, Peter 56
Berkowitz, L. 57
Billig, O. 98
Bin Laden, Osama 34
bin Nurhasyim, Amorzi 47
Björgo, T. 84
Blackburn, R. 69, 70, 71
Blida, Algeria 17
Bloody Sunday in Derry (1972) 29, 42,
87
bombs 9, 116, 117, 118
Bosnia 15, 16, 21
Bowyer-Bell, Joe 38, 39, 44
Breen, Suzanne 121, 122
Britain and Northern Ireland 72, 73

Brockner, J. 146
Bruce, Steve 38
Burgess, M. 93
Burton, Frank 38
Bush, President George W. 107–8

Cairns, E. 25
Canada: *Front de Liberation du Quebec* (FLQ) 63
Canary Wharf bombing 152
Carlos the Jackal 52, 60, 61, 67, 153
Carroll, R. 49–50
causes of terrorism 83–5, 166
Central Intelligence Agency 4
Che Guevara 5
children as targets 15–16
Clark, R.P. 97, 99
Clarke, R.V.G. 81
classification of terrorist groups 91
Clinton, President 152
Clutterbuck, Richard 39
Collins, Eamon 35, 36, 42, 123, 153
Colombian FARC 11, 115
commitment to terrorist groups 51, 66, 136–7
complexity of terrorism 109, 159
Conservative Party 3
Contemporary Research on Terrorism 26
Coogan, T.P. 42
Cooper, H.H.A. 31, 50, 52, 61, 67
Cordes, B. 88, 89
Cornish, D.B. 81
Corrado, R.R. 63
counter-terrorism 6, 158–9, 161, 162, 167
Crelinsten, Ronald 27, 29
Crenshaw, M. 44, 54–5; difficulties of personality research 74; and disengagement 151; identity formation 61–2; normality of terrorists 64–5; terrorist memoirs 35–7, 45
crime and terrorism 1, 8, 28, 111
criminalitycauses 83; 'positivism' and free will 53, 63; rational choice theory (RCT) 81
Crossmaglen, Co. Armagh 14
Cusack, Jim 121, 122
Cusson, Maurice 112

data for psychological studies 35, 37
Debray, Regis 123, 151

definition/characteristics of terrorism/ terrorists 27–8, 108, 159
dehumanization of the enemy 130, 132, 133–5
deindividuation in terrorist groups 133
della Porta, Donatella 38
Denny, L.M. 91–2
Dingley, James 141, 156
'Direct Action Against Drugs' 28
discipline in terrorist groups/movements 111–12, 125, 132–3
disengaging from terrorism 140–57; and group organization 151–2; and group pressures 144–5; implications 152–4; physical disengagement 150–1; psychological disengagement 144–9; and research 140–1, 154–6
Doherty, Martin 50
Drake, C.J.M. 71–2
Dworetsky, J.P. 133

Egyptian Islamic Jihad 135
Eichmann, Adolf 132
Elliot, J.D. 64
Enniskillen 19
Erikson, Erik 61
Ervine, David 73
European ideological terror 141, *see also* German 2nd June Movement; German Red Army Faction; Greece: Italian Red Brigades

Falkenberg White, T. 98
family influences on terrorists 62
Faranda, Adriana 97–8, 128–9, 145, 148
Ferguson, N. 93
Ferracuti, F. 45, 57, 58, 65–7
financing terrorism 111
Frank, Robert 56
Freud, Sigmund 60
Friedland, N. 3, 4; terrorist personality 56, 57, 58, 70, 71
frustration-aggression hypothesis 57–9, 76

Geneva Conventions 11, 20
genocide 132
Germany2nd June Movement 35, 144; Baader-Meinhof group 60, 63, 145; Red Army Faction 91, 98, 114; research on German terrorists, 1981 54, 62, 70; students 58

GIGN (Groupe d'Intervention des Gendarmes Nationales) 6
Gilmour, Raymond 35, 36
Gordon, Avishag 27
Greece: November 17 group 141
Guantanamo Bay 108
Guerin, Veronica 122
guerrilla warfare 10, 12
Gurr, T.R. 58

Hague Regulations 11, 20
Hamas *see* Palestine Hamas
Handler, J.S. 70–1
Harbinson, H.J. 64
Hassan, N. 91, 100, 129, 131
Herrhausen, Alfred 114
Heskin, K. 7, 8, 28, 52, 55, 64, 132
heterogeneity of terrorism/terrorists 30–2, 54, 74–5, 160; and individual psychology 74–5
Himmler, Heinrich 127
Hoffman, B. 7, 8, 11, 16
Hollywood, I. 93
Horgan, J. 15, 21
Hubbard, David 56
Hutchinson, Billy 73

identification with group/community 90–5, 99
incidents *see* terrorist event cycle
inclination to terrorism101–3, 105, 165
individual psychology 77, 82, 164–5; and heterogeneity of terrorism/ terrorists 74–5
individual terroristsin groups/ movements 82, 89, 90–5, 100, 109, 125; and terrorist attacks 109
interviewing terrorists 37–8, 39–43; in prison 40–1
involvement in terrorism *see* becoming a terrorist; being a terrorist
IRA *see* Official IRA; Provisional IRA; 'Real' IRA
Iranian embassy siege 1980 6, 36
Iraq 115, 118, 119; Fallujah 134; Mujahideen fighters 135
Ireland, Republic of 10, 41; Adare, Co. Limerick 120; 1918 Dáil Éirann 12; Kerry 115; murder of Garda Jerry McCabe 120–5; Republicans 14–15, *see also* Northern Ireland; Provisional IRA; Sinn Fein

Islamic Jihad 12, 28
Islamic Reistance Movement 91
Islamic Salvation Front 17
Italian Red Brigades 66, 91, 131; becoming a terrorist 97–8, 99; commitment 136–7; leaving 145; normality of terrorists 63–4; obedience to authority 128–9

Jackson, William 120
Jäger, H. 54
Jamieson, Alison 38, 63–4, 97, 98, 148
Japanese Red Army 144, 153
Jemaah Islamiyah 47
Jenkins, B.M. 3, 7
Johnson, Paul 119
Jongman 7
justification of terrorist activity 130–2

Kampf, H.A. 58
Kaplan, A. 61
Keane, F. 15
Kellen, Konrad 36, 38–9, 52, 60–1, 66, 67
Kelman, H.C. 127, 132
Kerr, Alex 45
Khaled, Leila 35
Khalistan Liberation Force 152
Klein, Hans-Joachim 60–1, 153
Knutson, J. 62
Kosovo 16

Lacqueur, W. 31, 38–9
leaders 33–4, 70, 125
Lee, R.M. 42
Lewin, Kurt 132
Liberté 17
Linn, R. 12
logistics of attacks 117–19
lures of terrorist groups 90
Lyons, H.A. 64

McCabe, Jerry 120–5
McCauley, C. 63, 71, 97, 144
McGarry, Philip 64
McGartland, Martin 35, 36, 123
McGuinness, Martin 142, 151
McMichael, John 73
MacStiofáin, Sean 35
Madrid, train bombing (2004) 110
Mafia 8
Maguire, Maria 35

Mahler, Horst 97
maintenance of dread 14
Mallin, J. 36, 39
Manchester bombing (1996) 9
Mandel, Paul 56
Marighella, Carlos 151; *Minimanual of the Urban Guerilla* 35
Marseilles airport hostage rescue 6
martyrdom 100, 102, 131
media accounts 23–4
Meinhof, Ulrike 60, 97
Merari, Ariel 3, 30–1, 57, 70
methods of terrorism 8–10, 158
Milgram, Stanley 126–7, 132
Miller, A.H. 25–6
Milliken, George 45
Morf, Gustav 56, 63
Morrison, Danny 154
Mujahideen fighters 135

Nafi, Basheer 28
narcissism 54, 59–60
'nationalist-separatist' groups 91
NATO in Kosovo 16
Nejad, Ali 36
Nelson, Sarah 38
Nicaraguan Contras 7
9/11 *see* September 11 attacks
normality/abnormality of terrorists 47–8, 56, 62–9, 75, 159
Northern Ireland 4, 10, 28; Ballynahinch, Co. Down 116; Bloody Sunday in Derry (1972) 29, 42, 87; commemorative events 137; Crossmaglen, Co. Armagh 14; Enniskillen 19; interviews with activists 93–4; Loyalist terrorists 51, 142; Omagh bombing 1998 117; peace process 142–3, 151; Royal Ulster Constabulary 116; state violence 29; terrorism in the 1960s 58; Ulster Defence Association (UDA) 73, 93, 94, 116; Ulster Volunteer Force (UVF) 45

obedience to authority 126–30, 140
O'Brien, Edward 115
O'Callaghan, Sean 35, 36, 42, 148–9, 153
Official IRA 148; *Reporter's Guide to Ireland* 39, 40, 96–7
Oklahoma City bomb 9

Omagh bombing (1998) 117–18
O'Malley, Des 121
OPEC oil ministers' meeting (1974) 153
organization/recruitment in terrorist groups 95–7, 103, 125
O'Sullivan, Ben 120, 121
O'Toole, Fintan 36

Palestine Hamas 11, 28, 91, 102, 131; Hizbollah 91; interviews with militants 91–2; *Intifada* 48, 101; Islamic Jihad 91, 102, 129; Izz a-Din al Qassan 91; Liberation Organization (PLO) 35
Pastika, General Made 47
Pearce, K.I. 52
Pearlstein, Richard 59–60
personality assessment 77
personality of terrorists 48, 53–79; frustration-aggression hypothesis 57–9, 76; identity formation 61–2; narcissism 54, 59–60; normality/abnormality of terrorists 47–8, 56, 62–9, 75, 159; psychodynamic accounts 60–2; psychological disorder: persistence of belief in 65–9; psychometric evaluation 69–70; psychopathy 49–53; trait measures 69, 70, 71, 75–7, 160
personnelchoice of 114–15, 164–5; training 15
Philippines, Abu Sayyaf 115
Pluchinsky, D. 36
political violence and terrorism 7
Post, Jerrold 32, 55, 59, 91–2, 146–7
predisposition to terrorism
process model 80–1, 104, 165
profiles 70–1, 160
Provisional IRA 3, 9–10, 11–12, 14–15, 16; attempted assassination of Margaret Thatcher 3; ceasefire 1994–6 72, 142; choice of personnel 114–15; commemorative events 137; commitment 129–30; decommissioning of weapons 34, 142–3, 153, 154; deindividuation 133–4; and disengagement 151–2; Good Friday agreement (1998) 151; Green Book 127–8, 131; and history 30, 31; and identification of terrorists 28–9; justification 130–1; leadership 33–4, 123–4; moral authority 130;

murder of Garda Jerry McCabe 120–5; as 'national-separatist' group 91; obedience to authority 127–8; and 'punishment attacks' 49–50, 151–2; raising money 111; reasons for involvement 86–7, 97; recruitment 95–6, 97, 98, 102; and research 39–45, 55; and Sinn Fein 141–3; survival of 141–3; training 115, 152; and warfare 18–19, 131–2

psychodynamic accounts 60–2

psychological warfare 3–4, 13–17

psychology and terrorism 32–5, 158, *see also* becoming a terrorist; being a terrorist; personality of terrorists; research

psychometric evaluation 69–70

psychopathy 49–53, 64

Quayle, E. interviewing terrorists 39, 45; involvement in terrorism 88, 104; Loyalist terrorists 51; responses to terrorism 6, 7–8; theories of terrorism 74

Rand Corporation 4

Rand-St. Andrews Terrorism Chronology database 5

Rapoport, David 25, 36

Rasch, W. 63

Raufer, Xavier 23, 31, 119

Reagan, President Ronald 7

'Real' IRA 117–18, 151

Reich, W. 32, 56, 58

religion 2, 94

Remembrance Day bombing, Enniskillen (1987) 19

research 25–7, 29, 35–46, 53–4, 167–8; difficulties of personality research 69–79; and disengagement from terrorism 140–1, 154–6; on German terrorists, (1981) 54–5, 68; inconsistencies in psychological research 65–9; interviewing terrorists 37–8, 39–43, 55, 141; methods 34–7; terrorists' attitudes to 39

responses to terrorism 22, 159, 166–7

Restorick, Lance Corporal Stephen 14

Richardson, Louise 1, 4

right/left wing terrorists 71

role models 92, 93

roles in terrorist groups 100–1, 109–10

'Root Causes of Terrorism' conference, Oslo, (2003) 83–4

'routinization' 132

Royal Ulster Constabulary 45, 116

Rubin, J.Z. 146

Rumsfeld, Donald 107

Russell and Miller 71

Ryder, C. 64

Sands, Bobby 5

Sarajevo 15

SAS (Special Air Service) 6

Schleyer, Hans Martin 98

Schmid, Alex 3, 7, 18, 19–21, 22, 38

security services 112–13

security of terrorists 136

Segal, M.E. 97, 144

September 11 attacks 2, 5, 8, 24–5, 118–19, 168; group dynamics of terrorists 34; and identification of terrorists 107; and terrorist personality 48

Shallah, Ramadan Abdullah 28

Shigenobu, Fusako 153

shooting 15, 118

Shqaqi, Fathi 28

Silke, Andrew 52, 62, 68–9, 93–4, 133

Singh, Kuldip 152

Sinn Fein 16, 28, 34, 141–3; and Marxism 141

skills acquisition 99–100, 105

Sluka, Jeffrey 38

sniping 15

social activity of terrorists 135–7

social/cultural context of terrorism 74, 102, 105, 166, 167

Spain 110–11, *see also* Basque ETA

Spire, A. 145

Sri Lanka, Tamil Tigers 11, 110

States/governments 11, 162; as sponsors of terrorism 115; using terrorist tactics 12–13, 21; using violence 2, 29

statistics 4–5

Stern, Susan 60

Stewart, Alisdair 26

Strentz, T. 71

suicidal terrorists 100, 102

Sullwold, L. 54

Symbionese Liberation Army 60

targets 3, 9–10, 71–2; children 15–16; immediate and overall 2; military targets 12; selection of 110–13
Taylor, M.: becoming a terrorist 88, 104; Bosnia 15, 21; interviewing terrorists 39, 45; Loyalist terrorists 38, 51–2; personality of terrorists 60, 61, 69; profiles 71; and responses to terrorism 6, 7; theories of terrorism 74
Taylor, Peter 42
terrorism: complexity of 109, 159; definition/characteristics 1–6, 13, 159–60; as a form of warfare 17–21; and other crimes 1, 8, 28, 111; and *political violence* 7; as a process 163–6; as psychological warfare 3–4, 13–17; and responses 166–7; and warfare 10–13, 131–2
Terrorism and Political Violence (journal) 26
terrorist event cycle 109–25, 164–5; decision and targeting 110–13; event execution 117–19; murder of Garda Jerry McCabe 120–5; post-event activity 120; preparation 113–17; 'search' process 112–13
terrorist groups/movements 1–2, 34; classification 91; commitment 51, 66; deindividuation 133; and discipline 111–12, 125, 132–3; finance 111; and identity formation 61–2; and the individual 82, 89, 90–5, 100, 109, 125; leaders 33–4, 70, 125; and levels of activity 100; organization/recruitment 95–7, 103, 125; and propaganda 89; roles of members 100, 109–10, *see also* becoming a terrorist; being a terrorist
terrorist memoirs 35–6, 88, 156
terrorists: capacities of 24–5; definition/characteristics 27–8, 108, 159;

heterogeneity of 30–2, 54, 74–5, 160; identification of 28–30, *see also* becoming a terrorist; being a terrorist; personality of terrorists; terrorist groups/movements
Thackrah, R. 10, 13, 20, 25
Thatcher, Margaret 3
Tittmar, H. 57
training of terrorists 115
trait measures 69, 70, 71, 75–7, 160

UK: British Government and Irish Rupublicans 142; Canary Wharf bombing 152; PIRA bombing campaign 115, *see also* Northern Ireland
Ulster *see* Northern Ireland
University of South Florida 28
US Department of State 46; Patterns of Global Terrorism Report 1996 20, 31
USA 60, 71; Atlanta, Olympic Games 1996 116; Oklahoma City bomb 9
Usabiaga, Isidoro 110–11

Veness, D. 8
victims 17; distancing from 132; and opponents 2, 9–10; random choice of 6, 51–2
violence 161–2; attitudes of terrorists 54

War on Terrorism 13, 107–8, 159, 162–3, 168
Wardlaw, Grant 32
warfare and terrorism 10–13, 17–21, 131–2
weapons 9, 116
'Weathermen' 60
White, R.W. 29, 30, 37–8, 98
Wilkinson, Paul 26–7, 52, 168
Wilson, R. 25
Wittgenstein 1